ADELE

SEAN SMITH

HarperCollins*Publishers*

HarperCollins*Publishers*
1 London Bridge Street
London SE1 9GF

www.harpercollins.co.uk

First published by HarperCollins*Publishers* 2016
This paperback edition 2017

1 3 5 7 9 10 8 6 4 2

© Sean Smith 2016, 2017

Sean Smith asserts the moral right to
be identified as the author of this work

A catalogue record of this book is
available from the British Library

ISBN 978-0-00-815561-2

Printed and bound in Great Britain by
Clays Ltd, St Ives plc

MIX
Paper from
responsible sources
FSC™ C007454

ADELE

Also by Sean Smith

Kim
Tom Jones: The Life
Kylie
Gary
Alesha
Tulisa
Kate
Robbie
Cheryl
Victoria
Justin: The Biography
Britney: The Biography
J. K. Rowling: A Biography
Jennifer: The Unauthorized Biography
Royal Racing
The Union Game
Sophie's Kiss (with Garth Gibbs)
Stone Me! (with Dale Lawrence)

To Michael and Anna

CONTENTS

INTRODUCTION

THE O2, LONDON, MONDAY, 21 MARCH 2016

A picture of Adele's immaculately made-up eyes, tightly closed, with a striking pair of false lashes, illuminates an enormous screen behind the stage. Suddenly, without warning, the lights go down and the eyes open wide, creating a maelstrom of excitement and cheering. The Adele roar shakes the foundations.

'Hello … It's me!' And there she is, a formidable presence, six feet in heels. She appears not on the main stage, but on a small circular platform in the centre of the audience. 20,000 people are already on their feet. Her black silk Burberry gown is speckled with hand-woven floral sequins that are instantly lit by what seem like a million mobile phones as she launches into her iconic comeback song.

How did an ordinary girl from Tottenham inspire such adulation and acclaim, mixed with a generous helping of affection? My row is full of friendly and chatty Americans, who thought it would be 'fun' to fly over and see her, even though she will be touring the US throughout the year. I wonder idly if there is anyone from her old neighbourhood here tonight.

Everyone seems to know the words to 'Hello'. It's a wall of sound, but her voice is as big as ever, refusing to be over-whelmed by the backing music or our sing-along. The track has already broken so many records. The figures are mind-boggling in an age when there's so much choice. I read that it topped the iTunes chart in 102 countries when it was released in November 2015. I can't name 102 countries! The problem with this song is that it will always have to be the first number at her concerts. 'Hello' seems a bit ridiculous as an encore anthem.

She is flanked by her security as she walks to the main stage and launches into 'Hometown Glory'. The picture of her Dusty Springfield eyes on the big screen gives way to photo-graphs of London. It's a simple song, the first she ever completed, aged sixteen, and powerful in its youthful under-lying message of nostalgia and empowerment.

Before we can draw breath, the blockbuster beginning continues with 'One and Only', arguably the best track from the record-breaking album *21*. It's smoky and soulful. Close your eyes and you can imagine one of the great divas of the past singing it in a jazz club … maybe Ella Fitzgerald or Sarah Vaughan or, best of all, Adele's favourite singer, Etta James.

I've been listening to Etta a lot while I work on this book and her peerless recordings remind me so much of Adele. 'Fool That I Am' was on Adele's set list when she started out, and part of me wishes it still was, but, for me, 'One and Only' carries the hallmark of Etta. Adele is one of those great artists who carry their influences around with them like a favourite handbag.

She needs to pause after three power songs in a row. She takes a swig from a mug containing a honey drink to soothe her voice, and starts to engage her audience in that natural, easy manner she has. It's as if you were standing next to her in a checkout queue at Asda – although I suspect she shops at Waitrose these days.

Banter and interaction with the fans have become a feature of this tour. She started off in Belfast helping a female fan make a leap-year marriage proposal to her boyfriend. Unsurprisingly, he said yes and the story went round the world. In Manchester, she invited a twelve-year-old girl with autism to come on stage and sing 'Someone Like You'. She was brilliant.

Tonight she invites two little girls, aged seven and eight, on to the stage and has to apologise for using the F-word. I can't think of another star who does this. Later she asks a girl celebrating her sixteenth birthday to join her to sing a duet of the Bob Dylan classic 'Make You Feel My Love' from the *19* album. Adele is gracious, 'It was really lovely to share that with you. Well done.' This is the first time I personally have seen Adele duet.

As she says later, this is a show and not just a gig. In some ways, it's old-fashioned entertainment, like a summertime holiday special on Great Yarmouth pier starring the late Paul Daniels, or perhaps a Christmas pantomime in which the much-missed Cilla Black would continually chat to the audience. I can imagine Adele asking us what she should do with one of her ghastly ex-boyfriends. 'Feed him to the crocodile,' we would shout.

She has a rare gift among modern artists of making a connection with her audience. 'As soon as I say "Oscar", I sound like a dickhead,' she announces, before telling us how

'Skyfall' came about. At the time, she confides, she was trying to breastfeed, or 'pumping and dumping', as she describes it. She even encourages a Mexican wave, which is about as uncool as you can get, but emphasises her feel-good factor.

Having made sure we are on her side and part of her world, she launches into the song itself – the majesty of her voice contrasting sharply with her girl-from-Tottenham persona, all F-words and cackling laughter. I find myself looking forward to the Adele moments between the songs. She admits, 'I've made a living holding onto a grudge', and we all laugh.

She explains how she wrote 'Million Years Ago', one of the power ballads on *25*, immediately after visiting an old friend who still lives in Tulse Hill, a mile down the road from where Adele spent her teenage years in West Norwood. She was reminded about how, every night after school, she would hang out with her friends in Brockwell Park, just off the Norwood Road, and 'talk rubbish'. Looking back made her so sad, she wrote the song literally in minutes when she got home.

Perhaps the key moment of Adele sharing comes when she mentions Angelo, her young son, who was born in 2012: 'He has given me so much joy, so much purpose. It has changed my life.' I could feel she genuinely meant it.

The songs that form such an important backdrop to modern living continued, with 'Don't You Remember' and 'Chasing Pavements' standing out. Five years ago, she tells us, things changed overnight with the performance of 'Someone Like You' at the BRITs. Then, it was spine-tingling. Now, it seems strangely comforting, still poignant, but with that comfy familiarity songs have when they obtain classic status. Adele says the song was her friend at a bad time. 'It saved my life,' she declares.

'Fire to the Rain' closes the main set, with Adele, thanks to special effects, caught in a downpour without an umbrella. In the old pre-mobile days, we would all have got our lighters out and let them flicker away while she sang. Struggling to light a cigarette is supposed to have given her the inspiration for the number.

The encore begins with her popping up on the small stage again. Unseen, she is carted by roadies between the two stages in a sort of wheelie bin. She starts with 'All I Ask', my favourite track on *25* and certainly the saddest. Fortunately, there is no sign of the sound issues that marred her performance of the song at the 2016 Grammys. It's a breathtakingly difficult song to sing and, for me, the best of the night.

Before she sends us home happy with 'Rolling in the Deep', she sings another great ballad off the latest album. 'When We Were Young' is accompanied on the big screen by a selection of sweet, nostalgic photographs of Adele as a child – a toothless grin, a shot with her mother on the beach in South Wales.

It's a rare glimpse of the girl who grew up to be the biggest star in the world. The pictures are just snapshots, but what was she really like, both then as a child and now as a mum?

PART ONE

WHEN SHE
WAS YOUNG

1

A SURPRISE
ANNOUNCEMENT

The live video for Adele's 2016 single 'When We Were Young' is a relaxed and informal affair. She is dressed in a chic black outfit and sings the nostalgic power ballad perfectly in front of her band at The Church Studios, a state-of-the-art complex in an old Victorian church in fashionable Crouch End, North London. One hundred yards away stands The King's Head pub, a popular local boozer where, coincidentally, the Adele Adkins story begins.

These days the studios are owned by the acclaimed producer and long-time Adele collaborator Paul Epworth, with whom she co-wrote two of her best-loved songs, 'Rolling in the Deep' and 'Skyfall'. Back in the 1980s, however, the studios were put on the music map of London by Annie Lennox and Dave Stewart. As Eurythmics, they recorded their debut album, *Sweet Dreams*, on the top floor. They went on to become one of the most successful acts of the decade, eventually buying the building and playing host to many top names, including Bob Dylan, Depeche Mode and Elvis Costello.

Down the street, on the corner of Crouch Hill, The King's Head, which was also founded in Victorian times, became a popular and trendy bar for a young crowd keen to rub shoulders with musicians or perhaps catch a glimpse of someone famous nursing a drink in the corner. Downstairs was one of those tight, atmospheric rooms for comedy nights or for up-and-coming bands. If you were lucky, back in the day, you might have caught Dave and Annie jamming. You can imagine that Adele might have played there if she had been starting out then.

It was just the sort of place to attract an eighteen-year-old art student called Penny Adkins. She had travelled there on the bus from her parents' house in Tottenham for a night out with friends one summer night in 1987.

Penny was tall, slender, raven-haired and stood out from the crowd. She caught the eye of most of the young men in the upstairs bar, including a broad-shouldered, handsome blond window-cleaner called Marc Evans, who had moved to London from South Wales and was carving out a good living with his round in the upwardly mobile neighbourhood.

It wasn't love at first sight, but there was definitely some lust in the air as Marc sauntered over confidently for some light conversation and Penny's phone number. Marc, who was twenty-five, had all the chat as a young man and enjoyed a very high success rate charming young ladies during the year he had been in London.

He and his younger brother Richard had been brought up in the popular Welsh resort of Penarth, nowadays more a Cardiff suburb than the popular seaside town it was then. Their father, John, had spotted the need for a self-employed

4

plumber and soon was so successful he was able to buy his family a five-bedroom Victorian townhouse. 'My parents always owned their own house through good old-fashioned graft,' observes Marc proudly.

Marc's mother, Rose, was a devout Christian and for many years has been a respected member of the Tabernacle Baptist Church choir. Marc was a choirboy as a youngster – 'an Aled Jones-type until the old schmoogers dropped'. He sang at All Saints, Penarth, in Victoria Square, a ten-minute walk away. As a teenager, he harboured ambitions to sing and act and even wrote off to drama schools, but, in the end, went to a technical college in Llandaff for formal training as a plumber before joining his father's business. Richard, meanwhile, chose a career in the police force.

Marc was enjoying the life of a Penarth playboy with a sky-blue MG roadster and a gorgeous girlfriend. When that romance went sour, his best friend, Nigel, who was studying for a degree in London, invited him to stay. Nigel's parents were quite well off, so he wasn't living in halls of residence but had his own place.

The two-bedroom flat in Turnpike Lane was conveniently situated a couple of miles from Crouch End in one direction and Tottenham in the other. Marc soon found work as a shop-floor manager in the Edmonton branch of Wickes, the home-improvement chain.

One day an elderly man came in and asked him for some 'scrim', the durable cloth used to polish windows. They got talking and the man told Marc he was earning a 'fucking fortune' cleaning the windows of yuppie house owners. The conversation gave Marc the germ of an idea and a few days later, on a pleasant summer evening, dressed smartly in a shirt and tie, ladder on his shoulder, he was knocking on the doors of suitable houses in Crouch End and nearby Highgate. 'Good evening, sir. Good evening, madam, would you like your windows cleaned?'

It was £10 or £15 for twenty-minutes' work cleaning the windows of a two-up, two-down property. By the time he met Penny later that summer, he was well on his way to earning £20,000 a year, which was a tidy sum for a young man in the 1980s.

Penny was a North London girl, not originally from Tottenham at all, but from Islington, and lived in Chalfont Road, a mile from the old Highbury football ground that closed in 2006. Her large family were, unsurprisingly, big Arsenal supporters, even though her mother and father, Doreen and John, eventually moved into a council house on the Tower Gardens Estate, off the busy Lordship Lane in Tottenham.

John Adkins was earning his living as a lorry driver when Penny, the youngest of five children, was born, but by the time their daughter was at senior school, he and his wife were working on a fruit and vegetable stall at the New Covent Garden Market in Nine Elms.

Penny was an artistic girl who showed an early talent for drawing and painting. She was never happier than when sketching in her bedroom or playing her trusty acoustic guitar. She was determined to use her gifts by studying art at university and, as many students do, she enrolled in a one-year foundation diploma in art and design at a college in Barnet.

While Penny's family were very much working-class North Londoners, she didn't have the rough edges. Marc explained,

'Penny doesn't have that sort of cockney twang. She could walk into a pub anywhere and you wouldn't know she was from London. It's not so much that she is posher – she is more reserved.'

Even though he had a girlfriend at the time, Marc sensed there was real chemistry between himself and the teenager. 'She was a very, very attractive girl. She had lovely long dark hair, legs up to her neck and, what can I say, Bob's your uncle.'

He wasted no time in ringing her to arrange a date a few days later at his favourite pub, the Punch and Judy in Covent Garden. Although it was a chance to get to know one another properly, Marc quickly realised that she wasn't the sort of girl to jump into bed on the first date. 'She wasn't like that,' he recalled.

'It was not a big love story,' he added. However, they contin-ued to meet at the pub, which became 'their' place. Over the next few weeks, things between them got more serious and Penny agreed to stay the night at the flat in Turnpike Lane.

About two months after they met, they were passing the time at the Punch and Judy, when Penny suddenly blurted out, 'Marc, I'm pregnant.' He was shell-shocked at the news, but put on a brave face for his eighteen-year-old girlfriend: 'All right, babe. No worries. We'll sort it out.'

Despite her young age, Penny was to prove hugely resilient. There was never any question, or even discussion, about the possibility of her not keeping the child. The most pressing concern was telling Penny's parents, who, at this point, hadn't even met their daughter's new boyfriend.

Despite his bravado, Marc had been brought up tradition-ally and insisted that he would be there when she broke the news. Penny arranged for him to join them for a Sunday lunch. 'I told myself to "man up", and so I went along and explained to them that I was the father. They were shocked, obviously, and asked me what I intended to do. I told them I didn't know.'

A week later, he had made up his mind. Back at the pub, he asked Penny what she was doing for the next thirty years. 'Do you fancy getting hitched?' Despite being eighteen and pregnant, she said no, telling him they were too young. It was an early indication of her strength of character. Marc observed simply, 'She was a very tenacious young girl, a very strong woman. If she'd wanted to marry me, she would have said, "Right, you've asked me, now let's do it." It wasn't in the stratosphere, you know. She wasn't even thinking about it. She probably saw me as a bit of a Jack the Lad and thought that this wasn't going to work out.'

Marc still had the job of telling his own parents that they would be grandparents for the first time. He took the train back to Penarth and told them he had met a girl called Penny, who was now pregnant. His father John, a strong-minded, masculine man, wasn't a touchy-feely chap, but took it well enough.

During the next nine months, Marc and, particularly, Penny had some important decisions to make. He moved into a shared house in Crouch End, nearer his round, when his pal Nigel got a job as a surveyor with Tower Hamlets and moved to Chingford in North East London. Penny, meanwhile, decided to give up her college course and become a full-time mum. Fiercely independent, she left home and moved into emergency accommodation for unmarried mothers on

Queen's Drive, an unappealing street near Finsbury Park Station. She also received support from the National Childbirth Trust (NCT) charity.

Marc saw her regularly, but it would be stretching it to suggest they were a devoted couple. He wasn't the sort of man to hold her hand while she practised her breathing at ante-natal classes.

Two weeks before the baby was due, he was eating breakfast at home in Crouch End when the phone rang. It was Penny's mum Doreen. 'Congratulations, Marc. You are the father of a baby girl.' Despite being premature, there were no complications and the baby weighed a healthy 5lb 10½oz.

Marc dashed to the florists, bought an extravagant bunch of flowers and hopped on a bus to the North Middlesex Hospital in Edmonton, just off the North Circular Road, to see his daughter for the first time. It was 5 May 1988.

The new parents needed to decide on a name for their baby. Marc suggested Blue, his favourite colour. It was nothing to do with enjoying blues music; he just really liked the name. Penny considered that for a second or two before replying firmly, 'I'm not calling her Blue.'

She had, in fact, already made up her mind that her daughter would be called Adele. It was an unusual choice, which perhaps was the point. In literature, Adele features in the classic novel *Jane Eyre* as Rochester's young French ward. Jane takes the girl under her wing when she is employed as her governess. An art student might know that the Countess Adele was the mother of the Post-Impressionist master Toulouse-Lautrec.

For her second name, Penny chose Laurie, something suitable for either a boy or a girl. As a sop to Marc, she agreed that her third name could be Blue. He was delighted. Penny didn't appreciate it, however, when Marc started calling his daughter Blue. She would snap, 'Don't call her that. Her name's Adele.' Penny never shortened it to Addie or Della. It was unusual in both their families for someone to have three first names. Adele Laurie Blue was certainly something to remember.

Fortunately, Penny, who had been kept in hospital for only a day, didn't have to stay long in Queen's Drive either. She was rehoused in a two-bedroom council flat in Shelbourne Road, Tottenham. If the wind was blowing in the right direction, she could hear the Saturday roar from the crowd at White Hart Lane. The famous Spurs ground was less than a mile away down the ironically named Park Lane, which bears no resemblance to the famous West End thoroughfare that is a byword for opulence.

The sight of football fans wearing the black and white scarves of Tottenham Hotspur as they strode to the match was a familiar sight throughout Adele's childhood and helped generate a feeling of community in what was a drab neighbourhood. On match days, Shelbourne Road and the surrounding streets would be turned into one enormous car park.

The football club was somewhat in the shadow of neighbours Arsenal, but back in 1988 the prospects for the future seemed brighter with the signing of Paul Gascoigne from Newcastle for £2.2 million. Gazza helped them to finish sixth that season, but the champions were once again their North London rivals – much to the delight of the Adkins family.

Tottenham, at that time, would have won votes in a contest to decide the least attractive place to live in England. Much of the negativity came from the fallout from the notorious Broadwater Farm riots in October 1985. Penny was still a schoolgirl when the disenchanted young black men of the neighbourhood took to the streets following the death of local mum Cynthia Jarrett. She died from a heart attack when four police officers arrived unannounced to search her home in nearby Thorpe Road. During the subsequent unrest, which included the use of guns and petrol bombs, a policeman, PC Keith Blakelock, was hacked to death.

Marc helped Penny move in to an upstairs unfurnished flat in a street that had little to recommend it. It would be home to her and her daughter for the next nine years. An elderly couple, Henry and Jane Barley, lived downstairs and, in the years to come, they would watch Adele if her mother had to pop out. Marc wasn't living there at first. About a month after they had settled in, he gave up his own place and joined them.

Together the new family took the train to Penarth to introduce Adele to her Welsh grandparents. Penny could be forgiven for being apprehensive. She had never met Marc's parents before and here she was arriving on the doorstep with a baby in her arms. His mother, however, had a natural empathy with her. She'd had Marc when she was eighteen and understood perfectly what it was like to be a teenage mum. His father, too, appreciated the difficulties of being young parents starting out in life.

Marc recalled, 'My mum was very gooey about the baby, while my father was more like, "Oh, very nice", because all babies look the same, don't they? It was very daunting for

Penny, as you can imagine, but they are very easy-going and laid-back people and they made her very welcome. She was relaxed within an hour and they were the best of friends from then on.'

South Wales would be a home from home for Adele over the coming years. Her Welsh grandparents were important people in her life and the frequent trips across the Severn Bridge were among the best times of her childhood.

Back in London, Penny set about turning the flat into the home she wanted, grabbing unwanted furniture from her sisters or searching vintage shops for a bargain. Adele has often described her mother as 'arty' and their flat reflected her taste. It helped that she could fill the wall space with her own work. Marc had his window-cleaning round and, in the early years, Penny claimed the benefits she was entitled to. Adele didn't go short of the things that every baby needs. As Marc observed, 'Penny was never skint. She had a huge family, she had me, she had my parents and she didn't want for anything.'

Penny is particularly close to her sisters, Kim and Nita, who have seven children between them. She also has two brothers, Gary and John Anthony. In total, Adele had something like thirteen cousins living in the Tottenham area, so there were always playmates growing up. She has often joked that she would visit her relations and enjoy the chaos of so many children playing together and then go home to her neat bedroom, where everything was in its place. Her room was never that tidy though.

Everyone clubbed together to buy Penny an old Citroën 2CV, one of those timeless designs with the roll-top roof, which perfectly suited a young woman with bohemian tastes.

She could strap her baby in and be round at her mum's or elder sisters' houses in a couple of minutes.

Marc was proud to be the dad of such a sweet baby, who didn't give her parents many sleepless nights. He liked nothing better than to come home and find Penny playing lullabies on her guitar to her sleeping daughter. 'She was very talented with a guitar,' he recalled.

All should have been set fair for the couple, but the reality was that they were two young people thrown together more by fate than compatibility. 'I loved Penny,' said Marc, 'but after a few months the chemistry began to go.' Eventually, when Adele was nine months old, they split up.

It had never been a secret that Marc was Adele's dad, but he wasn't named as the father on Adele's birth certificate. Penny told him she had left the space blank. A practical woman, she may or may not have been influenced by her need to move quickly up the housing ladder. Her decision didn't have an impact on their break-up in any way; in fact, it probably made it easier for them to resume separate lives. They remained on good terms with one another.

Marc didn't go far. He moved into a house share near The Flask pub in Highgate. He would still see plenty of Penny and Adele and would frequently stay over in Shelbourne Road. He never had a formal agreement with Penny about supporting her. If he had a good week, he would hand over a wad of cash or come bearing gifts of clothes and toys. And his father, who was quite well off by this time, gave Penny a monthly allowance to help out.

When Adele was a bit older, Marc would take her to the London Zoo in Regent's Park, which she loved. He recalled,

'She loved the monkeys most of all. To a child, they are naughty, aren't they?' Marc used to tease his daughter: 'I shall never forget one day at the zoo when she went to the loo, came out and saw that I had a scratch on my hand.'

'What happened to you, Dad?' asked Adele.

He replied, 'Well, the lion jumped over the fence and had me.'

'She looked at me, eyes wide, and said, "Oh did he, Dad?"'

There was never any question of Penny and Marc getting back together. He started going out with a school teacher and their relationship quickly became serious. When Adele was two, Marc's father asked him to go back to South Wales for the summer and help him run a takeaway outlet that he had taken for the season on Barry Island, a few miles along the coast from Penarth. Where Marc and his father were based later became famous as the setting for the popular comedy series *Gavin and Stacey*. Holidaymakers would queue up at one of three counters for burgers, hot dogs, ice cream, candy floss or sticks of rock and then eat them strolling along the front.

The first year was not a success, perhaps because of the decline in visitors to the resort, so at the end of the summer season Marc went back to London to be close to Adele and his friends. He also kept in close touch with his brother Richard, who was happily settled in the capital. They used to meet most weeks for a pint and a catch-up at the Punch and Judy. The following summer, Marc's father decided they should have another go with the Barry venture. The lease cost £18,000 for the season, so it wasn't something to be undertaken lightly. He asked Marc to take charge while he continued to run the plumbing business.

Penny brought her daughter down to see everyone and they stayed at the house in Penarth. Adele, who was now three, loved playing along the promenade or going to Rabaiotti's for one of their renowned knickerbocker glories. It was a huge treat for a little girl living in Tottenham. If he had the time, Marc would take her swimming. He had already taught her to swim at the local leisure centre, within walking distance of Shelbourne Road, and it's the one sport she enjoyed.

At the end of the summer, Marc decided not to return to London this time. He wanted to see how things would work out in South Wales. Life had moved on for both him and Penny. She now had a steady boyfriend, so the days of casually dropping in to see his ex and his daughter were at end. Penny was still only twenty-one and had her whole life in front of her. She was determined that having Adele to care for wasn't going to stop her living her life. They were a team.

2

SPICE WORLD

———

Just a week before her fourth birthday, in the spring of 1992, Adele was hidden inside Penny's trench coat and smuggled into the Brixton Academy in South London. They were there to watch The Beautiful South in concert. Looking back, Adele observed, 'It was amazing – my clearest memory of when I was little.'

The Beautiful South were a wry and quirky, yet very popular band formed in 1988 by two former members of The Housemartins, Paul Heaton and David Hemingway, who were both from Hull in Yorkshire. Two years later, their best-known single, 'A Little Time', was their only number one, but it established them as one of the leading chart acts of the decade. It's a feisty break-up song and easy to understand why it was a favourite of Penny's, as it expresses the need for a little time to 'find my freedom'.

Penny loved them and wanted her daughter to share the experience. The Academy is a standing venue, so Adele couldn't see anything. That problem was solved when Penny asked a well-muscled, bodybuilder type if he wouldn't mind putting her daughter on his shoulders. Adele now had the best view in the hall. The man also came to her rescue when a host of balloons were released and the little girl failed to grab one: 'He walked through the crowd and knocked someone out who wouldn't give me a balloon.'

When Paul Heaton finally met Adele in the autumn of 2015, he was flattered that she remembered the concert so well all those years later. 'She owes me the price of a ticket,' he joked. 'Unfortunately, it was only about £2 then.'

Although there was no great musical heritage in the Adkins family, Adele's home was always filled with music. Her mum would play guitar along with her favourite chart tracks and encourage Adele to get up on the sofa and sing.

It's easy to forget how young Penny was and these were the years she might have been enjoying college if fate had dealt a different hand. Adele has always appreciated that: 'She just thought I was amazing. She could have been at university but she chose to have me.' She once described her as being a 'hippy mum'.

Penny never treated Adele as an inconvenience but always as someone to be included in whatever was going on. She always had plenty of friends round to socialise into the night with music and good conversation, and she liked her daughter to be part of these happy times. Fortunately, Adele wasn't shy and enjoyed staying up.

On Friday nights, that also meant letting her watch *Later … with Jools Holland*, which was broadcast at 11.15 p.m. The relaxed and informal mix of big names performing next to virtual unknowns would prove to be an enduring success. The Kinks, for instance, rubbed shoulders with cutting-edge rapper

Neneh Cherry and La Polla Records, a Spanish Basque punk-rock band.

Mother and daughter forged a lifelong bond through sharing so many experiences, especially musical ones. Penny had no hesitation in loading up the Citroën and taking her daughter, then eight, to the Glastonbury Festival were they sat in the mud and watched Radiohead and The Prodigy on the main Pyramid Stage.

That was by no means Adele's first experience of a festival. She was an old hand by then. Closer to home, just after her fifth birthday, in June 1993, Penny took her to a one-day pop festival, Great Xpectations, in Finsbury Park. The event was a benefit to support the campaign to grant a permanent radio licence to the XFM station.

Damon Albarn and Graham Coxon from Britpop darlings Blur sang an acoustic version of the band's latest single 'For Tomorrow'. Damon is one of those people who drift in and out of the Adele story, not necessarily in a good way, but this was the first time she came across him. He wasn't top of the bill, however.

That honour fell to The Cure, led by the charismatic singer and songwriter Robert Smith. The band are one of the great survivors of British music, still hugely popular thirty-seven years after they began in the post-punk era of 1979. During Penny's teenage years, they were renowned for their dark and gothic sound that culminated in their most successful recording, *Disintegration*. Penny went through a Goth stage and was a huge fan of the group. Adele was a little unsure: 'I used to be really scared of Robert Smith because he looked like Edward Scissorhands.'

The album provided the soundtrack for Adele's Tottenham years. In particular, her mother's favourite track, 'Lovesong', stayed with her and reminded her of those days. Ironically, on that unseasonably cool June afternoon, The Cure didn't perform it, although they did play probably their best-known hit, 'Friday I'm in Love', as an encore.

The number one record that month was 'Dreams', the breakthrough hit for Gabrielle, a young black singer from Hackney with a silky smooth voice. Louise Gabrielle Bobb was refreshingly different. She wrote her own songs, had one of the most distinctive soulful voices in pop and was very much her own woman in a male-dominated industry – and she wore a sequinned eye patch to hide a drooping eyelid.

With her distinctive short black hair, she didn't look like your average pop star. She built the foundation of her career by singing in nightclubs. She explains, 'If there had been talent shows like *The X Factor* in the early 1990s, I would have done terribly! So, when success did come it was a real victory because I don't think anybody really expected it.'

Adele loved Gabrielle's eye patch so much that Penny knuckled down like any dutiful mother and made her daughter one of her own. Adele had a bout of conjunctivitis and when it was time for her to return to school once she was no longer infectious, Penny presented her with her custom-made patch. She had bought one in Boots and sewn on sequins. Adele would jump up onto the table wearing her eye patch and deliver her own version of 'Dreams'.

Gabrielle wore her famous eye patch for eight months before abandoning it; Adele wore hers for even less time. Its appeal was greatly reduced when she was teased at school. At the earliest opportunity, it was put in a drawer, only to be worn for special performances at home. Penny encouraged her to sing in front of her friends, even arranging the lighting in the house so it would seem as if the spotlight was on Adele while she sang.

The story of Gabrielle's life and career is fascinating, almost spookily so, when compared to Adele's. Her Dominican-born mother raised her and her three younger half-brothers as a single mum and chose not to name Gabrielle's father on the birth certificate. Gabrielle had regular contact with him when she was a child, but that dwindled as she grew older.

Gabrielle always had issues with her appearance, not just because of her eye, but also her weight. She was never a skinny, model type. She had a son in 1995 and subsequently regarded being a mum as more important than fame or fortune, although she is a multimillionaire and would never need to work again if she chose not to.

She wrote songs that reflected her mood, was discovered when an independent label heard her demo, released only three albums in the first six years of her career and liked to be in control of her own destiny, not at the beck and call of a record company. 'I was notorious for taking three years between albums. I love making music, but not 365 days a year. I'm probably just lazy, but I can't force myself to write songs. I have to long to be back in the studio and feel good vibes when I'm recording.'

Gabrielle never saw herself as a celebrity, preferring to slip quietly out of the limelight when she didn't have a record to promote – in a fashion remarkably similar to Adele at a later date. Her 'disappearance' led to the public wanting her more, so when her third album, *Rise*, came out in 1999, it went straight to number one, as did the single of the same name. It is a break-up song tinged with sadness, but one that is ultimately uplifting, '... ready to rise again'. Most of her songs have an autobiographical edge – 'diary entries' as she calls them.

Adele went to the Coleraine Park Primary School, just round the corner in Halefield Road. She once said she was the only white face in her classroom of thirty local children. That may be a slight exaggeration, but not by much. She may well have been the sole white English child. It was a very diverse community. During Adele's time in the 1990s, there were some eight major ethnic groups, but by the end of the following decade, there were forty-two ethnicities, with something like twenty-six different languages being spoken in the school.

Adele was popular, not least because she hated bullies. Marc recalled, 'Tottenham is a rough place, but if another kid was being picked on, then she would be the one sticking up for them. She was also very protective of her friends.'

She didn't stand out in class, and one talent her teachers may not have been aware of is that she wrote a lot, doodling little bits of rhyme and poetry, almost from the time she learned to write her own name. She was forever writing her mother little notes, especially if she had been told off for not tidying her room. Then she would shut herself away and push a note underneath the door to let her mum know that she wasn't coming out for a year. From a very early age, she was putting her feelings down on paper.

Every couple of months, mainly in the school holidays, Penny would load up the boot of the Citroën and drive down the M4 so they could stay with Nana and Grampy in Penarth. If she needed a break, Penny always knew she could leave Adele there, and her daughter would be loved and well cared for by her grandparents, whom she adored.

Grampy John became a father figure in Adele's life, simply by giving her so much time and attention. He doted on her. Marc explained, 'Adele would spend much of the summer with my parents and most of that time my dad would be playing with her, talking to her, showing her the sights.'

John was only in his mid-forties when Adele was born. Fit and energetic, he was a big man with a darker, more Celtic appearance than his two sons. He may not have looked like a traditional grandfather figure, but he held conventional values: 'He was a very hard-working man, my father – a very honest, straight-up sort of chap. He really was a lovely guy.'

John was also very fond of Penny. 'He just loved my mum,' recalled Adele. John and Rose didn't always wait for them to visit Penarth. Sometimes the proud grandparents would travel up to London and stay in a local B&B so they could see them both.

Adele was very fond of her mother's big family, but in Tottenham she was one of many, while in Penarth she was the centre of attention. Sometimes Adele would come down to visit with her best friend, her cousin Cema, who was Aunt Kim's daughter. Kim had married a Turkish man called Ahmet in 1982 and subsequently had four children, Bren, Cema-Filiz, Erol and Erden.

Occasionally, Penny and Adele would spend Christmas in South Wales, where the young girl was spoiled rotten. One of her earliest Christmas presents from her father was a red toy guitar, which she loved. She would often try to play Penny's grown-up guitar, but she was too little for that; here was something of her own.

These were happy times that Penny, in particular, always made fun for her daughter. One Christmas Eve, when Adele was asleep and Nana and Grampy had gone to bed, she carefully cut up a newspaper in the shape of feet and placed them on the stairs. When her daughter awoke in the morning, she said, 'Look, Adele, it's Santa's footprints. He's been.'

The great treat for Adele was in summer, when her grandparents would leave Penarth in their caravan. Marc, who would go too if he wasn't working, recalled, 'My mum and dad were very keen caravaners. They had a close group of friends. They were all caravaners and always had a laugh and a sing-song. My dad could be the life and soul. Adele loved it. She was a kid, wasn't she, and it was an adventure.'

They didn't go far, but it seemed like the open road to a girl from Tottenham. They would drive down the coast to stay at Three Cliffs Bay in the beautiful Gower peninsula or further along the coast at the Kiln Park camp in Tenby, one of the loveliest resorts in Pembrokeshire.

Adele was a kind and pretty, blonde-haired little girl with green eyes, and she made friends easily in South Wales. Many of the men and women that Marc had known all his life now had young families and they were very welcoming to the youngster from London. Her proud father observed, 'She was a lovely kid. She was one of those kids who, if she had a bag of sweets, would give them all away and keep one for herself.'

She tended to be on the skinny side, even though she wasn't sporty. She was not a girly girl. 'She was funny and very sociable,' said Marc. 'She was more of a tomboy type than a girl with dolls. She was a scruffy yo-yo.'

Not everything was idyllic. On one memorable day in Tenby, Adele went missing. One moment, she was bouncing away on a trampoline; the next, nobody could see her, which prompted a frantic search. Marc had been windsurfing at the top of the beach. When he got back to his parents and his girlfriend, he asked, 'Where's Adele?' She had vanished.

Marc panicked. 'Imagine your child has gone missing on a packed beach. It's terrifying, isn't it? My mum is crying and screaming. There were sand dunes behind us and there were two old winos there and so I marched straight over and demanded to know where my daughter was. It was mayhem. So then I went straight to the nearest chip bar and I said, "Can I use your phone?" So I dialled 999 and fair dos to the police, they were there in five minutes.

'Everybody was panicking now. So I sat down, took a deep breath and I thought, "Where is the little bugger?" Then I remembered the boat. We were on a boat trip the day before, so I made my way towards there. This woman came up to me and said, "Are you looking for a little girl in a yellow and pink dress?" She pointed me towards the landing point for the boat and there was Adele, just playing by the seaside. I picked her up and as you do out of fear and relief, I smacked her arse for her. And she cried and cried. She didn't speak to me for days.'

While Penny was filling her home with the cool sounds of the time – 10,000 Maniacs and Jeff Buckley, as well as The Cure – the young Adele was falling for the acts that were causing a ripple in the playground. In the summer of 1996 that meant only one group for young girls: the Spice Girls.

Adele was soon dancing around the bedroom singing 'Wannabe', the band's first record-breaking number one in July. Adele was among the millions around the world who could sing the song word perfectly without having any idea what 'zig-a-zig-ah' meant. She proved the point nearly twenty years later when she sang a spontaneous version with James Corden for his chat show's 'Carpool Karaoke' feature.

For a while, the Spice Girls were the biggest band in the world, effortlessly breaking America with their energy, pin-sharp image and consumer-friendly brand of Girl Power. In Geri Halliwell, they found someone with a drive and flair for publicity that was completely new for female pop stars. Adele was transfixed by her fire and energy: 'I just remember seeing Geri and being like, "Fuck it, I'm going to do that. I want to be Ginger Spice."'

Ginger was Adele's favourite, although, when she left the group, Adele switched her allegiance to Mel B (Scary Spice), who was equally mouthy and in your face. Despite being so young, Adele was inspired by the whole 'Girl Power' movement. The Golden Rules of Girl Power as defined by the Spice Girls were:

Be positive.
Be strong!
Don't let anyone put you down.
Be in control of your own life and your destiny.
Support your girlfriends, and let them support you too.
Say what's on your mind.

Approach life with attitude.
Don't let anyone tell you that you can never do
something because you're a girl.
Have fun.

They could easily be the principles of Adele's own life. To this day, the Spice Girls remain Adele's favourite group. They did shape their own destiny, wrote their songs – or at least had important co-writing credits – and earned a huge amount of money very quickly. 'Wannabe' remains the biggest-selling single ever by a girl group, shifting more than seven million copies. It was number one in twenty-two countries, including the US, where it was top of the charts for four weeks.

The Spice Girls were a manufactured group, however, in much the same way as Girls Aloud and, more recently, Little Mix and One Direction, except for the fact that their audition process wasn't televised for a TV talent show. There was another aspect that would catch the attention of Adele: three of them went to stage schools or 'fame academies', as they were popularly known. Before she became Posh Spice, Victoria Adams had attended Laine Theatre Arts in Epsom. Melanie Chisholm (Mel C/Sporty Spice) was sixteen when she was accepted at the Doreen Bird School of Performing Arts in Sidcup. Emma Bunton (Baby Spice) was given a scholarship to the Sylvia Young Theatre School in Marylebone. They would probably have all ended up at the BRIT School if it had existed in 1990.

Her father was unimpressed when Adele visited South Wales and told him of her enthusiasm for the Spice Girls: 'They were her heroes but I used to take the mickey out of her about it. I used to say they were terrible, bloody awful.' Fortunately, his lack of enthusiasm for Girl Power didn't discourage his daughter.

By this time, the dynamic of Adele's visits to Penarth had changed. Her grandparents were still there to fuss over her, but her father had a son, her half-brother Cameron. This time Marc was included on the birth certificate, although subsequently Cameron took the surname of his mother, Siobhan O'Sullivan. Marc set up home with them in Llantwit Major, a small resort seventeen miles west of Penarth.

Adele was thrilled to meet her little brother and, despite an age gap of seven years, has always been fond of Cameron in the manner of a big sister who's the boss. 'He looks like my twin,' she happily observed. 'We're identical, same hair and everything. It's bizarre growing up in a completely different city but then, when you see each other, it's as if you've spent every day of your lives together.'

Adele got on fine with her father's new family and occasionally would stay with them, but more usually she remained in Penarth with Nana and Grampy. Her legion of cousins grew even larger when Uncle Richard, who was still in London, started a family and had a son called Jasper, whom she also saw from time to time.

Marc, meanwhile, flitted from job to job. He worked another season in Barry before setting up a flower stall in Penarth. He subsequently went back to plumbing – this time on his own in Llantwit Major, not the family business.

Penny and Adele were on the move too: they relocated to Brighton. Adele still refers to herself as a Tottenham girl, but she hasn't lived there since she was nine years old. Leaving

Tottenham was one of two important events in Adele's young life that would spell the end of her childhood. She commented, 'I had a great childhood. I was very loved.'

Bizarrely, they cleared out of the flat in Shelbourne Road so abruptly that they left all sorts of possessions stashed away in the loft, including Adele's electric guitar, suitable for ages six and up, which had a 'special singalong head microphone for a really professional performance', a keyboard, her tricycle and her birth card from the National Childbirth Trust.

It was a dramatic move for them both, leaving behind the security of close family in Tottenham. It meant an end to whiling away afternoons strolling on the banks of the River Lea to visit cousins. The river, which rises in the Chiltern Hills near Luton and flows through Tottenham on its way to the Thames, figured large in Adele's childhood memories and is the title of one of the songs on the album *25*. 'It's a filthy river,' she once said with some affection.

Penny thought they would be happier in the trendy coastal town, which enjoyed a reputation as a centre for artistic pursuits. She had met an older man who owned a furniture shop and she went to work there, not only serving customers, but also taking a keen interest in furniture design.

Mother and daughter settled into a large flat in a Georgian house in East Drive, right next to the agreeable Queen's Park, which boasts a large pond, ideal for feeding ducks, and a ten-minute walk from the seafront. Brighton should have been ideal for Adele, especially as she was so fond of Penarth. She hated it, however, complaining, 'The people seemed really pretentious and posh, and there were no black people there.'

She was delighted when her mother embarked on a much more serious relationship and moved back to London. They settled in Brixton, near the border with Streatham in Cotherstone Road, an unpretentious urban street. They moved in with Penny's new boyfriend, Simon, who worked as a computer programmer and became the stepfather in Adele's life. He had been brought up in the Home Counties before starting his career in London.

Penny took him and Adele to meet the Welsh side of her daughter's family and he impressed everyone with his easy-going, friendly nature. Marc Evans thought he was 'a lovely, lovely chap'. He observed, 'He was a really mellow guy. Nothing would faze him. He would just let it go over his head – he was that type of fellow.'

Adele was much happier back in the city until a second significant event occurred that was the most traumatic of her young life to date.

John Evans, her beloved Grampy, had been diagnosed with bowel cancer and the prognosis was poor. He was admitted to the Velindre Cancer Centre in Whitchurch, Cardiff, just before her eleventh birthday in May 1999.

Penny drove Adele up to see him several times during the last weeks as he slipped away. It was very hard for the young girl to cope. She recalled, 'I was so uncomfortable with it that I nicked his wheelchair and was just going up and down the hospital corridors because I couldn't face the fact that the love of my life, my granddad, was dying. I wish that I'd sat with him on the bed and given him a cuddle and told him how much I loved him, but I was just too overwhelmed.'

He died, aged fifty-seven, on 23 May and Adele was absolutely devastated. She said, movingly, 'I painted him as this Jesus figure in my life. I loved him so much, more than the world.'

Despite being so grief-stricken, Adele bravely went with Penny to the funeral at the Tabernacle Baptist Church in Penarth. She wanted to be there not just for herself but also for her grandmother: 'My grampy and my nana had always been my ideal relationship – ideal friendship, companionship, everything. Even though I'm sure there's loads of shit I don't know about, as their granddaughter it was bliss, just heaven. I was so, so sad.'

Even though she coped well on the day, Adele didn't seem to be able to get over her sense of desolation. After a few weeks, her worried mother decided to seek professional help and took Adele to see a counsellor experienced in dealing with bereavement in children. Adele, it became clear, was a far more sensitive girl than people realised. She needed time to work through her feelings. It perhaps goes some way to explaining her heartfelt and intense response to the trauma of breaking up with people she loved – a mixture of anger and regret at being left and a heightened sense of loss.

Seeking something positive from her unhappiness, Adele told her mother that she was going to be a heart surgeon. She revealed her ambition: 'I wanted to fix people's hearts.'

3

THE MISEDUCATION OF
ADELE ADKINS

———

Adele's ambitions tended not to last long. Her mother was used to her wanting to be all sorts of things as she grew up. She had as many passing fancies as any other girl. At various stages, she wanted to be a weathergirl, a ballet dancer, a fashion writer and a saxophone player. Her mum would try to find a local class that might help, only to discover, as many parents do, that the following week it was all forgotten. Adele appreciated the support and encouragement: 'She has always said, "Do what you want, and, if you're happy, I'm happy."' She was certainly more content in an urban environment where she could make friends easily.

Adele may have wanted to be a Spice Girl, but she was never one to announce loudly in class that she was going to be a star. Her musical taste was evolving, however. Simon came home one day with a present for her – a video of the movie *Flubber*, starring Robin Williams. It was great fun, but after watching it a couple of times, the invention of a magic gel began to lose its appeal. At the same time, he had brought Penny a copy of the ground-breaking album *The Miseducation of Lauryn Hill*, the first solo album from the acclaimed singer of The Fugees. Penny played it constantly and soon Adele found herself singing along with the help of the lyrics sheet: 'I remember having the sleeve notes and reading every lyric and not understanding half of them and just thinking, "When am I going to be that passionate about something to write a record about it?", even though at that age I didn't know that I was going to make a record when I was older.'

Her mum heard her singing Lauryn's break-up song 'Ex-Factor' one day and asked her daughter if she understood what it was about. Adele had to admit that she didn't have a clue. She did, however, understand the anguish in certain love songs: 'I always loved the ones about horrible relationships. Those were the ones you could relate to and that always made you cry.' Ironically, the song expressed painful sentiments that she would come to appreciate all too well in her future relationships, especially when Lauryn exclaims that 'no one's hurt me more than you and no one ever will'.

Adele was growing up fast in her inner-city surroundings. She and Penny had moved with Simon to a bigger flat in Tierney Road, close to the South Circular Road in Streatham Hill. They went less often to South Wales. Marc Evans explained, 'She didn't like to come to the house in Penarth so much after Dad died.' She still kept in close touch with her beloved nana – and would continue to do so – but her memories were still very painful. She had seen less of her father during the previous couple of years, largely because he had a new family and a young son to support.

In any case, Marc was struggling to deal with his own series of traumatic events. Shortly after his father passed, his best friend Nigel died suddenly, aged twenty-nine. His relationship with Siobhan came to an abrupt end, so he left the home in Llantwit Major and, by his own admission, drowned his sorrows in far too much alcohol. He could offer no support or care to his daughter.

He took over the family business for a while, before taking a job fitting pipes on cruise ships. He grabbed the chance to see the world at a painful time in his life. He sent his children postcards from around the globe – South Korea, Malaysia, Singapore, Canada, the USA and the Mediterranean. It sounded glamorous that their dad was sailing down the Indian Ocean, especially when they heard his tales of pirates roaming the high seas. He always made sure he brought them back souvenirs from his trips away.

Back in South London, Adele was mixing with a much cooler group of friends. Until the age of eleven, she was influenced by what was in the charts – a top-ten girl listening to Britney, Backstreet Boys and Take That, as well as her favourite girl group. But as senior school approached, it became trendier to embrace R&B and Adele discovered new sounds in Penny's collection – black artists with big soulful voices. As well as Lauryn Hill, she liked Mary J. Blige, Faith Evans, Faith Hill and, most of all, Beyoncé. During break time, she and her friends would have sing-offs, belting out 'Survivor' and 'Say My Name' at the top of their voices. She admitted, 'I used to try and sound like Beyoncé and I would sing her Destiny's Child songs all the time. Running with an R&B crowd was the easiest way to fit in and be considered hip.' In the comfort of her own bedroom in Tierney Road, though, when there were no friends to impress, she would still have a sneaky listen to 'Wannabe'.

There was a chance of a last hurrah for Adele Adkins, heart surgeon, when she began Year 7 at the Chestnut Grove School in Balham, a mile and a half away. She was enthusiastic about biology lessons, anxious to gather as much knowledge as she could for her chosen career. But she was surrounded by apathy and negativity and soon preferred to hang out with her girl-friends or simply play truant. 'I gave up on it. My heart wasn't in it,' she remembered with unintentional humour.

Chestnut Grove is now one of the best and most in-demand academies in the area, but then it was much rougher. It was a 'crap comprehensive', according to Adele. It progressed rapidly under the leadership of head Margaret Peacock, who oversaw it becoming the country's first visual arts college and achieving 'Outstanding' status in a 2008 Ofsted Report. You would have thought its emphasis on the arts would have been perfect for Adele, but she has stated in no uncertain terms that she hated it: 'There were no aspirations and no encouragement there for anything other than getting to the end and getting pregnant.'

Such disenchantment is not what her deputy headmaster, Dominic Bergin, remembered about her: 'She was just a very nice girl. I first met her in Year 8 and she was a real lively girl. She was friendly and she was bubbly. She was always a big personality. My wife Claudette used to teach her English and said she was kind, hard-working, motivated and academically able.'

Mr Bergin does, however, remember Adele as being a bit grungy. 'She used to wear big canvas late-Nineties grunge trousers,' like many girls at the time. That may have been her fashion of choice, but she also wore brand new Nike trainers and a baseball cap.

Chestnut Grove, undeniably, didn't spot Adele's potential. Mr Bergin concedes they would have done more to nurture her if they had. One of her complaints was that she wanted to sing and perform at school, but wasn't encouraged to do so. Instead, she was told that she couldn't become part of the choir without taking clarinet lessons. She recalled, 'They gave me a really hard time.' This doesn't sound like the whole story, because Adele was showing signs of being musically proficient, more than just vocally. Learning the clarinet would actually serve her well in the future.

She was becoming more of a 'street' girl. Despite her natural desire to want to belong in her home patch of Brixton and Streatham, Adele never went off the rails. She gave the gang culture a wide berth and, as she has stridently asserted, 'never touched an illegal drug in her life' – not even a sly puff of something aromatic at a party. Her explanation for resisting the everyday vices of urban life is disarmingly simple: 'There was never anything I was embarrassed about with my mum, which I think is the reason I never rebelled. We always spoke about everything.' Another good reason was that she didn't want any news of misbehaviour to reach her nana's ears in South Wales. Drugs were a particularly sensitive subject: 'We had a family death from heroin when I was younger and it frightens me, the whole thing.' She has never elaborated on this out of respect for those most affected by the distressing turn of events.

The one temptation Adele did give in to, at the age of thirteen, was smoking – she loved it. She liked nothing better than gathering with her friends in Brockwell Park, which was a mile or so away, to talk and smoke her preferred 'rollies' before drifting home. Adele smoked a lot.

Penny was young and enlightened enough to want Adele to find her own feet, so she didn't judge or interfere when her daughter was, at various time, a grunger, a rude girl, a skater and a nu-metaller. She was more concerned when Adele was sent home from school for fighting – a spat about *Pop Idol* of all things.

The autumn of 2001 saw the first series of the talent show that launched Simon Cowell on the nation. Unusually for a young teenage girl, Adele was instantly a huge fan of Will Young, not Gareth Gates, who had pin-up looks and was clear favourite to win. She recalled, 'I was obsessed. Will Young was my first proper love.'

Tensions were running high in the corridors of Chestnut Grove, especially as Adele seemed to be in a gang of one where Will was concerned: 'The Gareth Gates fans were horrible to me and I wasn't having any of it. We had a fight and I was called into the head teacher's office and sent home. It was serious.'

At least Adele had the satisfaction of seeing Will pull off a surprise win in the competition. She eventually met him when they appeared on the same bill in 2007: 'It was so embarrassing. The first thing that came out of my mouth was "I voted for you 5,000 times."'

Adele was in danger of drifting aimlessly through her teenage years, her future threatened by poor attendance at school and a lack of direction and purpose. All she knew was that she wanted to pursue music professionally.

She had no desire to follow in Will Young's footsteps and try to win *Pop Idol*. She may have thought he was terrific, but she was unimpressed by much of what she saw on the show. The problem, as she saw it, was that kids were being given false hope by their parents. It even made her mistrust the nice things Penny was saying about her singing.

'You've got all their parents, and they're like, "Yeah, she's the next Whitney, the next Mariah." And then they go on and they're shit. So when my mum was saying that, I was like, "Oh yeah, you're trying to con me. You're trying to get me to make a fool of myself."' In any case, as the rules stood at the time, she was too young and would have to wait a couple of years.

Adele was still only thirteen, and doing her best impression of a bolshie teenager, when someone whose opinion she valued praised her. A friend of her mother's, who, according to Adele, was an 'amazing Faith Evans-type singer', heard her singing one night at the flat. She was sufficiently impressed to insist that Adele should pursue her singing seriously. Adele didn't need much persuading. She was well aware that music was the only career she wished to have.

Penny was enthusiastic, but wasn't sure how to proceed. As Adele explained, 'While my mum is the most supportive mum on Earth, she wouldn't have known how to channel me. With her I'd probably have gone the classical music route, or maybe Disney, or musical theatre.'

Fortunately, the solution was a short train ride away in a suburb of Croydon called Selhurst. The BRIT School was the only free performing arts school in the country and it would change Adele's life for ever.

4

TRUE BRIT

Adele's reaction was forthright when it was first suggested she might apply to the BRIT School for Performing Arts & Technology. 'I'm not going there!' she bellowed. 'It's a fucking stage school. I can make it on my own.'

She might, at a pinch, have considered going to the Sylvia Young Theatre School on the grounds that Emma Bunton had blossomed there. That was a non-starter, though, because her mother couldn't afford the fees. Further investigation revealed that the BRIT School cost nothing, although you needed to pass an audition to be accepted for a place. It was basically a state comprehensive with a twist. It would mean she could leave Chestnut Grove – and that was certainly a good thing as far as she was concerned.

The BRIT School was founded in 1991, but, a decade later, was hardly the household name it is today. It was the brainchild of an educational entrepreneur, Mark Featherstone-Witty, who saw the possibilities for a charitable performing arts school in London after watching the Oscar-winning 1980 film *Fame*. Alan Parker's invigorating and inspiring tale of life in the New

York High School of Performing Arts was so popular that it gave rise to a TV series that ran for five years. Cast members formed The Kids from *Fame* and had a number one album.

Featherstone-Witty persuaded George Martin, the celebrated producer of The Beatles, to back his idea. Martin's support and enthusiasm proved so influential in getting things up and running that he was described as the 'Godfather of the BRIT School'.

The other key figure was Richard Branson, whom George Martin brought on board. In the early days, the boss of Virgin was the public face of the project, initially called the London School of Performing Arts and Technology. He insisted that other record companies, as well as his own, contribute to the new venture.

Politically, the time was right for such a school and the Conservative government backed the idea for state funding as part of their City Technology College (CTC) scheme. The impetus it needed came when the record industry signed up as its sponsor.

The British Record Industry Trust (BRIT) gave the school its catchy name and has contributed in excess of £7 million during the last twenty-five years. The school is partly funded from the profits from the annual BRIT Awards, which makes it rather fitting when old pupils clean up on the night. It also raises a great deal of money through student performances at venues including the Roundhouse in North London, a favourite of Adele's because it was close to the vintage stalls of Camden Market.

The school principal when Adele submitted the long and detailed application was Nick Williams, a career educationalist who mostly left the teaching to his artistic faculty. His task was to disprove the famous observation of Margaret Thatcher that she didn't want a 'school for unemployed artists'.

Perhaps perversely, his job at a school that many perceived to be a fame academy was to dampen aspirations: 'Students think that you expect them to want to be famous. It's just a view that has something to do with celebrity culture or with what a fame school is, and we aren't any of these things. We almost have to say to pupils, "We don't expect you to be successful." We get their feet on the ground and make them realistic.'

The priority for Penny Adkins was to make sure her daughter was happy and had the opportunity to do what she wanted. The BRIT School might be the answer, but first Adele had to be accepted. Competition was fierce even before it could boast of alumni who were household names. Her application was strong enough to be selected for the next part of the process. The school had been impressed by the articulate and mature way she described herself as 'someone who is dedicated to music purely through love and passion for it'.

She wrote that she was willing and able to explore different styles of singing, playing and performing. She told the school that she was interested in arranging music, because it would 'help me to build on my songwriting both musically and lyrically'. This was not the work of a typical thirteen-year-old. Her personal insight shone through when she described herself as someone who will 'keep trying until I am completely satisfied with what I have created'.

She was invited to an open day in the autumn of 2001. The BRIT School then consisted of two main buildings. A red-bricked former high school for girls, built in 1907, housed the classrooms for the core curriculum subjects, such as maths and English. The music department was across the recreation ground in a more modern pavilion with an inviting glass-fronted atrium, which students would drift into at 9 a.m. to start the day.

As is often the case with open days, Adele was assigned a student in the year above to look after her and chat about life at the school. She was shown around by an aspiring singer called Beverly Tawiah, from Battersea, who filled her with enthusiasm. 'She really encouraged me and she was a brilliant singer. I thought, "That's it. I'm coming here."'

Tawiah may not yet be a star, but she is a much-in-demand singer, working with, among others, Mark Ronson. It is a fact of the music business that it is far harder to be noticed as a black female soul singer, however excellent, than it is as a white one.

The open day was one part of the process; her audition interview was the next. A couple of hundred applicants were chasing twenty-four places. The new deputy head of music, Liz Penney, remembers that Adele, thanks to alphabetical order, was the first prospective student she interviewed when the admission process began in January 2002. She had no idea what general standard to expect.

Adele, who was not yet fourteen, sang 'Free' by Stevie Wonder, one of the lesser known, soulful ballads on his 1987 album *Characters*. It's not an easy song to perform, requiring vocal dexterity and a strong lower register. She then played 'Tumbledown Blues' by James Rae on the clarinet, a classic study piece. She wasn't in love with the instrument, even though she had progressed to Grade 5. This was a decent achievement, but nothing that made her stand out from the crowd.

'I didn't see her play the clarinet after that,' says Liz, 'but I remember thinking she can play as well, so she must have had a little tuition. But when she opened her mouth to sing, I thought, "Well, that's a larger voice than you would expect from a thirteen-year-old." I immediately said to myself, "Oh yes, she's in."' Liz asked the teenager why she thought she should be given a place at the school. 'Because I am creative,' responded Adele.

Penny came along to support her daughter and immediately impressed Liz: 'I remembered meeting her mum on that first occasion because she is called Penny and my surname is Penney. So we were the two Pennies. And she is, I think, exactly the same age as me, so it was a bit like, "This could be my daughter." It was clear she was going to be a supportive parent. She knew exactly what Adele was applying for. It wasn't just an idea of "Oh, I want to go to the BRIT School". Her daughter was here to learn her craft. Sometimes you sort of build a relationship with some parents and not with others. Penny was one of the former. She came to every show.'

Adele's stepfather Simon would join them for parents' evenings and he encouraged her throughout her four years at the BRIT School, even though his relationship with Penny was coming to an end. The teachers always thought he was Adele's real father.

The BRIT School takes pupils either at fourteen or two years later. For Adele, it would mean two years of mostly ordinary school, with Thursdays devoted to pursuing her specialist strand. The options included theatre, musical theatre, dance, film and media or visual arts and design. For Adele, the choice was always going to be music.

She began the new phase of her life in September 2002. On the home front, there was change as well. Penny and Simon split up and she and Adele moved to West Norwood, no more than one and a half miles away, two minutes round the South Circular Road. Simon was still very much part of their lives, but he and Penny no longer lived together.

West Norwood is one of those districts of London that you need a sat nav to find. Nobody really knows where it is, although it is in the main catchment area for the BRIT School. It's actually between Streatham and Dulwich in SE27. Soon after Penny and Adele moved to the area, there was some amusing banter in the newspapers about local residents pretending that they lived in Dulwich Village, less than a ten-minute walk away. Nothing could be further from the truth. All over London, million-pound neighbourhoods stand shoulder to shoulder with impoverished streets and bleak estates. Nowhere is this more starkly evident than in this enclave of south-east London.

Tom Utley of the *Daily Mail*, who has lived there for many years, described West Norwood as reeking of 'failure and frustrated hopes'. He continued, 'Everything about the place – its uneven pavements, carved up by the cable-television companies, its net curtains, peeling paintwork, weed-infested gardens and its whiffy kebab shops – is shabby and suburban.'

Penny first found a flat in a building containing four apartments in Chestnut Road, one of the streets of large detached houses off the Norwood Road. These were the streets that appealed to young couples with growing families who had aspirations for something better. One attraction of their new neighbourhood was that they were close to the overground station and it was easy for Adele to commute to school.

They stayed only a few months before Penny found a larger flat above the Co-op on the main road. It wasn't exactly a step up. The security guard at the store told women in the neighbourhood to take care at night because the area was a 'war zone'. He wasn't exaggerating.

The gangs would drift down to the main road from the notorious York Road estate to deal and take drugs outside the Texaco petrol station next to Adele's building. On any given day, a local shopkeeper might be the subject of 'steaming', when one of the gangs would rush into a shop, stripping it of everything they could lay their hands on.

The seedier side of the neighbourhood was represented by a 'massage parlour' close to the railway station. Always there was the undercurrent of violence and menace. In one grisly incident that became the subject of local legend, someone was stabbed to death in a fast-food restaurant and his body left in the freezer.

On any given morning, commuters waiting on platform 1 at the overground station in West Norwood would see a young teenager in a Goth studded collar and parachute pants giving her full concentration to *heat* magazine or the latest edition of *i-D*, the style bible for modern youth culture. It was Adele on her half-hour commute to school.

You wouldn't see her every morning. In the aftermath of her unhappy time at her first high school, she still had trouble getting out of bed. Gradually, the BRIT School and, most importantly, the other students won her round. She explained, 'Whereas before I was going to a school with bums and kids that were rude and wanted to grow up and mug people, it was really inspiring to wake up every day to go to school with kids that actually wanted to be productive at something and wanted to *be* somebody.'

Her favourite day of the week was Thursday, when five solid hours were dedicated to music. At the BRIT School, it wasn't simply a case of there being no fees: all the equipment, the musical instruments and the rehearsal rooms were free as well. So when classes were over for the day, it meant personal time to get on with projects and practice.

Liz Penney noticed Adele's commitment right from the start. Liz was forever passing her in the corridor 'working by herself, writing lyrics, picking up her guitar and learning to accompany herself'.

Simon had bought her a 'really nice' Simon & Patrick acoustic guitar. Hand-crafted at the Godin factory in Quebec, Canada, it was a superior instrument. Pete Townshend, one of the greatest of all pop guitarists, strummed a few chords when she let him try it a few years later. 'It's a beautiful guitar,' he told her.

She wasn't sorry to give up the clarinet, and for a while took up the saxophone, which she found easy to play. She enjoyed belting out a tune and would take it home to practice. Her next-door neighbour, who happened to be a singer, was impressed when she heard Adele rehearsing.

Shingai Shoniwa, by coincidence, was a former BRIT School pupil. She had studied theatre, but switched to music when she joined forces with another student, guitarist Dan

Smith. Together they formed a band called Noisettes. They built up an enthusiastic live following before landing a record deal in 2005 and finally releasing their first album two years later. They had a chart breakthrough in 2009, when the single 'Don't Upset the Rhythm (Go Baby Go)' reached number two.

The two South London girls became firm friends, sharing a love and enthusiasm for music, even though Shingai was more than six years older than Adele. Shingai looked like an African supermodel. She was fashionable and flamboyant, but had a voice that Adele thought was terrific: 'When she was rehearsing, I used to press my ear against the wall to listen.' When opportunity allowed, she would pop next door to see Shingai and they would spend the evening jamming together. By this time, Penny and Simon had bought Adele a piano and sometimes Shingai would bring some drums over to hers. It was part of Adele's musical education. The older woman joked, 'Awesome days. They should put up two blue plaques!'

Adele stopped playing the saxophone when she found too many rollies weren't helping her breath control. In any case, she preferred using her guitar to compose her own songs, which pupils at the BRIT School were encouraged to do.

Liz Penney was by no means the only teacher who appreciated that Adele had something extra. Stuart Worden, the current principal, but then assistant to Nick Williams, recalls noticing Adele for the first time in a Year 10 history class: 'I popped my head in to see what was going on and they were studying the civil rights movement. I mentioned Billie Holiday's "Strange Fruit" and this girl said: "I love Billie Holiday." No fourteen-year-old loved Billie Holiday! I wondered who this girl was, listening to such sophisticated music at such a young age.' Adele then engaged Stuart in conversation, telling him she was also a fan of Eminem. He thought it was a nice mix for her to be a fan of classic jazz and 'a rapper with a spark and anger about him'.

As a teenager, Adele was far more intelligent and culturally aware than she likes to let on. One of her classmates observes, 'She was very smart!' Liz confirms, 'She was very bright. She always looked older than she was, so it was easy to forget that she was pretty much the youngest in her year. You might think she'd struggle and be behind the others, but she did not struggle at all. She is very quick witted. Some of the students were very able performers but struggled with the academic, literacy side of things, but Adele didn't.

'The thing about Adele is she was quick. She didn't need telling loads of times. She would just go off and, you know, do it. She also had very grown-up handwriting. Her work always looked like a sixth-form student rather than a thirteen- or fourteen-year-old.'

Adele didn't turn into a nerd the moment she went through the doors of the BRIT School. As Liz Penney tactfully put it, 'Sometimes she worked hard and sometimes she worked not so hard.' In other words, she embraced being a teenager with gusto.

She made friends easily with other students who were older than her. She already knew Tawiah from the open day and the elder girl would try to watch out for her: 'Adele was always cool and shit. She was like my little one.'

Tawiah would look for Adele at Clapham Junction when they changed trains in the morning. Often she would be with another girl, Kate Nash, who was also in the year above but specialised in theatre. She would be destined for great things in a career that mirrored Adele's for a while. At this stage, the two girls, who were only nine months apart in age, simply made each other laugh.

Adele's best friend, however, was an extroverted teenager from Brixton, down the road from her old stamping ground. Laura Dockrill, also a close friend of Kate's, is two years older than Adele, but they shared the same approach to urban life and embraced its unpredictability. Laura observed, 'I love the pure mix-up of people; you can never stereotype a road in South London.'

Laura's favourite childhood memory was of her father driving the family to Battersea Park, where everyone would 'pour out with bikes and breadsticks'. Her father was a prop man and she loved the ever-changing view of people as he whizzed about collecting and picking up all manner of objects around central London, people watching and eating crisps in cheap cafés.

Laura had an imaginative view of the world and, crucially for her friendship with Adele, the two teenagers weren't in competition to become the world's greatest singer. Laura studied theatre with Kate. She is a talented artist, performance poet and writer, and an example of the diverse nature of students at the BRIT School. She found her inspiration walking around her beloved hometown, declaring, 'I love watching, listening and thinking.' It's easy to imagine such an outlook on life having a significant influence on her younger friend.

The two teenagers shared a love of vintage clothes and big dangly earrings – the kind made famous by Pat Butcher in

EastEnders. They didn't agree on everything, however, particularly where designer labels were concerned. Adele, for instance, loved Burberry, but Laura preferred clothes that were one-offs.

With her new set of friends, Adele enjoyed what London had to offer. A trip to watch the first UK tour by the American singer Pink at the Brixton Academy proved an eye-opener. It was the first time she was impressed by the sheer power of a live performance. Pink had a fine voice but sang songs that were accessible to chart followers. Adele explained, 'I had never heard, being in the room, someone sing like that live. I remember sort of feeling like I was in a wind tunnel, her voice just hitting me. It was incredible.'

While the Pink show had a profound effect on Adele's understanding of performing live, an even more significant event in her musical development occurred when she was mooching around Oxford Street one Saturday afternoon and drifted aimlessly into the HMV store.

She received £10 a week pocket money from Penny, so, after investigating the new chart CDs that she couldn't afford, she rummaged through the bargain bin, emerging with two for a fiver. She didn't know it then, but one of them would be of huge importance to her.

The first CD was by jazz great Ella Fitzgerald and the second by Etta James. Etta was one of the most lauded and influential female singers of the past fifty years, but Adele had never heard of her. She chose it for two reasons: first, she was careful with money and loved a bargain – a trait she had inherited from her mother when they had to watch the pennies; secondly, she thought Etta had beautiful cat-like eyes and fabulous hair, although it was one of the blonde wigs she invariably wore.

Adele pictured herself with hair like that and figured that if she took the cover photograph into the hairdresser's, they could copy the style. It seemed like a good idea at the time, but when she got home, she idly tossed the albums onto a shelf and forgot all about them.

About a year later, when she was fifteen, she finally got around to listening to them. She liked Ella, because it was impossible not to, but she absolutely loved the rasping, raw power of Etta James: 'I found that her delivery was just so sincere that she really could convince me she was singing directly to me. Which is something I had never ever found in any other artist.'

Adele looked at the ordinary London girls she loved growing up, such as Gabrielle and Emma Bunton, and believed she could be them. There wasn't much she shared with Jamesetta Hawkins, who changed her name to Etta James when she recorded the defiantly risqué and subsequently banned 'Roll with Me, Henry' in 1955.

Etta never knew her father, although she suspected he was the famous pool shark Minnesota Fats. Her fourteen-year-old mother gave her up for adoption, but when she re-entered Etta's life, she turned out to be a hustler who ended up in jail. Violence, prejudice and serious drug abuse became the staples of a hard life. It didn't help that Etta was continually ripped off by unscrupulous record company executives. As the *Guardian* put it, 'She was addicted to heroin and bad men.'

By the time Adele listened to Etta, the latter had finally received the acclaim she deserved for some classic songs, including her signature ballads, the sensuous 'At Last' and the emotional 'I'd Rather Go Blind'. But it was the despairing 'Fool That I Am' that had a profound effect on Adele.

It wasn't just the sentiment of regret and final parting – 'This is goodbye, but I still care' – it was the way she conveyed her feelings. Adele became obsessed with the sincerity in her voice: 'It was the first time a voice made me stop what I was doing and sit down and listen. It took over my mind and body.' Surprisingly, perhaps, Etta didn't write the song, she just had total empathy with it. It was written in 1946 by Harlem-based songwriter Floyd Hunt and recorded initially by his own quartet, featuring jazz singer Gladys Palmer. The peerless Dinah Washington recorded a smoky interpretation a year later, but it suited Etta's distinctive vocal style perfectly and she released her definitive version in 1961.

When Adele came home from school at night, she would chill out on her bed listening to Etta for an hour. She knew nothing of Etta's troubled personal history or her feisty personality. While she was cosseted in the comfy world of the BRIT School, Etta, at a similar age, was a hard-drinking delinquent with a penchant for smoking weed and skipping school.

Adele was by no means the first artist to be influenced by the style of Etta James. The famous white soul singer Janis Joplin copied her raucous quality, as if she were always singing with a chronic complaint, but it is Adele who does Etta most justice.

'Fool That I Am' is the blueprint for Adele's vocal style. The two women have a very similar pitch with a deeply resonant lower register. Adele extends the end of a note in an identical way to Etta, making one word become two. Unsurprisingly, she sang 'Fool That I Am' so much that it became a staple of her early live performances and featured on the B-side of her re-released single 'Hometown Glory'.

Adele could match the intensity of an Etta James vocal, but perhaps at this stage in her life, she couldn't convey the same inner anger that one critic described as a 'raging bull quality'. That would change dramatically once Adele had experienced her share of unhappy relationships.

Etta won six Grammies, a star on the Hollywood Walk of Fame and was portrayed memorably by Beyoncé in the film *Cadillac Records*. She wasn't impressed when Beyoncé sang 'At Last' at the inauguration of President Obama in 2009, publicly stating that she should have sung it and would have done a much better job. A year later, Adele finally saw her live at the B.B. King Blues Club & Grill in Times Square, New York, when the seventy-one-year-old Etta could still belt out a song with attitude. She was scheduled to appear with Adele at the Hollywood Bowl, the last night of the *An Evening with Adele* US tour, but cried off at the last minute.

When she died in January 2012, Adele wrote a personal thank you in an online blog, graciously praising Etta's originality and breathtaking voice. Her true feelings are better described in this poignant observation about her biggest influence: 'I feel her pain.'

5

MISSING THE TRAIN

———

One of the secrets of the BRIT School was that it made students feel comfortable in their own skin – happy with who they were. Physically, Adele changed a lot when she became an adolescent. She was tall, a characteristic she inherited from both her mother and her father, eventually ending up at 5ft 9in. But whereas Penny was always slim, Adele was big boned like Marc, becoming a comfortable size 14–16 as a teenager. Sometimes she would need to reach for the size 18 in a fashion store.

She didn't help her figure by having a predilection for chocolate digestives and pizza, providing it didn't have anchovies on the top. 'I can't stand to have anchovies in my mouth,' she declared. 'I think they are disgusting. They remind me of sea monkeys. When you are a kid and you can go and buy them dry little fish and you can put them in some water and they survive for a little while. Not that I have ever eaten a sea monkey, but anchovies are just salty and yuk! I don't like them.'

She was unbothered by her size, however, and never threw herself into PE or a faddy diet to be MTV thin. She was content eating lunch rather than going to the gym, as long as it didn't affect her health or any potential relationship. None of her close girl friends was obsessing over their weight. In fact, it was the boys in her set who were most conscious of the way they looked, favouring lettuce leaves over pasta. She exclaimed, 'And they're not even gay, they're straight. Trying to be skinny indie boys …'

Adele was very interested in the latest fashions and would spend many happy afternoons scouring vintage shops with her mother to find a bargain they could afford. One of the reasons she enjoyed reading glossy magazines was to see what the celebrities were wearing. She enjoyed getting dressed up, but chose clothes more for comfort than anything else, even though she was surrounded by fashion plates at the BRIT School.

The short walk to the school from Selhurst Station was like an elongated catwalk in suburbia. One writer memorably described it: 'Follow the teen wearing bright yellow drainpipe jeans, a leather motorcycle jacket and bird's nest hairstyle. The school is no more than a five-minute strut from the station.'

One of the advantages of being a big girl was being able to get into places when she was underage. She had no trouble gaining admission to a club in Holborn, where she used to go with her friends. After a night out when she was fourteen, she came up with the idea for 'Hometown Glory', now a classic, but then the idle ramblings of a drunkenly swaying girl trying her hardest not to step on the cracks in the pavement. She told Q magazine, 'I was really pissed, wobbling all over the place. This French woman comes up to me and goes, "You need help, dah-ling?" And I went, "Nah, it's me hometown, luv."'

At this stage, she filed away the promising song to bring out again at a future date. She wasn't yet fully focused on song-writing and many of the thoughts she had at this age would have to wait to be developed. Another one became the 2016 single 'Send My Love to Your New Lover', which she first sketched out when she was even younger – only thirteen.

Adele may have looked mature for her age, but she was more a schoolgirl than a music student. She was enjoying herself. She still couldn't get out of bed in the mornings, which almost led to the ultimate reprimand. The teachers were despairing of her commitment when she rolled up to classes four hours late, even though she always said that she wasn't 'bunking', just sleeping. She genuinely wanted to go to school each day.

The final straw occurred when she was selected as one of the twenty most promising students to travel to Devon to perform at a West Country festival. They were all due to meet at Clapham Junction to catch the 9.30 a.m. train to Exeter. Adele was one of the closest to the station, just a short hop from West Norwood, but as departure time approached there was no sign of her. The teachers weren't surprised she was late. She was always late. The Director of Music, Tony Castro, phoned her and asked, 'Are you on the way?', expecting a 'Yes, sorry' response, but she had only just woken up. She had no chance of making the train. She told *Rolling Stone*, 'My heart exploded in my chest. It was pretty horrible. I almost did get kicked out of the school for that.'

Liz Penney had thought she would turn up at the last moment. She confirms, 'She was so upset.' A few years later when Liz saw Adele, her former student remembered the day clearly and was still distressed about it. 'I am so gutted,' she said.

It was literally the wake-up call Adele needed. She was beginning to understand the massive opportunity she had. Superficially, she was still the same old Adele, always the life and soul, but her older friends were contemplating what they might do when they left school and she, too, was beginning to think about her future.

The BRIT School was becoming famous. For more than a decade, nobody really knew it existed. That changed for ever when Adele was in her second year. At last a pupil had achieved enormous success and would test the school's policy of playing down the desire for fame.

The breakthrough was achieved, not as many now think, through the efforts of Amy Winehouse or Leona Lewis, but thanks to a stunningly pretty girl from Eastern Europe called Ketevan Melua. The record-buying public knew her better as Katie Melua.

Katie was another example of the diversity of the BRIT School. You could find yourself sitting next to a streetwise girl from West Norwood living with her mum or a middle-class daughter of a heart specialist from Georgia. Their artistic talents brought them together under one roof.

Katie, whose mother was Irish, spent her early childhood in Georgia, then part of the Soviet Union, before her parents moved to Belfast and subsequently to Surrey. A bright, studious girl, she began attending the BRIT School, aged sixteen, after taking her GCSEs.

At one of the school's showcases, she was discovered by the multi-talented songwriter and producer Mike Batt, a man who has never lived down forming The Wombles pop group. He remortgaged his house to release Katie's debut album *Call Off the Search* in November 2003 on his own Dramatico label. His gamble proved to be a shrewd move, because the record went to number one and sold more than 1.2 million copies in the UK within the first five months of release.

Much of Katie's apparent 'overnight' success was due to the enthusiasm of Terry Wogan, who played her enchanting first single on his Radio 2 show. 'The Closest Thing to Crazy' was a slushy love song that was unlikely to feature on Adele's mixtape.

Katie Melua was the biggest-selling female artist in the country in 2004 and 2005. Her teachers were amazed at how quickly it had happened. One minute she was one of the most academic pupils at the school, happily studying for her A Level in music; the next she was sharing a stage with Brian May at a Nelson Mandela benefit in South Africa.

This was a huge deal for the BRIT School. Katie was an ideal role model for students – an accomplished musician writing much of her own material. She also became very wealthy, and was listed as the seventh-richest musician under thirty in *The Sunday Times* Rich List of 2008. Her fortune then, at the age of twenty-three, was said to be £18 million.

Katie's boyfriend at school was Luke Pritchard, who formed the successful indie band The Kooks with two other former pupils, Hugh Harris and Paul Garred. She wrote the poignant title song of her second album, *Piece by Piece*, when she and Luke broke up.

Adele was too young to know Katie, who was nearly four years her senior. She has never cited her as an influence on her singing or her career, but did once say she thought her 'lovely'. Katie's melodic combination of jazz and blues owed more to the legacy of Eva Cassidy than to the powerful voiced, soulful or in-your-face singers that Adele preferred.

Amy Winehouse, however, was an altogether different matter. This was a young woman constantly on the edge of pain and regret, with the most emotive voice of her generation. Oddly, Amy and Katie never had much to do with one another, despite being at the BRIT School at the same time, probably because Amy studied musical theatre, whereas Katie stuck to music.

Their debut albums came out at the same time, but while Katie was number one, Amy's *Frank* languished in the lower reaches of the charts in January 2004. It was a slow burner, eventually selling a million and becoming hugely influential.

They were almost polar opposites as stars. Nick Williams observes, 'The one thing Kate and Amy have in common is that there isn't anyone exactly like them. They're not factory farmed. What we do is attract people into the school who are creative – that means things will happen.'

Superficially, Adele was treading a similar path to Amy. Both were working-class girls from North London. Amy's father Mitch was a taxi driver. Both were influenced in their vocal style by black big-band singers: Adele by Etta James and Ella Fitzgerald; Amy by Sarah Vaughan and Dinah Washington. And both wrote songs that honestly conveyed love and loss – as the title declared, they were both frank. Adele was nearly five years younger than Amy, and her personal life had still to develop, but the choices she made were never remotely as bad or shambolic as the ill-fated legend.

If you were in the mood for angst-ridden reflection, you wouldn't choose the romantic sounds of Katie. For Adele, it would always be *Frank*, an album she admired hugely, claiming it was this 'amazing' record that 'made her pick up a guitar'. That statement shouldn't be taken too literally. Adele gushes about so much music, it can be difficult sometimes to find something that she doesn't like.

She could, of course, already play the guitar, but it would be increasingly important to her when she took writing songs more seriously. That coincided, at sixteen, with becoming a full-time music student. Eighty per cent of her school time would be devoted to music once she waved goodbye to the national curriculum.

Although she had no trouble with her GCSEs and had achieved a distinction in her music GNVQ (General National Vocational Qualification), she still had to go through another audition process at school in order to be allowed to continue at what was its equivalent of a sixth-form college. If accepted, she would study for a BTEC qualification in music. Existing students, like Adele, were competing with a fresh set of applicants from outside. Fifty places were available to 400 hopefuls.

Again, Liz Penney was in charge of the audition, but other teachers were on the panel this time, which made the process more nerve-racking. They listened to Adele sing before she joined rival students to sit a written exam on 'When I'm Sixty-Four' by The Beatles. Two weeks later, she was relieved to learn that she had been accepted, although in her case it had been a formality.

The very first day of what was, in effect, a new school,

clearly demonstrated that Adele had a fresh determination about her and provided a rare insight into the character and dedicated mindset that would sometimes stay hidden behind her larger-than-life image. The music students were now split into two classes of twenty-five. Each of them, in turn, had to get up and perform something – a guitar solo, violin piece, saxophone break, some jazz on the piano. Adele sang, of course. One of her classmates remembers, 'She did a great performance and then sat down in her chair and was furious because she thought she had done a really bad job. That was our very first day performance.

'Adele was kind of, you know, an absolute perfectionist. She always had one thing on her mind and that was succeeding over anything else – over social life, over everything like that. That was her main focus.'

Adele has given the impression that she had a carefree attitude at the BRIT School. In reality, that was not the case.

In the canteen, there was a jukebox that had an eclectic mix of 45s for the students – anything from the Beach Boys to Mary J. Blige and Will Young.

One of the favourites during Adele's first senior year was a forgettable pop song called 'Leave (Get Out)' by American singer JoJo. Whenever the track came on the 'artists', as Stuart Worden liked to call the students, would break into song.

Everyone seemed to know the words of this particular cheesy break-up song about a cheating dog of a boyfriend, especially the anthemic chorus. One of Adele's friends and contemporaries observes, 'It was a bit like *Glee* but less contrived. It was just a case of jamming together – all of us. It was a very creative place.'

Adele would join in, as would another shining talent, a fantastic dancer and actress called Jessica Cornish, from Romford. At the BRIT School she was known as Jessica, although some of her class in musical theatre called her Jess. Now the whole world knows her as Jessie J.

She wasn't a bit like the superstar we all know today. One of Adele's smoking buddies recalls, 'She was very, very quiet. She would sometimes come and stand in the music room during breaks and stuff. I often thought it was a bit strange, because she was so quiet all the time and didn't make much of an impact. It's really weird to see her now; how big and confident and out there she is, because she wasn't like that at all. Adele, on the other hand, comes across very much as she did at school.'

In fairness, Jessie J was one of those students who lit up like a streetlamp when she was performing. She was already a practised performer in West End musicals, including the role of Brat in Andrew Lloyd Webber's *Whistle Down the Wind* when she was eleven. But, although she was a very fine singer, she wasn't as accomplished vocally as a specialist like Adele.

Jessie J literally found her voice at the BRIT School. She had to change from being a stage singer to being natural and relaxed in front of a microphone. She explained in her autobiography that her time as a student was all about 'gaining confidence, character building and finding out about myself'.

She and Adele did know each other at school, but weren't part of the same set. Occasionally, they would join forces in the canteen for a little jam and a song. Sometimes Ben Thomas would play guitar. Jessie J recalls those times with affection: 'We're so common when we're together. It's hilarious.' Best of all, she remembers the Adele laugh, which already was becoming her trademark: 'You could hear her laugh from a mile down the corridor. She was very kind of loud and everyone knew her, and she was the girl everyone loved and was up for a laugh.'

One of the myths about the BRIT School is that all its stars were there at the same time and all sat in a row in a classroom. Most of the better-known former students barely knew one another. Adele did know Kate Nash, whom she thought hilarious. She also knew future star Katy B (Kathleen Brien), who spent four years at the school, but specialised in theatre, in the year below. Soon after Katy joined the school, the Year 10s and the Year 11s were put together in groups for practical music classes. Adele and Katy were in the same group, although the older children would boss around the uncool newbies. When Katy was asked what she could do, she nervously said she could sing and proceeded to demonstrate that she could. 'You *can* sing.' Adele shouted to Liz, 'Miss, she can sing!'

Adele didn't remember *The X Factor* winner Leona Lewis: 'That Leona Lewis must have been a quiet horse as I can't remember her at all, and I know everyone there.' In fact, Leona had already left by the time Adele arrived. Only Jessie J, of the more famous alumnae, was in the same year.

Liz Penney, who was the musical director for her end-of-year show, the musical *Sweet Charity*, recalls that she cast Jessica as Charity: 'She was an incredible performer. But she was like Adele in that she wanted to learn. She would watch me do a vocal warm-up before her class and, at the end, she would be the one who came up to ask me to show her again so that she had it right. She was the consummate professional – and so was Adele.'

Both Adele and Jessie J thrived in the relaxed environment of the BRIT School. Jess is famously bisexual and there has never been any indication she hasn't been comfortable with her sexuality. Adele has surrounded herself with many gay friends and can be camp in a theatrical way, made charming by her persona as the cheeky chapette from Tottenham.

A mutual gay friend explains, 'It was all to do with making the space comfortable and safe. It wasn't a big thing to come out at the school. There were just as many gay boys as there were straight boys – and gay girls as there were straight girls. For the first time, you were able to look around and think, oh, I could date you and I could date you.

'You had the freedom to develop as a person and that is hugely important in creative arts. It was such an eclectic range with great personalities but no edge. Some of the people were suburban and some of them were real London urban kids with no money, did terribly at school but had an amazing singing voice or could draw like no one else could draw, an amazing graffiti artist or a brilliant actor.

'You put all these people together – black, white, fat, thin, gay or straight – and this safe, unthreatening setting taught you how to make friends with people you might not necessarily ever meet. From that point of view, it wasn't a normal environment at all.'

Adele made many of her friends in the smoking area. It wasn't cliquey. She liked nothing better than chilling behind the canteen, where there were a couple of tables and benches to sit, chat and enjoy a rollie – or sometimes just lark about. Wherever she was, Adele was mouthy and full of laughter and spirit. Another classmate, Allan Rose from Wandsworth, recalled, 'She was bubbly, fun and very outgoing. She was very popular.'

It suited Adele that there was hardly a drug culture at the BRIT School. A few smoked weed, but any bad behaviour was more likely to be caused by drink. 'Everybody was pretty well behaved,' observed a friend. 'We all pretty much wanted to be there, so there wasn't much cause for discipline.'

At lunchtimes, she would join in when the students trooped into Sammy's café for a bacon and egg sandwich, and after school it would be down the White Horse for a pint before catching the train home or grabbing a lift if someone was heading back into town. According to a drinking pal, the White Horse was an 'absolute dump'. 'It was a really rundown, horrid pub, but we would go in there because we could get served, even though we weren't eighteen.' Adele wouldn't socialise there that much, preferring to hook up with friends away from the small world of Selhurst.

Closer to home, she would join her older friends for a smoke in the park or go swimming at the Latchmere Leisure Centre in Burns Road, Battersea – a particular favourite because it boasted a wave machine. 'It was a huge part of my youth,' she observed.

When she was sixteen, she used to go to watch a newly formed South London indie band called The Maccabees play at the now defunct Bug Bar on Brixton Hill. They had mutual friends, which always makes a gig more fun. Adele was given one of their early CDs in a cheap and cheerful photocopied and stapled-together packet. One of the songs was called 'Latchmere' in honour of the pool.

The following year, the song was the band's second single release and last year, in 2015, she was thrilled to see them again at the Glastonbury Festival. They performed 'Latchmere', which brought some happy memories flooding back. It reminded Adele of how everyone had to swim in lanes and boasted the easy-to-remember chorus 'Latchmere's got a wave machine'. 'They're lovely boys,' she said.

Throughout most of her teenage years, Adele needed a Saturday job to fund her nights out, tobacco and the odd bottle of cider for drinking with friends in Brockwell Park on a warm summer evening. She worked weekends for her Auntie Kim in the Riverside Café, next to the River Lea in Stamford Hill, a couple of miles from her old Tottenham stamping ground. It was in a lovely location and popular with ramblers taking a walk by the river.

Adele had little opportunity to admire the view, however, as she was stuck in the kitchen most of the time, doing the washing up and complaining her hands were becoming prunes. Kim did the cooking and sometimes her daughter Cema-Filiz would help out as well, which made it jollier. The two teenagers remained very close chums and always had a laugh together.

Adele loved it. Every Sunday they would listen to the chart rundown, singing along and dancing around the tables as they cleared the plates. It could have been the setting for a sitcom.

When she decided she needed more money to save for a handbag she had her eye on, Adele started working as a shop assistant at a Gap store. 'I thought I'd be on the till or something or in the changing rooms helping people find their clothes. But all I did was fold jumpers for twelve hours a day.' She hated it and walked out after four days without even collecting her first pay packet.

6

DAYDREAMER

'Hometown Glory' is a sophisticated song for a sixteen-year-old, both lyrically and musically. It is a curious mix of whimsical nostalgia and anger. In this, her first completed song, she articulates the everyday life that makes even a humdrum day in London so special. She is, as she declares, just 'wandering'.

She begins the lyric with avoiding the cracks in the pavement, which is what had sparked off the original idea for the song, staggering outside the club in Holborn two years before. It's one of those childish things that is fun to do at any age.

This is not a song paying homage to London in the way that the classic example 'Waterloo Sunset' does. There's no mention of West Norwood Station, Brockwell Park or White Hart Lane – or any of the other landmarks in Adele's life. Instead, she is conveying a general feeling of affection for the 'wonders of my world'.

For a teenager who proudly stated she didn't have a great many words at her disposal, she manages to find a place for 'opaque' in the second verse. When the song became famous, Fraser McAlpine wrote in his BBC Online review, 'You've got to love a song which correctly uses a word like "*opaque*", haven't you? It's a great word, and you just don't hear it often enough in modern popular song.'

Adele used it to create a mood. She conveys a stifling summer's day when the girls are sunny and carefree in their short skirts and shades. But when the listener is ready to indulge in their own memories of London life, she completely changes the mood and has a rant at the government in a 'them and us' sort of way, declaring in no uncertain terms that the people are united and we aren't going to take any shit. She had been moved the previous year by the sheer scale of the anti-Iraq War demonstrations, when a million people took to the streets of London in February 2003 to protest against the now discredited invasion.

It's this contrast that makes the song especially memorable. Adele ended up writing it in rapid fashion after a row with Penny at home in West Norwood. Her mother, who had missed out on university, was keen for her daughter to grab the opportunity and continue her education at the Institute of Performing Arts in Liverpool. The college had a strong link with the BRIT School, having been co-founded by Mark Featherstone-Witty and Paul McCartney.

The Institute offered a three-year honours degree in music or other performing arts. Adele was certainly bright enough, and the BRIT School generally encouraged the 'artists' to go on to university or music college.

Adele had already met Paul McCartney, sort of, as a star-struck fan, when she had been awarded a *Fame Academy* prize. A proportion of the profits from the telephone voting on the BBC's short-lived talent contest of that name went to pay for a scheme that aimed to promote musical excellence by funding young music-makers. If you wanted to be considered for a bursary, you had to write off explaining why you should be awarded one. Adele wasn't one of the five main winners, but she was given a home four-track digital recorder, which was very useful for a budding songwriter.

McCartney was a trustee of the scheme and guest of honour at the celebration event held in St Luke's Church, Islington, a regular BBC venue. Adele went along with the two Pennies – her mum and Liz, who was pleased to learn that Adele was a fan of The Beatles too. 'A lot of people her age might not have been, but she understood the significance of him being there.'

The first big excitement was when they spotted the other big name at the event, Bruce Forsyth. Adele and Liz made sure they had their picture taken with him, and for a while it had pride of place on the fridge in the kitchen in West Norwood.

Sir Paul turned up for only about five minutes. Liz recalls, 'I was just talking to Adele and her mum, when suddenly we were aware the room had gone quiet and it was like a swarm of bees just gravitated towards him. So Adele and I ran over, pushed behind him, so he had to walk past us as he left through the back door. So we thrust our hands out at him and got our hands shaken by Paul McCartney. I haven't washed mine since!'

At first Adele was amenable to her mum's idea of further education in Liverpool, but it wasn't long before she realised how much she liked the life she had in London, with her friends and family, and the music, the bars and the parks she knew and loved. She swiftly changed her mind – hence the row and the inspiration to write 'Hometown Glory' in her bedroom on her Simon & Patrick guitar.

At school, Adele had many lessons dealing exclusively with composition, and songwriting became as important as singing. A classmate explains, 'We learned all about the different types of music and how to compose it – dance music, film music – you name it, we did it. We were trained in how to use Logic Pro, a professional kind of composition computer program. We were taught how to use all that. And we would write *a lot* of music.'

Other students became used to seeing Adele in the corner playing her guitar. They didn't appreciate how hard she practised and the time she spent improving, like a top-quality sportswoman. Karis Anderson, one third of the chart-topping group Stooshe, was also at BRIT School in the year below. 'My favourite memory of Adele was seeing her in her tracksuit bottoms in the foyer, playing her guitar. Everybody was just like, "Oh, there's Adele playing another song." It was just a nice vibe – not a care in the world.'

But Adele did care.

The students were taken through the A-to-Z of the musical process – from developing an initial idea, completing a song, learning and rehearsing it, then setting up and recording it in the home studio on the premises and, finally, performing it live. As well as Liz Penney, Conor Doherty was the expert in world music, Tony Castro helped with composition, Chris McInnes was in charge of sequencing or computer-based music and Declan Cunningham ran the BRIT School studio and taught Adele all about sound recording. She was like a sponge.

Adele and her fellow students rehearsed in a shabby outhouse on site called The Shed. One of those who joined her remembers, 'It wasn't at all glamorous, but then it didn't need to be. That was essentially the ethos of the school. It was not the state-of-the-art equipment or fancy furniture that mattered; it was the teachers and your fellow students.'

He recalls that everyone had the chance to hear her songs live at a grim but much-loved venue called The Cartoon Club in London Road, West Croydon. The students, with fake IDs at the ready, would swarm into the dimly lit venue with graffiti on the walls.

'It was pretty gross. But I remember hearing "My Same" for the first time. And we all went home singing, "We do-oo" at the tops of our voices.'

Adele wrote 'My Same' about her best friend, Laura Dockrill. It's an ironic title, as it affectionately chronicles their differences – a little like the George Gershwin classic 'Let's Call the Whole Thing Off': 'You like to-may-to and I like to-mah-to …' In this case, Adele says they are completely different but somehow match. Apparently, cautious Adele likes to sit on chairs, while adventurous Laura prefers the floor. It could almost be a love song if you didn't know it was about her closest friend.

Ironically, after Adele wrote a song celebrating their friendship, the two promptly fell out badly. She says she can't remember what it was all about – a likely story. The two girls didn't speak to one another for several years, until they were reunited thanks to the singer Jessie Ware, who had been writing with Laura.

She saw Adele at a New Year's Eve party and told her, 'I'm spending so much time with Laura and she really misses you. Adele was like, "I miss her too."' Encouraged by Jessie, Adele rang her former friend and, in a tearful conversation, arranged to meet. The two picked up where they'd left off, as if nothing had happened. She was so pleased, she thanked Jessie and made Laura take a bow when she was on stage at the Royal Albert Hall in 2011.

The third memorable song Adele composed while at the BRIT School was called 'Daydreamer' and was about a boy whom she describes as having eyes that make you melt. Looking back, her friends are confused about Adele's love life. She definitely had a big crush on a very good-looking boy studying music in the year below her. Nobody was quite sure if it was ever anything more than that.

One friend explains, 'As far as I knew, she never seemed to kiss boys or anything like that. She was always sort of eternally single. As far as I'm aware, she never had a boyfriend the whole time she was there.'

Adele was besotted with the younger boy in a teenage sort of way, trying to catch his eye in the canteen and wondering what he was doing after school. The problem she faced was that the boy seemed to be bisexual. Adele found it hard enough being in competition with other girls without having to beat off men as well.

Eventually, at a party, she plucked up the courage to tell him how she felt and was delighted when he seemed to suggest he was attracted to her too. She recalled what happened next: 'He kissed one of my best boyfriends and I was like: "Get lost!"' She could laugh about it later – but not at the time. 'I was like, "We're not even going out yet and you've cheated on me already!" "Daydreamer" is about everything I wanted him to be … the daydream of him.'

She subsequently wrote the song flat on her back, guitar pointing at the ceiling. She had slipped a disc while on a special school outing to the BRIT Awards at Earls Court – one of the perks of being at the school that bore the same name. She also came down with a bad bout of flu and couldn't stop sneezing, so it's quite surprising the song ended up being written at all.

The result is quite folksy and whimsical in the manner of 'Hometown Glory'. You could imagine Adele casually sitting on a stool in The Shed making sure she was note-perfect. The lovelorn lyric is not bitter or even melancholy; it is more wistful about what might happen in a perfect world. She is describing 'what I'm hoping for' – a boy to put his arm round her and look after her. The best thing about the unfortunate infatuation is that it gave rise to one of the songs that led to her breakthrough.

Stuart Worden didn't see much of Adele day to day, but first realised she had an extraordinary talent as a singer when the music department staged a production of Pink Floyd's classic 1973 album *The Dark Side of the Moon*. Adele sang the wordless vocal on the beautiful and ethereal track 'The Great Gig in the Sky'. It's one of the few Pink Floyd songs to feature a female voice. There are no lyrics, but it requires a singer of enormous power and sensitivity, as it drifts between loud and soft. On the original album, it is sung by Clare Torry. Adele matched her note for note.

Stuart was most impressed. 'It was not the kind of thing you expect from Adele, but there she was, having this big moment and I thought, "She's got range!"'

Ben Thomas, who was at her side as her guitarist right from these early days, observed, 'Everyone would be completely silent and in awe when she performed.'

Adele was improving, both as a performer and as a song-writer. Everybody on her course was getting better for the simple reason that they could devote so much of their lives to their music. Adele was now established as a solo singer – one who would take the lead whenever there were group projects. There were many opportunities for the students to perform live, either in the small concert hall at the school or at The Cartoon Club.

Exposure outside the school was limited, however. That was about to change, thanks to a student on the media course. Lyndon Blue was well known as 'Mr Myspace' because of his enthusiasm for the relatively new vehicle for promoting unsigned artists with ambitions. He also had the funkiest hair-cut in the place.

He and Adele had become firm friends in the smoking area. Lyndon was very popular and did his best to champion Adele. He first posted a pretty average recording he made on his phone of her singing 'Daydreamer', wearing one of her trade-mark cardigans with her hair under a woolly hat. The sound quality is not great, but it was 2006 and it did convey the sweet appeal of the song.

She made a demo of her three songs in the recording studio at the BRIT School, plus a jazz version of 'My Same'. Lyndon persuaded Adele that Myspace would be the perfect showcase for her songs and proceeded to post all the tracks online.

Adele was very computer literate. In her opinion, she could use a computer better than her stepfather Simon and he built websites for a living. She certainly saw the Internet as the way of the future for young people wanting to be noticed and she intended to be one of them.

It was time to take stock. Soon she would be leaving the BRIT School. It had been like having a soft, snuggly duvet around you every day. One thing the school did not do for its students was actively sort out their next moves for them. Instead, it provided them with all the tools they would need to make their way in the field of creative arts. In Adele's case, the school wouldn't be helping her to find a record deal. She had learned how the industry worked, and from time to time record company people would come in to chat to the class about what they were looking for and the best way to approach them, but that was as much advice about the future as she received.

Adele wasn't the only talented BRIT School leaver. Hers was a very high-quality and impressive year. Two of the guitarists, Ben Thomas and bassist Tom Driessler, would later form the core of Adele's touring band. Freddie Smith stood out as a virtuoso violinist. As vocalists, Charlene Soraia and Kimberly Anne were widely expected to do well. Kimberly Anne is now a respected live performer, while Charlene Soraia's claim to fame is her cover of The Calling's 'Wherever You Will Go', which featured in a Twinings TV ad and went to number three in the charts. Most tipped for stardom, however, was Rox, a half-Jamaican/half-Iranian singer with an outstanding soul voice, but she too needed to be patient and wait until 2010 for the release of her first album, *Memoirs*.

These three girls, Charlene, Kimberly Anne and Rox, were very photogenic and looked like pop stars. Adele didn't. A classmate sums it up, 'She definitely stood out. She had a very individual voice in comparison to some of the others. Her music was always kind of original and different. I never really thought she would be a huge star and I guess that was maybe down to image, but she was always very good and oh so dedicated.'

Ironically, it was the BRIT School's attitude to image that would be the ace for Adele. Unlike other stage schools, it didn't teach image. The students learned everything else, but the school encouraged them to be natural and not contrived. That would ultimately pay huge dividends for Adele, who had the biggest voice *and* the biggest personality.

Just before she left, Adele entered 'Daydreamer' in the school's annual songwriting competition. The Paul Rich Award for Musical Composition was sponsored by his son Clive in honour of the late musician and music publisher. Kimberly Anne won and Adele came only third. Shortly afterwards, she was chosen to be one of the performers at The Best of … show, which was the final, prestigious performance of the year.

Stuart Worden remembers she casually shuffled on to the stage in a black baggy cardigan, clutching a mug of tea, and announced, 'All right, mates', before picking out the melody of 'Daydreamer' on her guitar. He believes she was wearing a pair of old slippers, but that's probably a fuzzy memory, as Adele was always rather fond of nice shoes and trainers.

Liz Penney has never forgotten it: 'It was the first time I had seen her sing and play guitar on stage. I have been a teacher for many years and I don't say "that was amazing" very often. But when she sang, you could hear a pin drop.' Everyone agreed it was a special moment. Even Clive Rich, a respected media and music lawyer and entrepreneur, dined out for many years as the man who didn't spot Adele as a winner.

To mark the end of their time at the BRIT School, it was a tradition that the students who were leaving would pile into the White Horse with all the teachers for a farewell drink or two. Penny was the only parent who went along. Liz observes, 'With Adele, it was never the teenage thing of "How shameful my mum is here." It was very much, "Well, of course Penny is here." She had been part of it all the way through.'

Basically, at school Adele had learned how to take a musical idea through to the final recording. She has never been slow in giving credit. She told *Blues and Soul* in 2008, 'I do owe it *completely* to the BRIT School for making me who I am today.'

Adele was well aware of the old cliché about moving on from being a big fish in a small pond to a small fish in a big pond. She had reached a watershed in her life. Things were about to move very fast indeed.

PART TWO

SOMETIMES IT HURTS

7

XL CALLING

―――――――

One of Adele's favourite stories is that when opportunity came knocking, she thought it was an Internet pervert. She was seventeen when a top A&R man called Nick Huggett got in touch in early 2006. He had heard about her through one of his talent scouts and watched her three-song demo on Myspace. Even though he was in Barcelona with Dizzee Rascal, who was supporting the Red Hot Chili Peppers, he decided to act straight away: 'I just heard a really amazing voice and I thought, "Wow, there's something special about this girl."'

You never know in the music business when you are going to miss out on something good because you put it off until tomorrow. Nick emailed her through the site to ask, 'Are you signed?' Adele, when she tells it, recalls, 'I was like, "signed to what?" And he said, "Have you got a record deal?"' He suggested they meet up at the offices of his record company, called XL Recordings, in Ladbroke Grove, when he was back in London.

According to Adele, the only record company she had ever heard of was Virgin and that was because it was the label of the Spice Girls. She decided to take Ben Thomas along in case her worst fears were realised and this wasn't a proper appointment. 'He's puny, Ben, looks like a dwarf, but I'd never heard of XL, so I thought I might be on my way to meet a perv or something.'

It's a fun tale and typical Adele – one that deserves to be accompanied by one of her trademark chortles. Dealing with record labels was one of the aspects of the music business she had learned about at the BRIT School. It's hard to believe that someone as switched on and ambitious as Adele wouldn't have looked up XL online. She would have seen it was a leading independent label which, in 2006, was already riding the crest of a wave with the White Stripes, Dizzee Rascal and, most significantly for the BRIT School hopeful, M.I.A.

Nick Huggett stumbled into A&R when he was working in a record shop in London and met James Lavelle, the boss of Mo' Wax records, who offered him a job. When that label was absorbed into XL, he stayed on, enhancing his reputation as a man who rarely went to gigs, but used his ears to identify a sound that might sell. He used his ears with Adele.

XL has very individual artists on their books. Nick was adept at spotting prospective talent that offered something a little different. He had signed Dizzee – an East London teenager called Dylan Mills – after he heard his self-produced white label disc 'I Luv You' on a local pirate radio station: 'I was struck because it was the first time I heard someone rap with a cockney accent.' Dizzee was only nineteen when he won the Mercury Music Prize in 2003.

Nick shrewdly thought Adele was a one-off. He picked Adele and Ben up from the Tube station and drove them to the office as planned. She was still uncertain about what was going on, but Nick explained patiently that he was very impressed by her music and would be keen to sign her. He was very persuasive. Adele observed, 'That was when we got fucking excited!'

Nick was surprised that, unusually, Adele had no manager. So often wannabe stars have foolishly been trapped in a contract that would prove to be completely unsuitable in the long term. He realised she needed someone to guide her through the process of getting a deal, and who better than his old friend Jonathan Dickins to ensure that everything went smoothly and that she signed with XL when the time was right. Jonathan and their association would prove to be highly significant for Adele.

Few people were better connected than Jonathan. Everybody in his family is in music. As he puts it simply, 'I grew up in it; it's all I knew.' Jonathan's grandfather, the entertainment entrepreneur Percy Dickins, co-founded the *New Musical Express* and invented the pop charts in 1952 – an inspired idea that transformed pop music. Until that time, everything had been based on sales of sheet music, but he devised a top twenty based on record sales just before rock 'n' roll revolutionised things.

Rob Dickins, Jonathan's uncle, has been one of the leading executives in the music industry since the early Seventies. He was chairman of the giant Warner Music UK for fifteen years and was recognised as having a Midas touch after signing artists such as Enya and The Corrs. He was a supporter of the BRIT School through his work on the council of the BPI (British Phonographic Industry). Jonathan's father, Barry Dickins, made his name as booking agent to The Who in the bad old days when they used to smash up their equipment on stage. He remains one of the country's top music agents, working with many famous artists, including Bob Dylan, Neil Young and Paul Simon.

Uncle Rob gave Jonathan a start in the A&R department at Warner's WEA Records, and during his time there he started his own small label called Showbiz. The first record he put out as an independent was the hypnotic electronic dance track 'Galang' by the multi-talented visual artist and rapper M.I.A., which stands for Missing in Acton and not for her real name, Mathangi Arulpragasam. Musically, she could scarcely be further removed from Adele, but indirectly she has had a huge influence on the younger woman's success: she pioneered a path followed by Adele both in the UK and the US.

Of Sri Lankan origin but born in Hounslow, M.I.A. is only nominally a West London girl. She was brought up in northern Sri Lanka, where her father was a Tamil militant, and eventually returned to the UK as a refugee a week before her eleventh birthday.

Jonathan pressed just 500 vinyl copies of 'Galang' in 2003, but it was enough to get the single noticed in the clubs and dance halls, as well as receive precious airtime on Radio 1. The song was inspired by her observations of life in London, but it was nothing like 'Hometown Glory' – it was hard-edged and more about survival. Galang is Jamaican slang for 'Go Along', roughly meaning 'Behave!' It's a word that lends itself to a dance track. *Time Out* magazine listed it as number twelve in their 100 Best London Songs in 2012. 'Hometown Glory' was one place higher, with The Kinks' 'Waterloo Sunset', unsurprisingly, at number one.

In the summer of 2004, 'Galang' was uploaded onto Myspace and is widely acknowledged to be the groundbreaker in creating musical impact digitally. *GQ* magazine wryly commented that the song went viral before 'anyone was even using the word *viral*'. It proved to be the ideal advance publicity for the single's mainstream release on XL in November 2004. While the song was not a huge seller in traditional terms, it helped M.I.A. to become an icon in modern Western culture. *Rolling Stone* magazine names her as one of the eight people who had defined the noughties in a list that also included Jack White and Radiohead – both on the XL roster. The independent record label, therefore, had three of the most influential musical acts of the decade.

'Galang' was critically acclaimed and featured in many 'songs of the year' lists. M.I.A. was one of the first artists to build an online fan base, a blueprint that would be followed by Lily Allen and Kate Nash. M.I.A., who was already thirty, was the sort of designer, film-maker and songwriter that the BRIT School would have loved.

Jonathan Dickins explained to *HitQuarters* that looking after M.I.A. meant he explored wider aspects of the music industry for distribution, licensing, copyright, radio promotion and even manufacturing. He didn't hesitate when M.I.A. asked him to be her manager and realised he had found his own niche in music, away from the shadow cast by his successful family.

In March 2006, he decided to set up his own company, September Management, initially in the spare bedroom of his house. His philosophy was to have a handful of artists and bring them along slowly. He had signed a few young London musicians, including Jamie T and Jack Peñate, who would both be important in Adele's career. Adele may have maintained she hadn't heard of XL, but she had come across these two promising talents through their presence on Myspace.

Two months later, Nick Huggett called to say that he had met this young singer called Adele and had mentioned Jonathan to her. Jonathan recalled, 'He said I should check this girl out. I just got a Myspace URL. We had one meeting and got on great. She was a massive fan of Jamie T. She was eighteen, just out of college, and wanting a career in music.'

Both Adele and Jonathan have different versions of how their first meeting went. She said he made her laugh – 'literally stomach cramps the day after' – and decided on that basis to go with him and has never regretted it. When she presented him with the Manager of the Year Award six years later, she said, 'He made me laugh and he made me a great cup of tea. I made my mind up he was going to be my manager before he made his up that he wanted to manage me.'

Jonathan, curly haired and youthful, confirmed that they hit it off right from the start: 'We just got on great.' But he was also mightily impressed with Adele's focus, mirroring the opinion of her classmates at the BRIT School. Time and time again her amusing flippancy masks her steely vision.

She and Jonathan talked about music and her ambitions. 'It's unbelievable how focused she is in terms of what she thinks is right for her career. So I listened and threw in some ideas and generally it just clicked. It wasn't about me going, "This is what I can do, blah, blah, blah."'

Adele was never like the star striker in a Premier League football team. There wasn't a queue of men in suits with fat chequebooks looking to sign her. She'd had a little email interest, thanks to Myspace, but nothing to get excited about. Not everyone was kind. Someone, who clearly thought a career in comedy beckoned, suggested that she was a test pilot for pies. As usual, she ignored this sort of barb. She was incredibly fortunate to find two people, who, right from the start, recognised her potential.

Now she needed to show Nick and Jonathan that she could perform away from the secure and receptive environment of the BRIT School. She was already very accomplished, thanks to the amount of time she devoted to her music, but she didn't spend her evenings gigging around the music venues of London, singing her songs to three men and a dog.

She decided the best option was to sing at her eighteenth birthday party at a pub in Brixton, a familiar place close to home and one she could fill with family, friends and one or two important people from XL, who wanted to know that she could sing live and not just on Myspace. She also invited her teachers, Liz Penney, Conor Doherty and Chris McInnes, from the BRIT School.

Liz recalls, 'It was like a big gig party basically, which was lovely. And her mum, Penny, and stepdad were there and I remember talking to them about how proud they must be of her because she had achieved what she set out to. She had transformed herself from a young girl who could sing to an accomplished songwriter.'

Liz and her colleagues gave her two pretty and expensive hardback notebooks for her lyric writing. In the front of one of them, she wrote, 'Happy 18th Birthday, Adele. This book is to inspire you to write your first album, to write lots of meaningful lyrics … so don't forget me when you are rich and famous.' Since then, Adele has always written her songs in high-quality notebooks – nothing from the pound shop for her. She was very meticulous about her craft and using the best stationery would remain part of her songwriting routine.

The party was a great success and Adele, not yet suffering from stage fright, sailed through her songs before the celebrations became too rowdy. It was the perfect bridge between school and the real world.

Adele didn't receive a big signing-on fee from XL – that wasn't the company's style. It attracted artists through its reputation and the names they had on their roster. The label described it as a 'very sensible deal'. The size of the advance has remained confidential, but it enabled her to do three things: first, she splashed out on designer gear from Burberry – a label she particularly liked; secondly, she ditched her rollies in favour of Marlboro Lights; and thirdly, she could give up working in the Riverside Café because she was now, officially, a full-time musician.

The size of XL's financial investment didn't turn Adele's head. It was more the amount of time the company told her they were willing to take nurturing her so that her first album would be worth the wait. It projected an image of friendly chats, laughter and creativity – a Shangri-La for its artists. This was a label that understood that development might take a year or even two; Adele would need nearly two.

She felt right at home from the start. Ezra Koenig, of the chart-topping New York rock band Vampire Weekend, which signed the year after Adele, observed, 'Their office in London is literally an old house. So when you walk in, you're in this cosy house, and it's, like, there's stuff all over the walls and, like, little murals. And it's very communal and Richard has this very big, kind of personally decorated office, but people are always having meetings in there and hanging out on the couches.'

The ethos at XL was similar to that of the BRIT School. It valued creativity above everything else. The label boss, Richard Russell, explained, 'We are here to work with artists and to discover, nurture, develop and make music with artists.'

Richard's breakthrough act was the controversial Essex dance band The Prodigy, who, in the days before Myspace, simply sent him a demo tape in the post. At that time, Richard was responsible for A&R at the label, which he combined with his more creative work as one half of the rave duo Kicks Like a Mule. As an artist himself, he had an intuitive connection with the people he signed. His biggest hit was called 'The Bouncer'. It was quite a classic of its time and a top-ten hit in 1992. He sampled a real-life bouncer saying the well-tried line: 'Your name's not down, you're not coming in.'

When he took charge at XL in 1994, he got on particularly well with The Prodigy's leader, Liam Howlett. He admired the musician's uncompromising vision of his own band and music. The group never appeared on television, for instance, preferring to reach their audience through their recordings alone. The strategy worked for them. Their third album, *The Fat of the Land*, was number one in the UK and the US, and sold more than ten million copies around the world. As a result, XL moved up a division, particularly in America, where there was so much money to be made.

Richard's reputation at the cutting edge of Nineties rave music was what attracted M.I.A. to the label in the first place, although she, in rather an Adele-like fashion, said it was because the office was round the corner from where she lived in Notting Hill. His own recording and production took a back seat when The Prodigy became so successful.

Richard's ability to avoid corporate pitfalls is to a large extent due to the influence and involvement of the fourth man in Adele's discovery and development. Martin Mills was very much the silent partner who owned the company that owned XL – or 50 per cent at least. He ran the Beggars Group and everything passed through his in-tray. He is a self-made millionaire, who retained his enthusiasm for music along with a flair for business. He explained bluntly, 'We just aim to put out great music and do it well.' Martin is soft spoken, grey haired, Oxford educated and extremely astute. The BBC described him as the mastermind behind the whole Adele operation. He was certainly the business brains, signing every cheque and concluding every deal.

He had already been in the music business for thirty years by the time XL signed Adele, progressing from record-store assistant to punk-band manager and subsequently to start a small independent label, Beggars Banquet. Named after a Rolling Stones album, the label grew into the Beggars Group, a conglomerate of independents that included XL. His breakthrough act was Gary Numan, who wandered into the shop in Earl's Court one day, although he also acknowledges the commercial importance of The Prodigy. Rather like his business protégé, Richard Russell, he cultivated a homespun office environment, controlling things behind the scenes from his desk in a small end-of-terrace Victorian house in Wandsworth. As the company grew, he didn't want to lose the feeling that this was a cottage industry, so he expanded by buying the house next door and knocking it through, continuing until he had bought the whole terrace and could fit upwards of eighty staff inside.

By remaining very much in the background, the independents within the Beggars Group could retain their individuality. For XL, that meant expanding a cutting-edge reputation. Adele was quite a surprising signing, therefore, because she was probably the most straightforwardly pop artist they had taken on. The label's other artists gave her instant cool.

She went to celebrate her new deal with friends and family at her favourite pub, The Duke of Wellington in Portobello Road, and promptly had a panic attack. Most of the time, Adele sails along, taking things in her stride, but on this occasion the enormity of what was happening suddenly hit her.

Over the years, The Duke would be one of those locations where she enjoyed the best and worst of times. She had seriously thought about moving to this part of West London, but she would to have to sell a few records first.

Instead, she went back to the old flat in West Norwood and to the home comforts that her mother provided and she enjoyed so much. The Co-op below had gone. In its place was a discount store called This, That and The Other, which boasted that most items were under £1. The slightly cringe-worthy shop name unwittingly summed up where Adele was with her songwriting. She had a handful of excellent songs, but they were disjointed and would only fill an EP. She needed to find some creative focus. Boyfriend trouble was about to provide it.

8

HEARTBREAK SOUL

Even before she signed her contract, Jonathan Dickins set about creating a buzz around Adele. The strategy was simple: she needed to be talked and written about and heard as much as possible. That might be on the Internet, the radio or by appearing at the small venues around London where trends are set and reputations made. Jonathan is a great believer in the importance of performing live in enhancing an artist's reputation.

He wasted no time in putting together a group of dedicated professionals who would become Team Adele. For starters, she needed a radio plugger, an agent and a publicist, who could all use their influence and connections to promote her.

First on the list was Brad Hunner, who set up his own company, Radar Plugging, in 2006 and had a desk in the XL offices in Notting Hill. Airplay is an essential part of breaking an artist and things got off to a great start with Adele when he persuaded Radio 1 to play 'Daydreamer'.

Jonathan employed his sister, Lucy Dickins, as agent to his clients. She had worked her way up through their father's business, ITB (International Talent Booking), from making the tea to assistant and then to fully fledged agent. She shared her brother's ability to befriend artists and make them feel they mattered.

Lucy had begun by planning and booking gigs for Jamie T. She would happily be on the door taking the punters' money. 'I'll get my hands dirty,' she said candidly. 'I don't give a shit. They're my clients, but they're also my friends and I'll do anything for them.' She derived huge satisfaction from watching an artist develop from venues with a capacity of ninety to bigger and better stages.

The publicist Jonathan had in mind for Adele had the advantage of once having been a pop star and therefore he understood some of the pressures a young performer would face. Carl Fysh was the keyboard player and songwriter with Eighties boy band Brother Beyond. He had headed the publicity department at Sony in the late Nineties, before setting up Purple PR with business partner William Rice in 2004.

With her ambitious team in place, it didn't take long for Adele to be noticed. In July 2006, she featured in the fourth edition of a new online culture monthly called *Platforms* magazine, a cutting-edge mix of all the arts for the Myspace generation. Not surprisingly, the magazine, which had only launched in April, had its own Myspace page. The bonus for Adele was that she could be heard, as well as read about. There was a link to her songs 'Daydreamer' and 'My Same', as well as a picture story to go with them. At this early stage, it seems that 'Hometown Glory' didn't sit at the top of her playlist.

The words, the very first of the million and more that would be written about her, described Adele as an up-and-coming 'soulful indie singer/songwriter'. The emphasis was on her flair for words and, considering this was eighteen months before the release of her first album, was intuitive about her appeal: 'Keeping the personal meanings of her songs to herself but telling you everything at the same time, she has a knack for making you feel you're the one she's writing about.' She was, said *Platforms*, 'one to look out for'.

Jonathan has never said whether he or XL thought Jamie T or Jack Peñate were a better bet than Adele for long-term success at this point. The other two were certainly further along the road, enjoying the groundswell of attention that XL wanted for Adele. So her new team followed the tried and trusted formula of piggy-backing one signing with another.

Adele became familiar to small club audiences simply by opening for Jamie and Jack at gigs booked by Lucy. Record company executives and music journalists now dine out on stories that they were among the first to see Adele on those occasions when she would shuffle on stage with a pint of beer, steel-stringed acoustic guitar round her neck, plonk herself on a stool and sing 'Daydreamer'.

Penny was hugely proud of her daughter's progress and would enthusiastically put up posters if her gig were being advertised. Scarcely a week would go by without her nipping to the coffee shop across the street from the flat in Norwood Road to put a flyer in the window.

Adele had four songs to perform: the three from Myspace and a fourth, also composed while she was at the BRIT School, called 'Painting Pictures'. It was still very much a composition for a girl with a guitar, but it didn't possess the resonance of the others – perhaps that was because it was a younger lyric that lacked a storyline. She talks about painting pictures with her mind and filling her heart with golden stories. It was pleasant and the guitar work was impressive, but her usual bite was missing.

The whole Thamesbeat scene, as the media called the latest line of London musicians that included Jamie T, Jack Peñate and Kate Nash, was a remarkably small world. This new crowd Adele was associating with were decidedly not from Tottenham or West Norwood, although they all seemed to sport a sort of Lily Allen Estuary accent – posh cockneys who didn't bother to say their ts. Even Adele, who had genuine working-class roots, began to sound as if she ran a market stall in Albert Square.

Liz Penney was very surprised when she first started hearing Adele being interviewed: 'I thought, "I don't remember her London accent being quite that strong." I'm from London and I always had the impression we had a similar sort of accent. Then, when she first sort of flashed into the limelight, I thought, "Blimey, why is she talking like that?", you know?'

There was nothing working class about Jamie T. In real life, he is Jamie Treays, the public school-educated son of a chartered surveyor from Wimbledon. Although managed by Jonathan Dickins, he was signed to Virgin and not XL. In preparation for the release of his first album, called *Panic Prevention*, his promotional single 'Salvador' was played on Radio 1. His first official single, 'Sheila', was released in July, when Adele hooked up with him. It made the charts at number fifteen. 'Sheila' is a twenty-verse epic song about London, a catalogue of the tragedies bubbling beneath the surface of the great city. It scraped into the *Time Out* list of the greatest songs about the capital – Adele and M.I.A. were top twenty. Jamie T, who came over like a cross between a young Billy Bragg and The Streets, was very current and trendy, and the ideal artist to give Adele some reflected publicity.

She sang 'Painting Pictures' at the 12 Bar Club in the summer of 2006, when she opened for Jamie T during his monthly Panic Prevention night. The venue in Denmark Street, Soho, was firmly established as one of the hipper spots, playing host in its time to Jeff Buckley, The Libertines and Katie Melua – perfect for Adele. It had the kind of relaxed, informal atmosphere that she enjoyed.

She felt at ease in a venue that was a natural progression from The Cartoon Club in West Croydon. Brixton Jamm on the Brixton Road was another cool place with a reputation for breaking in promising new acts. Adele's friends The Maccabees had played there and it almost felt like a home gig.

The Troubadour in Earl's Court was a more folky venue. In December 2006, she opened there for Jack Peñate. He was, said *The Sunday Times*, about to be 'huge', so it made sense for her to be included in his promotion for the time being.

According to Jack, they had first met at the 333 Club in Hoxton Square at the monthly Troubled Minds night. Jack's friend Caius Pawson, the son of celebrated Old Etonian architect John Pawson, ran the club in addition to being a leading A&R man at XL. Adele says she and Jack first got in touch with one another after liking each other's music on Myspace. What is not in doubt is that they shared a manager and a record label.

Jack, who is four years older than Adele, is middle class, well educated and comes from a large artistic family. His grandfather was Mervyn Peake, renowned artist and author of the Gormenghast Trilogy. Jack was born in Blackheath and privately educated at the expensive Alleyn's School in Dulwich – nothing remotely West Norwood about the grounds and buildings of this establishment. Alleyn's was popular among celebrities and famous former pupils included Jude Law, Pixie Geldof and Florence Welch of Florence and the Machine. From day one at the school, he was friends with singer Jessie Ware and she became part of his touring entourage alongside Adele.

Jack started taking music seriously in his teens and formed a band called Jack's Basement, which also featured a school-mate, Felix White, who in this very small world would become the lead guitarist with The Maccabees, as well as Jessie Ware's flatmate. Jack left the band to go solo when he went to University College, London, to read Ancient World Studies, but dropped out after two years to devote himself to music.

He is highly intelligent and quick witted, qualities that mirror Adele's own. When he opened for The Maccabees at Night and Day Café in Manchester, some wit in the crowd shouted out, 'Who are you??' He responded, 'A boy band from Milwaukee.' *AllMusic* described him as like Lily Allen minus the sarcasm and the party frocks. Adele was in the audience to cheer him on when he played the BBC tent at the 2006 Bestival on the Isle of Wight in September. Jack observed, 'We're incredibly close.'

Following the successful M.I.A. blueprint, Jonathan Dickins set about moving Jack to the next stage with the limited release of a promo single, 'Second, Minute or Hour', on a new label, Young Turks, set up by Caius Pawson as part of XL. The plan was for his profile to continue to grow throughout the next twelve months; a proper release on XL was planned for the following autumn.

He intended to pursue the same strategy with Adele, but she wasn't ready yet, although her image – or lack of it – was already taking shape. She sat or stood and sang, usually with a guitar: that was it. She sat as she played 'Painting Pictures' when she appeared at the trendy St James's Church, Piccadilly, in September 2006. One of the advantages of playing the guitar was that she didn't have to dance around or even move much.

She sat again when she played 'Painting Pictures' at the second birthday concert of Blue Flowers the same month. The music venue at the back of the George IV pub in Chiswick had been put on the map by members of the Thamesbeat group. It was small, almost intimate, with tables and chairs, but was well chosen to showcase Adele. She played there three times while she was establishing herself on the London indie scene. Chris Pearson, who ran the music nights, recalled, 'I knew Adele's manager, Jonathan, who had just taken her on and she was one of those acts that just amazed everyone with her voice.'

She impressed a journalist for the first time when she appeared at the White Hart in Bethnal Green. She was 'a chubby, slightly dishevelled girl in a patchwork floor-length skirt', who radiated a resolute eccentricity but wowed the audience of just twenty people when she began to sing. The wider reaction to Adele would be similarly positive.

She was still only eighteen and wanted to have some fun with her new friends and some money in her pocket. She wanted to drink beer in The Duke of Wellington and then go on to her favourite nightclub, the St Moritz in Wardour Street, for more drinking and dancing. She loved it because they would mix playing the latest hip-hop with Eighties Wham: 'It starts off all cred and by the end of the night everyone's dancing round their handbags.'

Sometimes, however, the edges became blurred between enjoyment and professionalism. She was booked to appear at another East London pub, but hadn't realised how late her spot would be and had lost track of her drinking. At 2 a.m., in front of family, friends and an expectant crowd of 300, she performed arguably her least successful gig: 'I played three songs. I forgot the words and I fell off my chair.' Fortunately, it was a free concert, so nobody could ask for their money back.

Most of the gigs were much more successful. Florence Welch was then another young singer struggling to get noticed on this demanding circuit. They shared a bill at a small London club one evening and Florence recalled, 'Something changed in the room when she started singing. Already, that voice! That was an amazing moment, seeing her.'

It had been an exciting six months for Adele, making a name for herself in London. Her Myspace blurb was still the same: 'Adele Laurie Blue Adkins is a future soul sensation. She doles out lilting melodies about crushes and best mates on an old acoustic guitar. Her songs include "Daydreamer", "My Same" and "Hometown Glory". Number of Friends: 5261. Celebrity Visitor: Mike Skinner (The Streets).'

She would have been dead chuffed about the last bit. When she was fourteen, she had moved on from Will Young and fallen for the Croydon-born rapper: 'I was so in love with Mike Skinner, I wrote him a letter.' If she had investigated more closely, she would have seen that his critically acclaimed debut album, *Original Pirate Material*, recorded in Brixton, was released on Locked On, a subsidiary of her own XL Recordings and therefore part of the Beggars Group.

The world surrounding Adele as she was steered to stardom was like a secret society with connections throughout the record business. It was a bit like the Masons without the funny handshake or Opus Dei in *The Da Vinci Code* by Dan Brown without the sinister overtones. It was certainly an octopus that locked Adele in its embrace with twice as many tentacles.

She needed to make more of a contribution, however. So far she hadn't been under pressure from her label or her manager, because they understood she was an eighteen-year-old girl and the groundwork and development had to be done. The more she thought about what was needed, the more 'overwhelmed' she felt. She knew that at some point she would have to go into the studio to make her debut album. The only problem was that she still had just four songs ready to go. She didn't exactly have writer's block: it was more a case of not having anything to write about. She was too young to have a lifetime of experiences on which to draw and she wasn't someone who could go for a walk in the country and write about daffodils. She needed inspiration from somewhere fast.

She found it in a 'rubbish boyfriend', who triggered an emotional turmoil she hadn't felt since her grandfather died. The subsequent mix of anger, regret and loss became the fire behind a new creativity she couldn't find while on the tread-mill of small-time gigging. 'I would have died for him,' she admitted.

Apart from the boy who had moved her to write 'Daydreamer', this was the first proper relationship she had experienced. It didn't go well. They had been dating for some three months when she discovered he had been cheating on her. His behaviour had a devastating effect on an inexperi-enced young woman. She marched into the all-night West End bar where he was having a drink, told him what she thought of him and 'punched him in the face'. She was swiftly escorted from the premises.

She explained that the wide and empty pavement of Oxford Street was laid out in front of her in the early hours of the morning: 'I got thrown out, and as I was running away, the phrase "chasing pavements" came to me. I sang it into my phone.' Everything might have been different if the straying boyfriend had run after her and they had made up there and then, but, thankfully for the creation of a great song, he didn't. She realised she was just chasing an empty pavement. When she got home to West Norwood, she made straight for her room and her guitar, roughed out three chords, and one of her most famous songs was born. Coincidentally, running along the pavements had also been the original inspiration for 'Hometown Glory'.

A few weeks later, the relationship spluttered to a less dramatic conclusion, when she sent an 'it's over' text from her favourite table in The Duke of Wellington. That provided fitting symmetry, as they had first met in the pub. 'Chasing Pavements' was about a universal choice in a bad relationship:

should I give up, or should I keep running after you when there's nothing there? It was exactly the dilemma that millions of women, in particular, could relate to in their own lives. Adele already had the ability to describe universal and timeless emotions. It was, she admitted, an intense yet flimsy teenage relationship, but it gave her something to write about. She had always been better at putting her feelings down on paper: 'Songs are how I feel and that is the only way I do get it out of me. It's for me, for my own peace of mind. In reality I can't really admit things to myself so I have to put it in a song.'

In isolation, 'Chasing Pavements' might not have been seen as quintessential 'heartbreak soul', as Adele called it. But in conjunction with the other emotional songs that ended up on the album, it had enormous resonance. Breaking up, it seemed, was always the most memorable part of a relationship and Adele figured that out.

She had discovered the secret of her creativity. Three weeks later, she had written nine new songs. Now she was ready for that first album.

9

LATER … WITH ADELE

Adele was a one-take wonder. Occasionally, she might need two. If she needed three, then she was probably ill. She wasn't the least bit fazed by being in a recording studio, thanks to the training she had received at the BRIT School. She wasn't looking around, wondering what everything was: she already knew. When it was time for her to sing, she would slip into her vocal booth in the corner and totally lose herself in the track. Jim Abbiss, the leading producer on her debut album, was impressed: 'She can be having a cuppa one minute, talking about *EastEnders*, but as soon as the recording light goes on, amazing music pours out of her.'

Jim met Adele when she came in to sing backing vocals on the track 'My Yvonne' for Jack Peñate's first album, *Matinée*, which he produced. The song betrayed Jack's literary education with an opening line reference to Meaulnes from *Le Grand Meaulnes*, the classic French novel by Alain-Fournier, in which the girl of Augustin Meaulnes' dreams is Yvonne de Galais. In effect, 'My Yvonne' is about the girl of your dreams. The acoustic song is sweet, a little in the style of Damien Rice.

While they were working on it, Jim suggested they needed a female voice. Jack said he knew somebody. Half an hour later, the studio door was thrown open. Jim recalled, 'This big, buxom cockney girl – Eliza Doolittle-like character, cig in one hand, can of beer in the other – falls into the studio. As soon as she started singing, my jaw dropped.' In truth, Adele doesn't do much in the finished article, but it would be the first time she was heard on a record when the album was released in October 2007.

By then, Jim Abbiss had produced eight tracks for Adele and managed to create something that was very nearly an old-fashioned concept album. He was impressed by her vitality and thought her a 'normal London girl'. His involvement was an early indication of how seriously XL was taking their young artist.

Jim had become much in demand as a result of his work with Kasabian and Arctic Monkeys, whose debut album *Whatever People Say I Am, That's What I'm Not* was, at that time, the fastest-selling debut album in UK history and won the Mercury Music Prize in 2006 and a BRIT Award the following year.

Originally a keyboard player from Peterborough, Jim had already accumulated twenty years' experience in the music business by the time he began working with Adele. His work with Arctic Monkeys and their frontman, Alex Turner, had already revealed a talent for harnessing creativity and originality.

The first song he produced for Adele was 'Hometown Glory', which almost didn't happen, because the original piano player pulled out at the last moment and Jim had to find someone else. He tried the respected jazz and session pianist Neil Cowley, even though he had never worked with him. Jim recalled, 'I knew of him, but she had never met him and it could have gone disastrously wrong, but we actually got it on the first take. It was an extraordinary thing to witness because he literally started playing and we used that take. It had everything.'

Jonathan Dickins isn't one of those managers who likes to be office-bound when there is creative work to be done. 'It really excites me to be involved in every aspect of an artist's career and development.' He made some telling contributions to Adele's first album. He ensured she was treated like a star and worked with the best people before she had even enjoyed any real success.

For 'Chasing Pavements', he brought in his friend, the acclaimed producer Francis White, better known profession- ally as Eg White, to work with her. He was already familiar to Team Adele through working with Carl Fysh when they were both in Brother Beyond. Carl played keyboards and Eg was the bass player. The two of them combined to write most of the group's songs.

Eg White provided the model for much of Adele's song- writing in the future: her original musical idea or concept would subsequently become a collaboration, using talented and established writers and producers. Adele wrote about 80 per cent of her debut by herself; much of the remaining 20 per cent was Eg.

He was less cutting-edge and more mainstream than Jim Abbiss. At the time, he was best known as the writer of the Will Young chart-topper 'Leave Right Now', for which he won an Ivor Novello Award in 2004. He also worked with James Morrison on his number one album, *Undiscovered*, released in 2006.

Eg was, in effect, a songwriter for hire who, when you passed him the ball, was odds-on to score a goal. He told the *Guardian* how he worked: 'Someone comes over at three, we have a cup of tea, chew the cud for a bit, go: "All right, shall we write a song?" And by six they've gone home and we've fucking done it. "Chasing Pavements" – that took two or three hours.' Adele remembers going along to his studio and watching him turn a few chords and a chorus into 'Chasing Pavements', which she thought had a Burt Bacharach feel to it.

For 'Chasing Pavements' and two other tracks, 'Tired' and 'Melt My Heart to Stone', Eg followed up his songwriting duties by tackling the production as well. His contribution on *19* softened Adele's persona as a lonely minstrel. The tracks, basically, were more middle of the road, which increased the commercial possibilities, particularly in the US.

That was in the future. While Adele took advice well, she was also strong in her own mind when it came to her music. She thought the album needed something more upbeat and danceable. She played Richard Russell the song 'Cold Shoulder' and, after he had told her how lovely it was, asked him to get Mark Ronson involved, because she wanted it to have rhythm. It needed Ronson's beats. She had been a huge fan of the musician/DJ since his debut album *Here Comes the Fuzz* in 2003 and thought he had produced one of the greatest albums of all time in *Back to Black* by Amy Winehouse in 2006.

Russell duly set up a meeting between Adele and Mark at the XL offices. The producer had forgotten all about it, which was understandable, as it was the day of the release of his second album, *Version*, in June 2007, which included the memorable cover of 'Valerie', featuring Amy.

By the time Mark had been reached and made it to Notting Hill, Adele was plonked in front of the TV watching *The Jerry Springer Show*, 'pissed off her face', chain-smoking her Marlboro Lights and generally fit for nothing. It was, she told *Blues and Soul*, the 'most awkward meeting EVER'. Despite that embarrassing first encounter, Mark was perfectly happy to be involved. In the credit notes for the album, she thanks Mark 'Don't Fall Over' Ronson for bringing the tune to life. Presumably, the 'don't fall over' remark is an in-joke, recalling what he said to the drunk teenager at their first meeting.

The album, it seemed, was now finished and good to go, but Jonathan still thought it lacked something – perhaps a track that would get everybody talking and back up the commercial appeal of 'Chasing Pavements' and 'Cold Shoulder', another radio-friendly song. He had long been an admirer of one of the lesser-known Bob Dylan ballads called 'Make You Feel My Love', which featured on the gravel-voiced maestro's 1997 collection *Time Out of Mind*. Adele wasn't particularly a Bob Dylan fan; in any case, she was unsure about covering another artist's work, especially one who was a legend. She felt that a song represented a personal commitment by the writer that would be impossible for another to replicate.

She changed her mind when Jonathan played her Dylan's version. She was so moved: 'They were the most beautiful lyrics that I had ever sung or read and they just kind of summed up everything that I had been trying to write in my songs about how I felt.' Dylan, always so poetic in his work, perfectly captured the desire to make someone love you.

The pianist Neil Cowley wasn't a Dylan fan either, but Jim Abbiss played the track to him in the studio and he sat down at the piano to work out how to transpose the song from the folky, free-spirited guitar-driven original to a lusher, soulful sound that suited Adele. 'Dylan was all over it, so we made it a bit stricter. It was always the same recording process. Adele was in the corner behind the glass and it was just two or three takes. I remember Jimmy saying, "Well, I think we have got it and I really like it."' Adele felt the song completed the album's shape: 'The album was kind of like a V and then when I did this song, it just became a whole circle.'

Other well-known artists had recorded the song, including Billy Joel and country star Garth Brooks, but they sounded nothing like Adele. Paul Gambaccini, the respected broadcaster, observed, 'She gave it her own twist and it was best of all the versions, including Bob Dylan's.' Listening to this particular track made him realise that Adele Adkins was a great singer.

Adele recorded her debut between May and September 2007. She couldn't take it easy, sing a couple of songs and go down the pub. Team Adele was making sure she kept busy to maximise the chance of her success. Up to that point, she had become known more by association with other people; now it was time for her to stand alone.

* * *

A month after Adele's nineteenth birthday, Jools Holland looked into the camera and, with his inimitable delivery, announced, 'And now making her TV debut, we welcome, from Brixton, Adele.' And there she was, trying not to display any of the nerves she was feeling, picking out the opening chords of 'Daydreamer' for what seemed like the millionth time.

Later ... with Jools Holland was into its twenty-ninth series and firmly established as a TV institution. Adele's management team had been lobbying hard for her inclusion and had sent the producer, Alison Howe, a demo tape of some of the early recordings with Jim Abbiss. She was immediately impressed: 'When we fall for somebody, we have to have them.' Nobody could remember the show presenting an unreleased act at any time in the previous fifteen years. Adele was flattered to be asked: 'You can't just blag your way on to *Jools Holland*!'

Before the recording began, she was interviewed backstage and said her music was 'acoustic soul', which was a nice and catchy description. She distanced herself from Kate Nash and Lily Allen by suggesting they were creating a genre, while she just wrote love songs. The audience was about to discover that she didn't sound like them either. There was nothing 'mockney' about her vocal style – a result of being influenced by the great American singers, not home-grown ones.

The studio was dark, except for a spotlight on Adele, legs crossed in a comfortable smock, flat shoes and red floral earrings. The leading fashion commentator Alison Jane Reid was impressed with what she saw as a carefully styled, understated look. She observes, 'I like the image. It's authentic. She is wearing the uniform of the singer-songwriter – a simple mini dress over leggings and her hair is worn in a low, messy bun. My impression is that this is a very professional job.'

Nothing about her appearance distracted from her voice, which was exactly the desired effect. In reality, she was shaking inside. She kept her eyes wide open, hoping she didn't look like a frightened rabbit, rather than close them, as she was used to doing when she sang.

Adele explained, 'They usually put you in the middle of the room, but for some reason they put me at the end, right in front of the audience, with Björk on my left, Paul McCartney on my right and my mum crying in front of me.' Penny was there to support her quietly and unobtrusively, as she always did. Adele reported that her mum was worried she would fall off her chair or 'fuck it up somehow'. She didn't meet Björk, who apparently was in a bad mood all day, but she did meet Björk's son Sindri, who was her age, and she thought 'very buff'.

She had already met Paul McCartney once, at the *Fame Academy* bursary evening, but he wouldn't have recalled such a fleeting moment. Then she had been a fan; now she was performing on the same bill. After the show, she walked past him in the corridor and had wanted to say something cool and casual like, 'Hiya, great performance there, Paul', but her nerve failed her. 'I couldn't do it and went to jelly, but he stopped me and spoke to me, which was so nice of him.'

Afterwards, Alison Howe was delighted and enthusiastic: 'She's a classic. She doesn't fit anywhere; she just has a great voice. I would hope that by this time next year she will have sold as many records as Amy and I don't see any reason why she shouldn't.' This was a very bold statement, as *Back to Black* was the biggest-selling album of 2007, with sales of 1.85 million. She would prove to be prophetic, however, even if her timing was a little awry.

When Adele was able to draw breath and reflect on her TV debut, she only had one reaction: 'What the fuck – this is ridiculous!' The hype surrounding Adele was growing. As well as TV, she featured on Radio 1 on Zane Lowe's evening show, online being interviewed by Pete Townshend and his wife, Rachel Fuller, for their 'In the Attic' webcast, and live on the Park Stage at Glastonbury. At the festival, she was among friends. Playing on the same day were Noisettes, Mark Ronson and Jamie T. On different nights, Amy Winehouse, Kate Nash, The Maccabees and M.I.A. appeared. To finish off some great exposure for XL, Jack Peñate was there too.

Finally, after all this attention, it was time for Adele to release a record. Despite 'Daydreamer' being the song that had received most promotion during her previous year of perform- ing, Jonathan Dickins and Richard Russell decided to go with 'Hometown Glory'. It did have an advantage over the other tracks on the album: it was about London and that was very fashionable. Part of the schtick of the new Thamesbeat was songs celebrating or chronicling the capital. M.I.A. with 'Galang' and the Jamie T single 'Sheila' had been part of that. XL, who had released Jack Peñate, got in on the act with 'Torn on the Platform', about catching a train at Waterloo. It had reached number seven in the charts in June 2007.

The best known of the London songs at the time was 'LDN' by Lily Allen, then the queen of this metropolitan movement. 'LDN', text-speak for London, had been released as a 500-copy vinyl limited edition and then re-released five months later as a mainstream single. Lily was the most successful of the Myspace artists and, while she was nothing like Adele, her profile meant female singers were very much in vogue in the mid-noughties.

Adele was part of this wave of London artists, but she didn't want to be associated too closely with a genre that might appear dated in a year's time. For the moment, 'Hometown Glory' was her only song about the city, so 500 copies were pressed and the very first Adele record was released on Monday, 22 October 2007. The acoustic feel of Adele's guitar-led early demo had been replaced by Neil Cowley's superbly romantic piano intro.

The B-side was 'Best for Last', another Jim Abbiss production recorded for the album and one that was more typically Adele. The lyric is a heartfelt poem to the boyfriend who won't return her love and it swings between anger and regret. She tells him directly that he is a 'temporary fix'. The song is a sophisticated blend of different rhythms with a strong bassline that Adele played herself. Jack Peñate contributed backing vocals, returning the favour for 'My Yvonne'.

The publicity blurb was the usual spin as far as new artists were concerned. Adele, it seemed, was born and raised in Brixton. Clearly, it was thought better to be born in the more edgy and trendy Brixton than in drab and uninspiring Tottenham. Streatham was unglamorous, while nobody knew where West Norwood was, so those locations were non-starters. Brixton seemed right. The idea she was from that part of London had already been planted when she was introduced by Jools Holland. The artist always goes along with this sort of rubbish, because of an overwhelming desire to succeed. Adele told Radio 1 DJ Steve Lemacq in her first radio interview that she grew up in Brixton before moving to Tulse Hill.

The quite expert PR material managed to mention London three times, as well as nine artists who had influenced her: Etta James, Jill Scott, Björk, Dusty Springfield, Billy Bragg, Billie Holiday, Jeff Buckley, The Cure and Peggy Lee. Peggy was a new one and was included in preference to Ella or Aretha Franklin. It continued, 'Adele is a truly unique new artist. With her mix up of rhythm, blues and soul, served up with a healthy dose of London attitude, she spins beautiful dark stories of loves won and lost and sometimes just daydreamed about.'

The atmospheric sleeve of the single featured Adele in pensive mood, sitting at a table in a London café, head resting on her hand, gazing into space. It was released on Jamie T's Pacemaker Recordings label, which he had started up the previous year to showcase his own music. Adele's debut was the only time another artist featured. Linking his two acts in this way was a masterstroke by Jonathan Dickins, because Jamie gave Adele credibility, while she, in return, was gathering a huge amount of interest, which would be a boost for his publicity.

The first thing Adele did was make sure all her friends and family shared her excitement. She sent some copies down to Penarth, so her nana, father and brother each had one. Perhaps because of that gesture, 'Hometown Glory' remains her father's favourite among all her songs.

Realistically, this was only a limited edition promotional tool, but it exceeded all expectations and gave an indication of Adele's future appeal. Both Radio 1 *and* Radio 2 played the track – the first XL release ever to feature on Radio 2. Adele couldn't believe how well the song did. She observed, 'I'm so flattered it was received so well because it was the first proper song I ever wrote.'

The music papers understandably paid her much attention, but the mainstream national press were interested as well. The *Daily Mail* mentioned her tour to support the single and the upcoming album; the *Daily Mirror* reviewed the song and, aligning Adele with Amy Winehouse – something she would have to get used to – declared they would be putting out banners to greet her in her neighbourhood. The *Sunday Mail* in Glasgow called it a 'gloriously, bluesy soulful track, sounding a bit like Amy Winehouse'. Everyone agreed that here was a special voice that one reviewer called 'supple, subtle and soulful'.

The *Daily Telegraph* pointed out that the 'stripped down, confessional' style of songwriting instantly carried an air of sincerity. The *Guardian* even sent round their respected music writer Caroline Sullivan to interview Adele at the flat in West Norwood. The two women munched Garibaldi biscuits at the kitchen table – an early example of how Adele was developing an unpretentious image. Now that she was flying solo, not on the coat-tails of other artists, she could project her own personality – funny, normal and natural.

Her live performances backed up the relentless publicity. She appeared with Mark Ronson at the BBC Electric Proms at the Roundhouse and opened for Will Young in November for one of the annual acoustic concerts known as the Little Noise Sessions. Over eight days, these charity evenings in aid of Mencap boasted a line-up that would have graced the

Pyramid Stage at Glastonbury. Keane and Snow Patrol featured the same week as Adele, and U2 turned up to the Union Chapel, unannounced, and played four numbers.

Adele is a great admirer of Mencap, especially because of her mother's interest in charity work. She also loved the beautiful Islington venue and said she would be back – a promise she honoured a year later.

Adele, Adele, Adele ... there was so much coverage of Adele that she was in danger of being so overhyped her album would turn out to be a massive disappointment. Even she admitted, 'I am getting a bit sick of seeing myself in stuff.' The big question was: could she deliver?

10

CHASING THE DREAM

Adele couldn't wait to tell her family that she had been nominated for a BRIT Award. She was even more thrilled when Jonathan Dickins corrected her and told her that she had, in fact, already won. She confessed, 'It's a bit weird getting a BRIT Award before you've done anything, innit?'

She had been chosen to receive the first Critics' Choice Award, voted for by leading pop writers who thought she was the artist most likely to break through in 2008. The excellent news for Adele was that she would be announced as the winner during the nominations' lunch in December, which meant there were two whole months to cash in on the publicity before the big night at Earls Court.

Those weeks would include the XL release of her first mainstream single, 'Chasing Pavements', and the long-awaited album a fortnight later. They had struggled to find the right title for the latter. Adele's favourite album names were *The Miseducation of Lauryn Hill* and *Debut* by Björk, but both of those were taken, obviously. She didn't want anything too obscure. She thought of *19* to reflect how she was feeling when she wrote and recorded the songs. She said she became 'a bit of a woman at that age'. She didn't have a crystal ball to predict that the title would be the start of her unique brand of age-related recordings.

Just before the announcement of her BRIT, she sang her new single on *Friday Night with Jonathan Ross*, then the biggest chat show on British television, with a weekly audience of more than four million. She sat on the sofa next to Renée Zellweger and couldn't believe how thin Bridget Jones was in real life. The headline guest was the American comedian Jerry Seinfeld. Adele had to hide the fact that she hadn't a clue who he was. At least she recognised home-grown television stars David Walliams and Matt Lucas and referred to them as the guys from *Little Britain*.

As if news of an impending BRIT Award weren't enough to brighten her New Year, she was also named as the one to watch in the remarkably similar BBC's Sound of 2008 poll to find the most promising new talent. Once again, 150 critics, music editors and broadcasters voted for the act they thought would succeed in the following year. For Adele not to have won one without the other would have been a surprise. There were a limited number of acts to choose from and in both cases the blonde Welsh singer Duffy was runner-up. The career paths of the two rising stars would intertwine for the next year or two.

The vinyl single of 'Hometown Glory' had done its job. Now, the mainstream release of 'Chasing Pavements' and the album made for exciting times, if a little nerve-racking because she had to show that the enormous amount of hype was justi-fied. Before that, though, she had to shoot her first video.

If you hadn't been at Glastonbury or crammed into Troubadour, then you needed a sense of the artist who was singing to you in such a heartfelt way. 'Chasing Pavements' was an emotional song that demanded a dramatic, thought-provoking film. XL brought in Californian director Matthew Cullen and told him they wanted something creatively ambitious. They gave him three weeks to devise, storyboard, choreograph and shoot the project.

Matthew was drawn to the theme of the song – continuing in a relationship that isn't working – and portraying that conflict. He chose the metaphor of a car crash, in which the two victims, a young couple, come to life to tell the story of their love affair. He shot it in Los Angeles, but made it seem like Hyde Park, even remembering to put a UK licence plate on the battered vehicle.

Adele didn't do much. She sat in a car looking sad and then strolled wistfully in the park, dressed in sombre black and brown. The dancers who played the crash victims brilliantly captured Matthew's concept. The trick is that they appear to be lying down on paving stones while they tell their story of meeting, embracing, falling in love and falling out of love in a series of graceful movements. At the end, ambulance crews wheel them away in different directions. The *Guardian* described it as 'very beautiful'. Kanye West, no less, was impressed enough to post the video on his blog with the comment, 'This shit is dope!!!!!!'

One of the paradoxes that really worked in Adele's favour was that she didn't look nineteen when she was promoting *19*. She always appeared older than she was, so it gave the effect that she was a woman speaking to you whatever age you were. Hers wasn't a silly 'then he kissed me' sort of message.

She sang 'Chasing Pavements' once more at the televised launch party for the BRITs at the Roundhouse. Again, she began a little nervously, before losing herself in the music and bewitching the audience with the power of her voice. She was unimpressed with her performance. 'That was awful,' she mouthed. She also embarrassed herself by giving a peace sign as she walked off stage. 'I can't believe I did that on TV – like Ringo Starr,' she cringed. Her self-criticism was a revealing throwback to her first day as a senior at the BRIT School when she was furious with herself while the other students were in awe of her singing. She remained a perfectionist.

The media had begun to realise that Adele was a fully formed, larger-than-life character, whose voice and demeanour were a welcome antidote to the clones of Mariah Carey that seemed to warble on *The X Factor* every week. Sylvia Patterson in the *Guardian* called her 'exuberant, bawdy, disarmingly honest, effortlessly funny, gasping for "a fag", devoted to her beloved music'.

Adele was concerned, however: 'I feel like I'm being shoved down everyone's throat. My worst fear is my music won't connect with the public.' Her concern was misplaced. 'Chasing Pavements' entered the charts at number two and stayed there for three weeks. She was kept off the top by Basshunter feat. DJ Mental Theo's Bazzheadz with 'Now You're Gone', which, coincidentally, was also a break-up song. The similarity ended there, because the number one was pop by numbers – a trite and juvenile club song with an accompanying video full of model types wearing very little. In comparison, Adele's debut had so much more substance; it gave an early indication that she was a class apart.

Not everyone liked Eg White's production, fearing that it was too chart conscious, but there was universal praise for Adele's vocal. Nick Levine, in *NME*, said: 'Adele's voice is a revelation, steering the big brassy chorus through its melodic twists and turns with consummate ease.'

The album did even better – *19* entered the charts at number one. The beautifully lit cover image by the cutting-edge London-based photographer Hege Sæbjørnsen is arguably the most atmospheric of all Adele images. She presents a youthful yet slightly mysterious look. Alison Jane Reid observes, 'It's like jumping straight back to Dusty Springfield and the Sixties. Even the black eyeliner is pure Sixties retro.'

In the accompanying CD booklet, Adele is liberal with her thank yous. Naturally, she starts by thanking her mum for everything, but second on the list is her stepfather Simon, 'for always being there'. Third is Jonathan 'professional' Dickins and fourth is Jack Peñate, for 'always making me smile. I love you very much.' The list is extensive, as is often the case with first albums. She doesn't forget Liz Penney, Conor Doherty, theatre teacher Imogen Brodie and Stuart Worden from the BRIT School, or old alumni and great friends, Laura Dockrill, Lyndon Blue and Shingai Shoniwa.

On a page of happy snaps, she includes a very young Penny with baby Adele and another jolly one of Jack Peñate with his right arm half strangling her and his left draped around Nick Huggett. She also includes a picture of John and Rose Evans by the sea in South Wales – a lovely reminder of how much they meant to her. She gives Nana and Grampy the biggest thank you in the text as well, calling them the 'original romantics', a touching reference to how her grandparents would stroll along the front in Penarth, always holding hands, even into their fifties. Although she mentions 'my little brother Cameron', the rest of her family, including her father Marc, aren't named, but receive a general thanks.

She didn't thank the boy who inspired much of the album. Everything she wanted to say, she had put down in the lyrics, from the anger and bitterness of 'Cold Shoulder' to the resigned sadness of 'First Love'.

His anonymity didn't stop speculation that he was a good-looking black actor and musician called Kyle Winfield, who also went by the name of Slinky Sunbeam. Adele was unimpressed by the rumours and, unusually for her, issued a strong denial: 'People keep saying I am/was seeing Slinky Sunbeam. I'm not and never have done. Whoever this "source" is, they're talking out their arse. He ain't my type.'

One of the sidebars to the *19* story came when her now notorious ex apparently demanded a cut of her royalties for inspiring the songs. He was, it seemed, deadly serious and kept calling about it for a week. Adele explained, 'He really thought he'd had some input into the creative process by being a prick. Finally, I said, "Well, you made my life hell, so I lived it and now I deserve it."' She did concede that his treatment of her made her an adult.

She chose not to 'out' her ex-boyfriend to the world, even though he had caused her so much emotional distress. That would have been cruel. Revealing his identity would also have destroyed the mystique of the album. As it stood, every woman could picture a broken relationship of their own and empathise with Adele's songs. Knowing what he looked like would have ruined that.

Despite all the excitement and the hullabaloo surrounding Adele's launch, she was already very careful not to share too much with the world – not only to protect herself, but also because she understood how unbearable life could become for the people close to her if they were hounded by press and paparazzi. 'I'm obsessed by celebrity,' she acknowledged. 'I just don't want to be one.'

She was a long way from being internationally famous, yet she already had very strong and intelligent views about the nature of celebrity and the constant spotlight. 'If I'm at an awards ceremony or out in Central London, it's fine to have them take pictures. But outside my mum's front door? I'm not having that.' This was an incredibly strident point of view for someone starting out.

She had a sixth sense that the media might not always be her friend and needed to be strictly managed. As if to prove the point, reviews of *19* were decidedly mixed, with many critics anxious not to jump on the Adele bandwagon. They deserved to be greeted with a one-word reaction: 'Ouch.'

The *NME* gave it 5 out of 10 and concluded, 'It's clear that, for all the hype, Adele is not yet ready to produce an album of sufficient depth to match her voice.' *Uncut* online was worse: 'Adele simply hasn't found her own voice yet. The acoustic tracks that open the LP are awful: "Daydreamer", about a bisexual beau, is ickily trite … It takes more than clubbing with Kate Nash and Jack Peñate to be a genuine contender.'

Even compliments were backhanded. Gavin Martin, in the *Daily Mirror*, said, 'A cover version of the substandard mawkish Bob Dylan song "Make You Feel My Love" stands out, highlighting the shallowness of her own navel gazing diary entries.'

Adele quickly gave up reading everything written about her. Considering her subsequent success, it seems bizarre that these initial reactions were so lukewarm.

Some loved it, however. The *Guardian* wrote perceptively, 'Rather than screaming for attention, there's an artistically focused stillness at the centre of so many bruising love songs.' Chris Long was enthusiastic on BBC Online: 'It's a genuinely touching, maturely considered and brilliantly sung opus that belies her titular age.' He highlighted 'Hometown Glory', 'Cold Shoulder' and the 'piano-epic' 'Make You Feel My Love' as being tracks that 'make Lily Allen and Kate Nash sound every bit as ordinary as they are'.

Clearly, it was a good career move to distance herself from the sounds of Thamesbeat, which looked likely to have a short shelf-life. Amy Winehouse, however, was a different proposition. The critics, almost without exception, name-checked the troubled singer in their Adele comments. People were genuinely worried about the brightest star of her generation, who seemed to have her finger on the self-destruct button. Chris Long hoped that Adele would, in the future, be better at handling astronomical fame than the 'crumbling' Amy.

Adele was always very gracious about Amy, maintaining that she didn't mind a bit being constantly compared to her. She'd almost invited the comparisons anyway, by including the track 'Right as Rain', which was quite Amy-like and might easily have found its way onto a Winehouse album.

'I love Amy Winehouse and I love her music as well. So I have no problem being compared to her. At least I like her. If it was someone like Joss Stone, I would be very unhappy. I do like Joss Stone. I liked her first two records. I thought they were amazing, but she has gone a bit doolally now.'

19 was at the top of the charts for only one week, but at least it gave Will Young the chance to give Adele the build-up she deserved when he introduced her at the BRIT Awards in February 2008. Her big night at the UK's most prestigious pop event of the year was the zenith of two months of enormous hype and reward. Will managed to read his autocue without being too put off by what seemed like a noisy hen party of BRIT School students. He explained what her award was for and made the point that the critics were already proved right, because *19* had gone to number one. He asked the audience to give a big cheer for the 'gorgeous' Adele, and the BRIT School students obliged.

She managed to avoid any F-words, but was, as usual, disarmingly honest: 'I am not going to talk for too long because I think speeches are really boring, but I would really like to thank some people … Oh God, my heart is beating, it's so fast.' Even in a short acceptance, Adele had the ability to make you feel you were part of her world. She was likeable as she named Jonathan, who had been there since day one, Alison Howe, everyone at XL and Beggars, Nick Huggett, Jamie T, Jack Peñate and the BRIT School, and, of course, her 'beautiful mum'. Penny, for once, had chosen not to attend, worried that she would make Adele even more nervous than she was already.

As many performers do, Adele managed to conceal her nerves from the audience − most of the time at least. She confided beforehand, 'I'm usually sick before a gig. I heave at small ones, so God knows what I'll be like at the BRITs. I'm cacking myself.'

Adele's first-ever performance at the awards was a low-key event in more ways than one. She sang the mellow Coldplay song 'God Put a Smile upon Your Face' as the first of a medley of Mark Ronson numbers from his album *Version*. She had to decide whether to sing in her high register and risk missing some of the difficult top notes or opt for low, which might be thought not 'wow-y' enough. She chose low, which was probably a mistake, because her performance was, for once, underwhelming and the track clearly didn't suit her.

She wasn't helped by being followed by a painfully thin Amy Winehouse, who closed Ronson's segment with a raucous and exciting 'Valerie'. Amy didn't win an award that evening, but Kate Nash kept the BRIT School flags waving by collecting Best British Female Solo Artist.

Arctic Monkeys stirred up some controversy when they accepted their award for Best British Group. Singer Alex Turner pointed to the students and said, sarcastically, 'We all went to the BRIT School. We remember you all. After we graduated, we formed the Monkeys and we've had a fantastic time since.'

The principal, Nick Williams, laughed it off when the media tried to suggest it was part of a BRIT School backlash. He described is as 'a bit of fluff' and a joke by Alex Turner, but did acknowledge there was some prejudice against his students.

Adele was more feisty and forthright in her response: 'Fucking idiots. Think they're working class. Their bloody mums are art teachers, aren't they?' She didn't get it quite right – Turner's mother taught German and his father physics and music.

11

AT JOE'S PUB

Adele admits she is a bad flyer, forever fretting about whether the plane is going to crash and hoping she'll have time to call her mum. Nevertheless, soon after the BRITs, she jumped on a flight to New York at the beginning of March for an important gig in front of only 184 prospective fans and record company executives.

It was a gamble to leave the UK when she was one of the hottest properties in music and make a start in the US. Originally, the plan was to wait a few months and take on America in the summer, but the popular celebrity blogger Perez Hilton had mentioned her in a New Year column and said she had a voice like honey. He became a champion of Adele and her music over the years, but his first recommendation was particularly significant in getting her name out there. She was well aware that millions read his column, even if they didn't have a clue whom he was talking about.

XL had a growing, if still small, presence in the US, thanks to the man Richard Russell had appointed in 2006 as vice-president in charge of A&R in America. Kris Chen was regarded as the sort of go-ahead person they needed and was well liked. He was known for his previous work as label manager with Domino Records, home of Arctic Monkeys, where he had also worked closely with BRIT Award-winners Franz Ferdinand. His job, and that of his handful of staff in the Beggars Group headquarters on Grand Street, was to give maximum attention to a very small output. They didn't have the resources to match the big labels when promoting a record, especially in the very important world of radio.

The success of M.I.A. was largely due to the deal that XL signed with the prestigious American company Interscope to release and distribute her records over there. While Adele was breaking through in Britain, M.I.A.'s rap record 'Paper Planes' was a huge US hit and on its way to becoming the second biggest-selling single ever for XL, eventually shifting four million copies.

Back in London, Richard Russell and Martin Mills wanted to arrange something similar for Adele. A deal with an American giant wouldn't guarantee success, but it would be a start. They had a fortuitous break when the man who 'discovered' her, Nick Huggett, left the company to become head of A&R at Sony's Columbia label in the UK. At least he could alert the American giant about her. Now, she had to impress the suits. Kris Chen's job was to arrange a showcase gig so that she could.

He rang Shanta Thake, the programme director at Joe's Pub in Lower Manhattan, and told her he was bringing a new singer-songwriter called Adele to the US and that she had been receiving a lot of positive attention in the UK. Shanta explained, 'It's often the case that people will be a big deal there and never come out big here. I think when we heard the songs from Kris, we were like, "Oh my God, this girl is amazing." But you hear that a lot.' She was certainly impressed enough to book her. Adele would be performing on St Patrick's Day, Monday, 17 March 2008. Tickets went on sale at $12 each.

Joe's Pub was part of The Public Theater complex on Lafayette Street and conveniently less than a mile from the XL office. Despite sounding unpretentious, it was far classier than most of the small venues around London that Adele had played while building a following in the UK. Named after the legendary theatrical producer Joe Papp, who founded Shakespeare in the Park in New York, it was widely regarded as one of the premier venues in the city. It was a place that would take a chance on an unknown and prided itself on helping to build reputations.

Adele's usual nerves weren't helped by having a cold – one of those typical bouts of sniffles you get after a long flight. She was worried that she wouldn't be able to sing at full power, so the staff at Joe's ran round getting the honey to put in her tea and lemon. Everybody, it seemed, realised that this was a big show for the likeable girl with the broad London accent. One of the ways she handles her anxiety is to prattle away in the manner that has since become her trademark. She walked on stage and declared, 'Forgive me if I start coughing up or something during a song', which she followed with her inimitable chuckle, and the audience were already half in love with her.

Adele had asked for one simple spotlight, similar to her request for her performance on *Later ... with Jools Holland*. She understood very early on that she was seen to best effect with just her guitar and her voice. Shanta recalled, 'When she opened her mouth to sing, we were like, "What is happening here?!" Seeing her live was, like, a phenomenon. She was just a clear superstar.'

Everybody was delighted and the memory of the reception she received would stay with Adele, who would always have a soft spot for Joe's. The executives were impressed and negotiations were swiftly concluded for her recording contract with Columbia. She appeared at Joe's again the following night. Before the concert, she signed her US deal in her dressing room.

She received her first American review two days later in the *New York Times*, which was helpful exposure, even if the review itself was pretentious and not exactly glowing. Under the headline 'Another British Invader Arrives, Guitar in Hand', the critic noted that she didn't 'deploy many melismatic runs' and thought the songs 'poised but callow'.

The reviewer, inevitably, raised the spectre of Amy Winehouse. If M.I.A. had provided the business model for XL to follow with Adele, then Amy's success and notoriety shone a light on female singers from the UK, especially those who also went to the BRIT School. Adele continued to be upbeat about the constant comparison, stating firmly that she adored Amy, even if privately she found it getting a bit boring.

By the time the *New York Times* hit the newsstands, Adele had moved on to California for her first-ever West Coast gig at The Hotel Café, an intimate venue in West Hollywood. Work behind the scenes meant this was another small but highly significant event. Jonathan Palmer, who was in charge of creating television licensing opportunities at Columbia, invited Alexandra Patsavas along.

Alex, as she is known, is one of the big hitters in the world of Hollywood music, responsible for the soundtracks of many top-rated shows through her Chop Shop company. She was impressed with Adele and, in particular, with 'Hometown Glory' and said she would try to include it in the hugely popular *Grey's Anatomy*.

She eventually scheduled it for the season finale, to be shown on 18 May 2008, three days before Adele would be starting her first proper US tour, *An Evening with Adele*, at the Roxy on Sunset Strip in LA. The timing was perfect. This sort of television exposure was gold dust for an artist and a further indication of how fortunate Adele was with the people working for her. They were clever and dedicated and understood what they needed to do to give her an edge. She had only just turned twenty, but a sign of her professional maturity was that intuitively she knew whom she could trust. It's why so many of Team Adele are still with her today.

She probably didn't have a group of TV doctors in pristine blue scrubs in mind when she wrote the song. They were conducting a graphic operation, while her music played in a tense episode that was watched by eighteen million people. Neil Cowley's haunting piano was perfect for the scene.

Before her US tour began, Adele warmed up with half a dozen shows around the UK. She had moved up a division from her short acoustic sets accompanied by Ben Thomas on guitar and her touring piano player Steve Holness. Now she had a full band; ten songs grew to fourteen; and much banter with the audience took a thirty-five-minute show over the hour. A souvenir programme featured the cover of *19* on the front. *An Evening with Adele* was born.

Her persona at bigger venues was well developed right at the beginning and has changed little through the years. She chatted away as if she were at a family get-together before the footie started.

During the opening night at St David's Hall, Cardiff, she waved to Rose, her Penarth nana, and pointed to her brother Cameron in the audience. Her father, Marc, was also there that night, but stayed backstage. Afterwards, the family grabbed a few minutes with the new headliner before she was whisked off into the night. Adele had rarely been to Wales after she had become a teenager and her life had changed so radically at the BRIT School, but she still kept in touch with everyone by phone. She charmed her audience by declaring that South Wales was her second home.

Many artists don't have the personality to communicate to a crowd, but that was never a problem for Adele. One minute she was chatty and chuckling, the next she could switch to being emotional and heartfelt when she sang. She apologised in advance for any high notes she missed during her cover of 'Fool That I Am' and then proceeded to struggle with one or two. Nobody cared. They liked her.

She seemed instinctively to know how to interact. At the Tyne Theatre in Newcastle, she sang the theme tune to the popular television series *Byker Grove* ('Ooo … Byker … Ooo … Byker … Byker … Grove'), which instantly had the audience in the palm of her hand. She didn't begin with 'Daydreamer' in the bigger arenas – that was better suited to smaller venues. Instead, she opened with the up-tempo 'Right as Rain'.

To give the tour a boost, XL released 'Cold Shoulder' as a single. It was probably the most commercially produced song on the album after 'Chasing Pavements'. These days, singles from albums tend to sell progressively worse with each release and the second from *19* barely scraped into the top twenty. The video was less ambitious than the first single, simply showing Adele in dark, subdued lighting in a room full of ice sculptures that are slowly melting.

The B-side, 'Now and Then', was arguably more interesting, in that it would have been the saddest song on the album if it had made the final cut. The lyric heartbreakingly conveys the sense of loss at the end of a relationship. Perhaps everyone thought it would be one Jim Abbiss–produced acoustic track too many on *19*, although for some reason it did surface on the extended Japanese version.

Strangely, it also didn't feature on the setlist for *An Evening with Adele*. Instead, she padded out songs from the album with three covers in addition to 'Make You Feel My Love'. Each was very different. 'Fool That I Am' is a smoky ballad; 'Many Shades of Black', a contemporary rock song by The Raconteurs, Jack White's new band, also signed to XL. Lastly, as part of the encore, she performed a bluesy version of the Sam Cooke classic 'That's It, I Quit, I'm Movin' On'. As she admitted, 'I have to do covers because I've only got one album.'

Being back in the UK gave Adele the opportunity to sort out her financial affairs. She had achieved a number one album and signed a lucrative American deal. She wanted power over her career and an important aspect of that was to have total control over her finances. She could turn to Jonathan Dickins or Martin Mills for advice if she needed it, because they both retained 100 per cent ownership of their companies. Her stepfather Simon had also run his own company and was able to give her advice on how best to proceed. At the age of nineteen years and eleven months, she had decided to set up her own company to manage her money. She wanted to call it something that would resonate with her personally and turned to her first album for inspiration. She chose her favourite track, the intensely emotional and poetic 'Melt My Heart to Stone'. She observed, 'I just love singing it. When I wrote it, I was crying.'

Melting Stone Ltd was incorporated on 4 April 2008 by accountants Morris & Shah, who specialised in acting for musicians. In its first year, the turnover was £1.2 million, with a net profit of £562,000 – not bad for a twenty-year-old from West Norwood. Adele is the sole shareholder, director and company secretary, and would exercise similar control as more companies were set up for her in the future. Neither Jonathan Dickins nor Penny was involved. It was an early indication that behind the façade of an ordinary girl with very real emotions was a formidable and smart woman.

Her life was a whirlwind, completely different to the days when she struggled to get out of bed. Now she was up at 7 every morning for an endless round of newspaper and magazine interviews, radio shows and photo shoots that she didn't much enjoy, but realised were a necessary evil. In the evening, she would have to go on stage and be a singing sensation and potty-mouthed Londoner, not seeing her bed again until 3 a.m.

That routine didn't change much when she returned to the US to start her North American tour, except her days now included airport lounges, a tour bus with 'six stinky guys' and hotel rooms for one. At least Jonathan had ensured that she had a full-time assistant with her, called Rose Moon, who worked for September and would become essential to Adele and, in effect, her day-to-day manager.

Jonathan was back and forth from London at least half a dozen times to make sure she was all right and, understandably, he was delighted with the reception she received from the fourteen concert dates that criss-crossed the US and Canada. He observed, 'The reviews were so good, it was like I'd written them myself.'

He must have been thinking of Jon Bream in the Minneapolis *Star Tribune*, who clearly had his crystal ball in good working order: 'The highly touted British newcomer delivered a knockout performance of acoustic R&B-tinged pop, one of those tiny shows that will become legendary years from now when she's a star.' He enjoyed the patter between songs. Adele complained of a migraine, moaned about the heat and whined about her wisdom teeth. She was refreshingly unstarry. Jon was probably the first critic to prefer Adele to Amy Winehouse, declaring she had more range and depth.

Her closing number was 'Chasing Pavements', which was released as her first US single in June. Time and again, Adele had to explain what 'Chasing Pavements' meant. 'I am starting to dislike it myself now,' she complained. 'Even my mum is, like, "I don't get it."' Even so, she would patiently, and with her usual good humour, explain that it was a metaphor, because obviously you couldn't chase a pavement. She was, in effect, chasing nothing, because there was no one there.

She managed to avoid re-recording the song, substituting sidewalk for pavements for the American audience. She had to laugh when it was pointed out that someone had posted to the Urban Dictionary online, defining the expression as a gay sex act. She told *Billboard*, 'The gay community thinks I am really dirty because it turns out as some really dirty sex position. But I never knew that and everyone thinks I am dirty but I am not.'

Apparently, some radio stations withdrew the song from their playlists because of the connotation, resulting in some extra publicity. Even a little controversy couldn't boost sales that were disappointing for both single and album. *19* entered the *Billboard* 200 at number sixty-one and spent the summer languishing in the lower reaches of the chart.

No British artist has a divine right to succeed across the Atlantic. Many of the biggest stars in UK pop history have failed to make any lasting impact in the US. Cliff Richard, perhaps most famously, never impressed American audiences. The roll-call of those who couldn't repeat their success in the US includes Kylie Minogue, Oasis, Take That and Westlife. Any success was fleeting and didn't reflect the efforts that were made. Robbie Williams tried very hard to make it, but is able to walk down the street in Los Angeles where he lives and not be recognised.

Jonathan Dickins was well aware of the challenge. At the time of the first Adele push, 97 per cent of the acts that broke through in the US were home-grown. Adele tried to be philosophical and maintained, as others had before her, that it wasn't the end of the world if she didn't make it. She explained in a television interview, 'I want as many people as possible to hear my music and that's why I want to come here and do the work and get my music out to a lot of people, but I don't think it is the end of the world if you don't do well in America.'

Adele had expected to be able to write songs for her important second album while on the road. She had time on her hands between shows, but airports and motels didn't provide her with any inspiration. She even toyed with the idea of renting an apartment in Brooklyn for the inspiration she was bound to receive from a magnificent view of the Manhattan skyline. It was all wishful thinking. Her lyric book remained resolutely empty. She poignantly described the universal predicament for pop stars: 'You play to 2,000 people who adore you and then go back to your hotel room alone.'

Perhaps things would change back in London, where the sights and sounds were more familiar and reassuring. She found herself surprisingly homesick and had fallen into a cycle of drinking too much between gigs. She missed her friends and family and, most of all, she was pining for a new love.

12

EARLY LIFE CRISIS

Throughout her teenage years, Adele had focused determinedly on her music and her career. She had an old head and a young heart. After a couple of unsatisfactory relationships – one a crush and the other a wretched experience – now, aged twenty, she embarked on a third that she acknowledges made her an adult. She was properly in love for the first time.

Ironically, the couple had met when the world's media were beginning to wonder who had inspired *19*. That boyfriend was very much old news as far as Adele was concerned. She had rid herself of him by putting the intensity of her feelings about him into her songs.

She was introduced to the man who would become Mister 21 by friends during a time in her life when the hype surrounding her was almost out of control and made it very difficult to start a new love affair. He was ten years older, cultured and artistic, and more likely to suggest what book she should read than what topping she should have on her pizza. He sparked her interest in film and literature, food and wine, travel, politics and history. Adele, a very smart woman, had grown accustomed to reading superficial magazines, but now she was more likely to pick up *White Teeth*, the acclaimed novel by Zadie Smith set in the multicultural environment of Willesden Green.

Quite simply, she was besotted. She was asked in an online interview about the pain of breaking up and perceptively compared it to the feeling she experienced starting a new relationship. She observed, 'You are still just as desperate and pathetic and confused as you were at the beginning.' When an American TV crew came over to film her in London, they were amused to find Adele checking her phone every few minutes to see if her new boyfriend had replied to a text.

At least the couple could enjoy a summer together in the flat she started renting above a shop in her favourite area of Notting Hill. She had plenty of money and was planning to buy as soon as possible, but, for the moment, this was blissful – a world away from West Norwood.

She honestly thought she had found her soulmate: 'We had everything – on every level we were totally right. We'd finish each other's sentences, and he could just pick up how I was feeling by the look in my eye, down to a T, and we loved the same things, and hated the same things, and we were brave when the other was brave and weak when the other was weak.'

Her new man wasn't a celebrity and was as unimpressed as she was by some of the more fashionable hang-outs, such as Nobu and the Ivy, which she once said was 'shit'. Her favourite nights were when they could slip unnoticed into the cinema and then have a low-key meal some place where she was left alone. In Notting Hill, they could eat Mediterranean at Ottolenghi or Asian at E&O, although these were both trendy and they ran some risk of being noticed. If they were going to the Ritzy in Brixton, then she most liked her secret Malaysian restaurant, where they would never be bothered.

She started staying in a lot more, learning how to cook and enjoying a cuddle on the sofa with a glass of red wine and one of the Al Pacino classics she loved – maybe *Scarface* or *The Godfather: Part II*. Adele is quietly a movie buff, enjoying gangster films in particular.

Not everything was bliss. She had an almighty dust-up with paparazzi when she spotted them loitering in the street outside her flat, waiting to snatch a picture – something she detested. Amusingly, they weren't interested in her at all, but in the supermodel Elle Macpherson, who, much to Adele's surprise, lived in the house next door.

At first, the new relationship didn't seem to be affecting her work in any way. She fulfilled July engagements in Berlin, Montreux and Amsterdam, before four more in London ended her summer obligations.

She sang in St John's Smith Square at the Black Ball charity event, a fundraising evening for Keep a Child Alive, which supports and fights for families in Africa living with the HIV/Aids virus. Adele has always been a keen supporter of children's charities, giving a monthly donation to Great Ormond Street Hospital in London, even when money was tight, because of the wonderful help they had given one of her cousins who had severe epilepsy. The Black Ball was hosted by Alicia Keys, a singer she had long admired. The two women got on well and Adele promised to sing again at the charity's annual New York night in November.

At the auction, Adele secured a painting by the controversial artist Stella Vine for £8,000. She could easily afford the purchase price. While she was shrewd where money matters were concerned, she wasn't in the least mean. She subsequently gave the painting to her mother, a particular fan of the artist, who had started off her adult life as a single teenage mum. Adele even toyed with the idea of commissioning Vine to paint a portrait of her and Penny together.

The cloud on the summer of love was that Adele was drinking too much – to the extent that it was becoming a problem. She had never been shy about admitting that she liked a glass or two at home in her bedroom and would prefer to pass out 'steamingly drunk' on her bed than on the sofa of a nightclub. Her new man was equally happy polishing off a bottle of Cabernet, so that didn't help her cut down. She didn't realise until later that her life was out of control for a while and she could admit then, 'I was drinking far too much and that was kind of the basis of my relationship with this boy.'

In the short term, a crisis occurred when she was due to fly back to the US for further dates and promotion in August and September. She didn't want to leave her man and so cancelled everything. Even at this early stage of her career, she was in total control of her work, even if it meant making a bad decision.

Officially, the reason for the cancellations was family problems. She elaborated on that in her Myspace blog: 'There's some problems at home I've had to sort out. I was looking forward to touring and throwing myself back into it. But my home life needs more attention. I apologise from the bottom of my heart for disappointing you all.'

Adele doesn't give a running commentary on her life. She prefers to leave it until well after the event before she says anything. That's why we had to wait a year before the truth came out, when she told *Nylon* magazine: 'I couldn't bear to be without him, so I was like, "Well, OK, I'll just cancel my stuff then" … I can't believe I did that. It seems so ungrateful.' She added amusingly, 'We refer to that period as my E.L.C., my Early Life Crisis.'

For two months the world heard nothing from Adele. She disappeared completely from view. She cancelled everything and told Jonathan and Carl Fysh that she was switching off her BlackBerry and didn't want any emails, interview requests or texts. She was having some time off. Revealingly, her management and record label did as she wished, shrewdly realising that she needed a reboot rather than a boot up her backside. She still saw her friends, but they were not overly impressed with Mister 21, believing that Adele was a different person when she was around him.

Adele was desperate to be part of a couple. She loved romance or, perhaps more accurately, the drama of romance. She wanted to be swept off her feet and taken to Italy, but as she told *Rolling Stone*, her man was more artistic than romantic. They did go to Italy, but she ended up making all the arrangements, booking a lovely hotel in Milan and paying for everything.

Unknown to her, back in Wales, her father Marc had also been suffering serious drink problems for several years, downing up to eight pints of lager a day as he tried to put his life back on track. Exactly how much alcohol problems are genetically inherited is a grey area, and Adele didn't grow up in a heavy drinking environment.

She had to pull herself together for the release of 'Make You Feel My Love', the fourth single from *19*. 'Hometown Glory' had been re-released in July and had much exposure on Radio 1 and 2, even if it only scraped into the top twenty. More importantly, it kept Adele's music out there by being featured on the popular soap *Hollyoaks*.

This strategy of product placement had worked well in the US and was replicated in the UK many times. 'Hometown Glory' was one of those songs that suited an elegiac, even sombre mood, and was soon a favourite on dancing and singing reality shows and programme trailers – it was often used for *Coronation Street*. Some numbers are classics without ever being huge hits and its use at funerals reveals how popular her first song became.

Sombre would describe Adele's mood when she filmed the video for 'Make You Feel My Love' in London at the start of September. She clearly was feeling sad and didn't want to be there. The director Mat Kirkby, who started in commercials before moving on to the pop world, had no idea what was going on in her private life: 'I know that she did seem very unhappy … when we sat down and talked out the idea for the video, we were trying to address that, you know. I didn't want to put her in a catsuit and have her doing cartwheels or anything.'

Instead, he placed her centre stage in a dimly lit room, singing the plaintive song, while hoping and waiting for her lover to respond to her mobile phone text. Ironically, it was the story of her life in her latest relationship. 'Make You Feel My Love' fitted the storyboard behind her lost love of *19* perfectly, and now suited her present unhappy love affair as well.

Adele wasn't a total mope, of course. To a certain extent, she was still the life and soul, giving it the 'full Sid James' as Mat describes it, within forty-five seconds of meeting, but things were obviously not right. He observed, 'I want to be diplomatic, but literally every take she did, she just disappeared for a fag and a bottle of beer. She seemed to be quite thirsty at the time, but, you know, hot lights – one gets thirsty.'

Amusingly, Mat made a huge gaffe by using his real mobile phone number as the one Adele texts on screen at the start of the video. As a result, he was plagued by calls – literally thousands of them – from 'little kids', as he called them. 'The first call they make, they usually hang up. The second call they make, they say, "Is that Adele?" And the third, they usually sing to me. Most of them think I'm her ex-boyfriend who has done her a terrible wrong.'

His video of 'Make You Feel My Love' has had more than 100 million hits on YouTube. The money and prestige Mat received from it helped him to finance his directorial debut, a short called, of all things, *The Phone Call*, which starred Sally Hawkins and Jim Broadbent. In 2015, it won the Oscar for Best Live Action Short Film.

The song only made number twenty-six in the charts, although it did push Adele back into the spotlight after her relatively brief time away. Unusually, the track reached number four two years later, when it featured heavily in *Comic Relief* and a series of *The X Factor*.

Adele had to return to the States or all the publicity and promotion, the interviews and the concerts she had undertaken there would have been for nothing. There were already rumblings that her US adventure had flopped, following the lukewarm sales of *19*. Columbia and, in particular, their English-born chairman, Rob Stringer, were not going to give up easily. He had liked Adele since the first time she walked into his office in New York with a cigarette hanging out of the side of her mouth and announced, 'Yea, this'll do.'

He used all his considerable influence to secure her a singing spot on the hugely popular television show *Saturday Night Live* on 18 October 2008. Adele is under no illusions: 'It was the night that changed my life.' By sheer fluke, it became the most watched episode of the programme for fourteen years, with 17 million viewers.

At the time, the US was totally absorbed by the presidential campaign involving Barack Obama against the Republican candidate, John McCain, and his vice-presidential running-mate, Sarah Palin. She was the controversial Governor of Alaska who proved to be a godsend to political commentators and satirists around the world. Chief among the latter was the acclaimed actress and comedienne Tina Fey, a former *Saturday Night Live* regular who had returned that autumn for a series of parodies that brilliantly and uncannily captured the election hopeful. Palin agreed to be on the show in person on 25 October, but at the last moment she switched weeks and so turned up on the evening when Adele appeared. The whole world, it seemed, tuned in to watch her in a sketch with Tina.

Adele knew about the Fey impersonation and managed to get the two of them muddled up. She explained, 'When I saw Sarah Palin I thought it was Tina. I was going "Tina, Tina!" then quoting lines from the movie *Mean Girls*, because she wrote it. The security guard had to barge me out of the way, thinking I was some fucking freak.'

Understandably, the security on the show was heightened on the night, with what seemed like a million Secret Service personnel checking everything. They walked into Adele's dressing room, where she was being made up, to check she was meant to be there, which she found hilarious.

Adele, who was in favour of Obama for President and had a badge supporting him, refused to allow Palin in her dressing room before the broadcast because of the candidate's views opposing same-sex marriages and civil partnerships. Many of Adele's entourage are gay and this would have been an awkward encounter. She did end up having a proper, formal meeting after the show, which wasn't much more than a hi–goodbye, but, joking apart, Adele thought she was 'a really nice lady', even if she didn't agree in the slightest with her right-wing politics.

During the show, Adele sang 'Chasing Pavements', remembering to change the last line to 'chasing sidewalks' in a slightly cheesy nod to her US audience. One big difference from her appearance at Joe's Pub earlier in the year was that she had ditched the guitar and stood in front of the microphone, employing her now familiar Dusty Springfield flowing hand movements. Behind her, she was supported by the glamorous Wired Strings, who gave the arrangements a much lusher sound, similar to Eg White's album production. She returned later in the show to perform a jazzier version of 'Cold Shoulder'. Her performance in front of such a huge television audience was immaculate. Endearingly, at the end of the song, she had wrung her hands together, as she habitually did in a self-effacing way, and said, 'Thank you very much.'

One member of the enthusiastic audience was the actress America Ferrera, star of *Ugly Betty*. She was already a fan, having bought *19* and played it repeatedly. She was singing along to the songs when she was asked if she would like to meet Adele backstage. She was thrilled to discover that Adele enjoyed her series: 'Come be on our show,' suggested America. 'And she was like, "I would love to!"' It was a show-business moment and Adele forgot all about it amid the general excitement.

It was a memorable night. Before *SNL* transmitted, *19* was number forty on the iTunes chart. The next morning, she was flying home to London. As she took off, she had risen to number eight. When she landed, she was number one. Adele wrote on her blog that she was 'chuffed'.

Another unexpected bonus was meeting the famous producer Rick Rubin at the TV studio. He had flown from Los Angeles especially to hear her. In fact, she spotted him for the first time while she was singing. He was a character you couldn't miss – his distinctive flowing hair and beard made him stand out as a man who might have been a roadie for ZZ Top. He was the founder of Def Jam Records and, at the time he showed up to *SNL*, he was also Co-Chairman of Columbia Records. He was one of the biggest names in American popular music, a multiple Grammy winner and the producer of, among others, Justin Timberlake, Shakira and Kanye West.

A couple of weeks later, Adele met Timberlake for the first time, when she flew back to New York and they both performed at the annual Keep a Child Alive Black Ball at the Hammerstein Ballroom in Manhattan. She'd had a small crush on him since her adolescent days, when he was a bleached blond singer in 'N Sync. She told the renowned columnist Liz Jones, 'I wanted to say, "I love you, let's get married and have children", but instead I just barked at him, "Woof". I always bark at boys when I fancy them.' She shared a table with David Bowie and his wife Iman, and sang a duet with Alicia Keys of 'Make You Feel My Love' and 'Hometown Glory'.

She was back in Notting Hill by the time the nominations for the 2009 Grammys were announced in Los Angeles in early December. Her appearance on *Saturday Night Live* had been fortuitous, because it put her in the forefront of everyone's mind a couple of weeks before the nominations were decided. She was lying in bed, still awake at 4 a.m. and googling to see if Leona Lewis was in the running for an award, when she received a text from Perez Hilton to tell her the good news. She had received four nominations. Three were for 'Chasing Pavements' and the fourth for Best New Artist, which would be a very good one to win. Leona was up for only three, as was Duffy, whom, it seemed, Adele couldn't shake off.

Adele had to go and lock herself in the bathroom for what seemed like an hour to take it all in. She was crying with emotion. Eventually, she woke Penny, who was staying in the flat, and told her what had happened. Her mother started screaming with excitement and then dashed upstairs to tell the neighbours, even though it was the small hours of the morning. Adele had so much to look forward to that her early life crisis seemed well and truly over.

13

EN VOGUE

Adele was ending the year full of resolve. She had decided to give up drinking on Boxing Day, after spending a jolly Christmas with her mum, when she cooked the turkey and the trimmings for the first time. The pre-New Year's resolution wouldn't last for ever, but it was an indication that Adele was going to take this latest recognition more seriously than anything that had gone before.

She accidentally put her foot in it by trying to be modest about her nomination. She announced that she wasn't sure an artist should be up for a Grammy after one album and was then horrified when it appeared in the press as an 'Adele doesn't want to win' story. That was not what she meant. She clarified matters by explaining that it was like winning an Oscar too soon: 'It puts a dampener on the rest of your career.'

Of course she wanted to win, even if she wasn't the favourite to do so. Disney heart-throbs the Jonas Brothers were the front runners. Her team impressed upon her that the Grammy Awards were a big deal, and that she needed to raise her game to take advantage of the exposure. She needed a makeover.

She had already come a long way since her teenage years at the BRIT School, when she was filmed by friends larking about with a cigarette and posing mischievously for the camera. Alison Jane Reid observes, 'You can see how pretty she is, with huge eyes and a naturally engaging, fun-loving personality. One picture with her ciggy is a typical attempt at girlish posing. Who hasn't owned a cheap pair of oversized gold hooped earrings or experimented with synthetic hair extensions or wigs that just look wrong? Poor Adele, she didn't expect the world to pore over her teenage snaps. The images from her student days suggest she is playful, fun and very normal.'

In the early days of her career, she had moved on, but there wasn't a complete transformation. Her hair was still her natural shade of 'ginger biscuit', styled into a short pixie crop, her eye make-up was reserved and not yet Sixties retro. For performing, she tended to wear little black smocks pulled down over jeans, although she would often try to add a touch of colour, as when she appeared on *BBC Unplugged* and finished off her monochrome look with bright red shoes that were remarkably similar to the pumps Judy Garland wore on her adventures in *The Wizard of Oz*.

Offstage, she didn't always get it right. She was photographed at the opening of the new H&M store in Regent Street two months before her twentieth birthday in a shapeless beige dress over black leggings. Alison Jane commented, 'She looked like a student wearing her mum's clothes. It was not at all glamorous – more an outfit for a casual night down the pub. Her hair is a disaster and she gives the impression that she has just got out of bed.'

On the red carpet for her big first night at the BRITs in February 2008, she is undoubtedly beginning to look more like a star and, in Alison Jane's opinion, showing signs that she is using a professional hair and make-up artist. Her panda lashes show her smoky green eyes to much better effect. The problem is the off-the-peg outfit that doesn't fit her properly. 'It's too fussy and quite unflattering on all but a stick insect,' says Alison Jane Reid.

Over the years, Adele's size and weight have been one of the principal targets of media interest. Mostly, questioners were looking for signs of insecurity, which she resolutely refused to give them. Right from the start, she expressed the view that she was comfortable in her own skin and that her weight wasn't an issue to her. She was forever being asked if she would pose for *Playboy*, which she thought was a ridiculous question. Her response was always blunt. The fact that she wasn't an MTV dolly worked in her favour, because she stood out from the crowd. She told *Vogue*, 'Fans are encouraged that I'm not a size zero – that you don't have to look a certain way to do well.'

Her potential caught the attention of one of the biggest names in the fashion world, Anna Wintour, the famous and sometimes infamous editor-in-chief of American *Vogue*. The editor, or one of her staff, had spotted Adele as a potential subject for *Vogue*'s Annual Shape Issue in April, which would hit the stands in March.

Anna Wintour is the British-born daughter of Charles Wintour, who was a long-standing editor of the *Evening Standard*. As a fashion journalist, Anna worked her way up to be in charge of British *Vogue* and then its American counterpart, and is credited with turning around the fortunes of the magazine. She is now so influential that *Forbes* magazine listed her at number twenty-eight in its list of the 100 World's Most Powerful Women in 2015 – one place higher than the Queen. She is acknowledged to be a perfectionist and a tough boss and earned the nickname 'Nuclear Wintour', which she probably didn't deserve and dislikes intensely. With her hair in the Sixties bob she has worn since she was a teenager and her customary sunglasses, she has been a fixture in the front row of the most prestigious fashion events for the past forty years.

Anna owes much of her frosty and biting reputation to her fictional portrayal by Meryl Streep in the hit film *The Devil Wears Prada*. The movie, which was based on the memoirs of a former personal assistant, made more than $300 million worldwide and was one of the big international hits of 2006. Adele had certainly seen it and imagined herself in a scene from the film as she waited patiently outside Miss Wintour's office.

The lure for Adele, as well as the excitement of being in *Vogue*, was that she would be photographed by Annie Leibovitz, one of the finest and most prestigious photographers in the world. Some of the most beautiful women in Hollywood wait years to be featured, and here space and prestige were being given to a young woman who bought her underwear in Primark and three years before was a Croydon schoolgirl.

The idea of the special edition was to boost the confidence of normal women who, obviously, were of every shape and size. The magazine explained, 'In our annual celebration of size and silhouette, *Vogue* singles out eight women that represent the very best of beauty in all its forms.'

The women photographed represented pregnant, thin, curvy, short, tall and athletic. Adele was curvy. Leibovitz pictured her in a Michael Kors evening coat in black and large white polka dots, lying on a bed with her face resting in her hand. She looked beautiful, although not exactly like Adele. Ironically, you can't really see what shape she is at all. She is lying in such a way that she doesn't look particularly curvy. She was expecting it to be an all-day ordeal when the session began in a hotel room at the swanky London West Hollywood Hotel in Beverly Hills; it took about ten minutes.

Wintour was pleased, though, hence the invitation to her office. Adele need not have worried about meeting her in person. 'She was so nice,' she said. But she had to blag it when she was asked what labels she liked: 'I was trying to make up these designers I was quite sure I had read in *Vogue* or something before.' Adele believes you can come across as a 'dickhead' by pretending you know something when you don't.

Wintour clearly took a shine to Adele – perhaps she reminded her of London – and wanted to style her for the upcoming Grammys. Adele didn't hesitate to accept the offer and so was shipped off to the New York designer Barbara Tfank, much liked at the magazine, for a custom-made dress and coat ensemble.

In the same way that singers sometimes need only one song to make it, Tfank had sprung to prominence when, working with Prada, she designed the dress Uma Thurman wore to the 1995 Academy Awards. The outfit appeared on the front page of *Women's Wear Daily*'s annual Oscar issue the following day. Many commentators cite this exquisitely made lilac dress and chiffon wrap as the one that changed the red carpet for ever. The then little-known but undeniably beautiful Thurman epitomised Hollywood glamour and high fashion. Tfank's creation featured in the book *100 Unforgettable Dresses* by Hal Rubenstein. The acclamation the dress received started the trend of more attention being given to what the stars wore than to the awards themselves.

Tfank subsequently enjoyed a reputation for craftsmanship, attention to detail and fine fabric. She and Adele had an instant rapport. 'She is a lioness,' said the designer, who appreciated that the singer had good instincts about herself and how she wanted to look – providing it was basically a black outfit. Tfank styled her as if she were starring in an old black and white movie.

For Adele, she adapted one of the black satin dresses in her latest collection. The original was sleeveless, but Adele wasn't enthusiastic about that, because she thought her upper arms were her worst feature. Tfank added sleeves, flatteringly cut to just below the elbow. Adele loved the swish of the silk mid-calf dress – not a length she was used to wearing. Tfank had also added a double-faced green chartreuse cocktail coat for the red carpet pictures. They finished off her outfit with a nineteenth-century floral diamond brooch, which she wore on her décolletage. In a different era, she might have sat for one of the great English portrait painters.

Team Adele was impressed. Jonathan Dickins gushed, 'I'm all proud', when he saw the finished effect in her Los Angeles hotel room before they set off for the awards at the Staples Center. Her marketing manager at Columbia, Doneen Lombardi, was so moved, she burst into tears. Adele loved the way she looked, telling the *Vogue* reporter Hamish Bowles, as she admired herself in the mirror, 'I feel so proper.'

Alison Jane Reid was also pleased with her progress. 'She is beginning to dress like a diva in bespoke fashion made to flatter her shape and size. It all fits beautifully, flatters her shape and shows that bold is beautiful. Her make-up and hair – by the LA-based celebrity stylist Kevin Posey – are flawless too.'

Adele didn't forget Tfank and turned to her for many important nights in the years ahead. The designer, a champion for the more voluptuous woman, observed, 'I love her and being involved in helping a young person develop their style so that in twenty years' time, they look back on their pictures and aren't embarrassed; it's about looking timeless and beautiful.'

On the big night, Adele gave her first interview to *Vogue* and prudently didn't mention that she once said she would rather be on the cover of *Rolling Stone* or *Q* magazine than *Vogue*. Instead, she was happy to talk about her love of Manolo Blahnik shoes, like the ones worn by Carrie in *Sex and the City*, one of her all-time favourite television programmes. She confided that she owned a pair in blue and another in silver, but didn't find heels comfortable to wear.

Adele's taste is a mixture of expensive and ordinary. On the one hand, she embraced the high-street shops H&M, Topshop and Miss Selfridge; on the other, she liked British designer labels Vivienne Westwood, Aquascutum and Burberry. She also loved rummaging through vintage shops, although these days she didn't have the time. Adele definitely had an inner fashionista that many misguidedly assumed she wouldn't have because of her size. She loves dressing up and the Grammys was a fantastic opportunity to do so. 'I'll go proper glam,' she had announced when trying to decide on the look she wanted.

Buried deep in the ensuing article was the observation that Adele had avoided all the shallow industry parties surrounding the Grammys in favour of going to the movies with her 'new beau'. Right from the start, she didn't enjoy these sorts of parties and mostly gave them a miss. Instead, she saw *Doubt*, starring Meryl Streep, *The Wrestler* with Mickey Rourke and *Milk* with Sean Penn, all of which would feature at the Oscars two weeks later. Adele's film date was 'a soft-spoken London lad with the looks of Michael York in *Cabaret*'. Mister 21, it seemed, was still on the scene.

Penny didn't travel with her, which was hardly surprising, because her daughter had hidden her passport. Instead, she stayed behind in London, decorating the flat Adele had bought before she left. She had purchased a one-bedroom apartment in a block on the corner of Kensington Park Road and Blenheim Crescent for £380,000. Her new home was only one block away from the Portobello Road and close to all the familiar Notting Hill haunts.

Adele had promised to ring Penny from the venue to tell her how she got on. It would be a bit of an anticlimax after all this fashion fuss if she came away empty handed. Whatever happened, though, the makeover was a success and a triumph for couture. Alison Jane Reid explains, 'The point about individual design is that it accentuates your good points and conceals your defects. The dress did all of that. It plays up Adele's hourglass curves in a frock that oozes glamour and prettiness. She has a great neck too.'

Grammy night was Adele's first full-on Hollywood experience. She half-thought she was in the middle of a dream and would suddenly awaken to discover it was all a big joke. She seldom looks nervous, but was a little worried that nobody would know who she was.

There seem to be a million different Grammy Awards every year. If you banged two dustbin lids together and recorded your dog howling, there would be a category for you. She won her first before she had set foot on the red carpet. Her manager Jonathan rang when she was in the car on her way to the Staples Center to tell her she had captured the Best Female Pop Vocal Performance.

The award for Best New Artist, however, was one of the major ones that was always televised. This year it was presented by British-born singer Estelle and Kanye West, wearing a silver jacket that looked as if you could wrap a turkey in it. Adele looked suitably surprised when she was announced as the winner, kissed Jonathan and made her way on stage. After embracing Estelle and awkwardly shaking Kanye's hand, she said, 'I think I'm going to cry' and gave a short speech thanking everyone – Jonathan, her mum, Columbia, XL, friends and family. She even took a second to mention her rival. 'Duffy, I love you, I think you are amazing,' she said graciously, which is always easier to do when you are the victor rather than the vanquished. She ended by quickly saying, as though embarrassed, 'All my friends, all of my family and Alex. Thank you everyone.' It was the first and only clue she would ever give to the identity of her boyfriend. She never mentioned Alex by name again.

Afterwards she phoned Penny, who was back in the new home, watching the ceremony on television. After much shrieking and whooping, her mother ticked her off for chewing a piece of gum, which did admittedly spoil the effect of all Barbara Tfank's work – a Gainsborough heroine does not chew. Adele's excuse was that she genuinely expected the Jonas Brothers or Duffy to win, so she wasn't prepared for the cameras to be on her suddenly.

She still had to perform. She ditched her painful Manolos and padded barefoot on stage to sing a note-perfect 'Chasing Pavements'. For the last chorus, she was joined by Jennifer Nettles, the dynamic country singer with Sugarland. Surprisingly, perhaps, the two voices blended together well. Jennifer is not a Dolly Parton-type, more a purer version of Janis Joplin. She had the power to match Adele, but with an entirely different vocal style.

Job done, Adele posed happily, minus gum, clutching her awards tightly for the photographers. That was quite enough and she decided to give any more posing a miss by avoiding the Woodstock-themed official Grammy after-party and the other trendy soirées she was invited to, in favour of a couple of cigarettes and a trip to In-N-Out Burger on Venice Boulevard. There, in a pair of comfy jeans, she kicked off her shoes for the night and had a milkshake.

PART THREE

FEEL MY LOVE

14

THE GUARD DOG

Adele's closeness to her mum was self-evident. She was forever praising Penny in interviews, calling her a 'massive idol' and letting everyone know how much she loved her and owed her. She even phoned her once by mobile phone in the middle of a concert and encouraged the crowd to roar hello. In 2009, she said she wanted to sell 20 million albums so that her mother could give up work. It was tongue in cheek and a figure she plucked from the air as an unobtainable dream. Needless to say, she followed it with a hearty laugh.

The first problem with that ambition was she needed to make an album in order to sell it. As with *19*, she had been thinking about new material for a year and written practically nothing – only a few rubbish songs on tour that would never see the light of day. Everyone was keeping their fingers crossed that she wouldn't fall victim to DSAS: Difficult Second Album Syndrome.

Rick Rubin was at the Grammys, naturally, as he was named Producer of the Year. He and Adele had met a couple of days before, when she sang at a tribute concert for Neil Diamond, an artist much associated with Rick, who was largely responsible for reviving his career. The event was a fundraiser in aid of MusiCares, which helps musicians who have fallen on hard times. The charity named the veteran singer-songwriter as its Person of the Year.

Adele sang the Diamond hit 'Cracklin' Rosie', which she thought was pitched too low for her. Her mood wasn't improved when she tore a nail before she went on and had to use a tampon to soak up the blood. She forgot she still had it on her finger when she grabbed the microphone with that hand during her performance, which was embarrassing to say the least. The tampon was literally right in front of her face. She was convinced she was the worst act of the night, even though Rick tried to tell her she was one of the best. 'I followed Jennifer Hudson and I just know I was shit. He tried to boost my confidence going, "It was brilliant. It was great."'

He and Adele had the chance to talk briefly and they discussed a shortlist of the writers she might work with on her next album. Columbia and, in effect, Sony wanted some input to move her sound forward from being quintessentially English to more universally commercial.

By chance, she met one musician on the list, Ryan Tedder, in the lobby of the London Hotel when she popped back to change after the Grammys. You couldn't miss her, he recalled, because she was carrying a huge bouquet of balloons and trying to navigate them into the elevator like a character from a Charlie Chaplin film. Ryan combined his work as singer in leading American band OneRepublic with co-writing some of the biggest hits of recent years, including 'Halo' for Beyoncé and 'Bleeding Love', the number one for Leona Lewis.

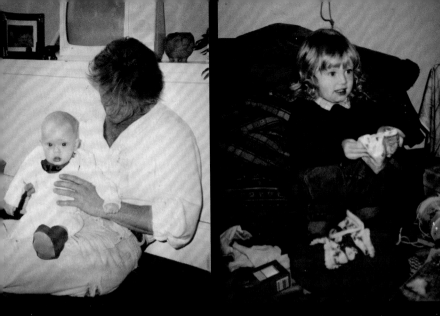

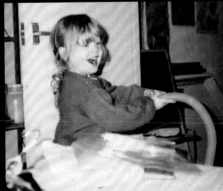

TOP LEFT: Adele Laurie Blue Adkins is held by her father, Marc Evans, when he was living with her mother, Penny, in a flat in Shelbourne Road, Tottenham.

TOP RIGHT: It's Christmas time in Tottenham and a smartly dressed little girl is opening a present.

ABOVE: On one of her regular trips to Wales, Adele visits the animals at the Amelia Trust Farm near Barry in the Vale of Glamorgan.

LEFT: After her mum and dad split up, Marc would still come to Tottenham to visit her.

BOTTOM LEFT: Happy times with her dad in Alexandra Park, Penarth.

BELOW: Getting interested in fashion, Adele relaxes in Nike cap and trainers at her nana's house in Penarth.

RIGHT: Adele loved her Pat Butcher earrings and wore them most days to the BRIT School.

LEFT: Chilling on the grass outside the BRIT School. The relaxed atmosphere helped to make her comfortable in her own skin.

LEFT: Like the other students at school, Adele learnt the art of performing live and was already accomplished as a teenager.

LEFT: Looking glamorous at her eighteenth birthday party at a pub in Brixton.

BELOW: Adele is having a laugh with Kate Nash, who was in the year above her at the BRIT School. They were both part of a Thamesbeat scene that flourished in 2006.

LEFT: Sometimes one is just too busy to chat: Adele, her manager Jonathan Dickins, on the left, and her great friend Jack Peñate are each in their own little worlds at the Black Ball charity gala at St John's Smith Square in July 2008.

LEFT: Adele was nervous at her first ever American gig at Joe's Pub, Manhattan, in March 2008. The audience of 184 loved her.

RIGHT: Even the incomparable Paul Weller didn't mind accompanying Adele at a gig for BBC 6 Music at the Maida Vale Studios in December 2008.

BELOW: Now that she had stopped playing the guitar on stage, Adele had a hand free to drink a trusty mug of her favourite tea at the O2 in 2008.

BOTTOM RIGHT: The sheer emotional power of her performance of 'Someone Like You' at the 2011 BRITs was unforgettable and changed her life.

ABOVE: Posing with Beyoncé at the Grammys in February 2013.

ABOVE: Later that evening, grabbing a cuddle with Katy Perry.

BELOW: Two weeks later … Three of the greatest together – Barbra Streisand, Adele and Shirley Bassey at the Academy Awards.

The premiership of divas.

ABOVE: Adele was over the moon when she passed her driving test at the first attempt in October 2013.

ABOVE: Her lovely dachshund Louie goes everywhere with her.

BELOW: Strolling with her man, Simon Konecki, when she attended the Glastonbury Festival as a fan in June 2015.

Adele performing joyously at Glastonbury 2016 – a beautiful woman

They exchanged the usual pleasantries and congratulations and promised to be in touch again soon. It would be more than six months before Adele had anything ready for him. She had been trying to write as she continued the *An Evening with Adele* tour around the US but, as before, she found no inspiration from life on the road.

For a while, her stock seemed to be higher across the Atlantic than at home. To her surprise, the casual invitation to appear on *Ugly Betty* was followed up when the programme got in touch to ask her to play herself in an episode called 'In the Stars', a reference to the action taking place in a planetarium. It's a brief cameo, in which she exchanges some dialogue with Betty, but it's not Oscar material. She says, 'Very nice to meet you' and 'Ta-ra, take care', before singing 'Right as Rain'.

Adele wasn't impressed with her efforts. She thought she sounded like Dick Van Dyke in *Mary Poppins*: 'I'm the worst actress of all time. I'm like a fucking cardboard box.' Any acting ambitions were put firmly on the back burner while she concentrated on her day job of singing.

She was nominated for only three awards at the 2009 BRITs and didn't win any of them. Duffy, for once, beat her hands down, winning four on the night, including MasterCard British Album of the Year for *Rockferry*, Best British Female Solo Artist and Best British Breakthrough Act.

While Adele had been having her early life crisis and spending much of 2008 trying to break through in the US, Duffy had risen to the top in Britain. Her polished debut, *Rockferry*, was the bestselling album of the year, shifting an impressive 1.7 million copies. Duffy was like the anti-Adele. She was slim, blonde and described by one critic as the Sienna Miller of pop. Her voice lacked the power and presence of Adele's, but suited the record's carefully crafted production, which coincidentally included a contribution from Eg White on three tracks.

The story of Adele versus Duffy is a bit like a morality tale or the Aesop fable of *The Tortoise and the Hare*. At first Adele was the hare, with all the hype surrounding *19*, which went to number one in its first week of release. Then Duffy, the tortoise, seemed turbo-charged, and *Rockferry* became the fourth biggest-selling album in the world in 2008.

The media tried unsuccessfully to stir up some rivalry between the two emerging stars. Adele even had to declare that she didn't hate Duffy when pressed on the show *Never Mind the Buzzcocks*. She did point out, though, that she, too, was actually Welsh.

As quickly as she rose, Duffy fell. Many put it down to a dreadful advertisement she did for Diet Coke in 2009. She rode around on a bicycle, singing the cheesy show tune 'I Gotta Be Me', which clearly didn't suit her voice. The ad finished with the tagline 'Hello You'. The commercial seemed completely fake. In comparison, Adele, who, crucially, has never advertised a product, seemed much more authentic. She was never going to be pedalling around London, swigging a soft drink: she was strictly a cabs-only woman.

In Duffy's defence, many artists have been well rewarded for soft drinks ads and the endorsement is quickly forgotten when a new, brilliant album comes out, but Duffy didn't have one. She fell out with her management team and her follow-up, *Endlessly*, released in 2010, was a flop, selling barely 200,000 copies. The lead single, 'Well, Well, Well', failed to make the top forty and she didn't release another. The one consolation for Duffy, as her career appeared to sink, was that in 2009 *The Sunday Times* Rich List estimated her fortune at £4 million.

Adele needed to avoid a similar fate with her second album. She had practically a month off from touring at the end of March, which gave her the chance to settle into the new flat and begin some serious writing. She turned again to Eg White, but inspiration was low, until they finished one song called 'Take It All'. He had literally played a single chord and she had started ad-libbing some lyrics. They turned out to be some of the most heartbreaking she had ever written, reflecting that all was not well with her relationship.

The magic at home had soon disappeared and she and her 'soulmate' spent their days bickering over nothing. They would argue about her lighter running out of fuel or not putting enough sugar in a mug of tea. She confessed, 'I was being an idiot and getting drunk …'

In the song, she questions why everything she can offer isn't enough. She is the 'crumbling fool', inviting her lover to walk away and take it all. The words certainly sound as if they are written by someone recognising they are on the verge of a hugely upsetting separation. Her boyfriend saw it that way when she played it to him that night. They didn't toast the song. They argued bitterly and split up for good shortly afterwards.

Adele had to fly back to the US to finish the tour, with The Script as her opening act. Not everything went smoothly. Her record company had to act when, for once, her chatty banter with the audience backfired badly. In Toronto, at the end of April, she told a jokey story about how she had bought two guitars earlier in the day from a rude pawn shop owner. She ended it by declaring that 'he wasn't Canadian, he was Jewish'. She immediately sensed that her throwaway remark had backfired badly with the audience and tried to make it better by declaring, 'I just meant he wasn't a rude Canadian … I'm digging myself deeper.'

Columbia Records were quick to issue her apology: 'What I said on stage in Toronto on Wednesday night at Massey Hall was not meant how it came across. But I completely understand how it was offensive. I sincerely apologise for being so naive and disrespectful! It was not my intention to be hurtful and I'm very sorry.'

A week later, much more happily, she spent her twenty-first birthday performing a set at the Roseland Ballroom in Manhattan. As she was telling the audience the story behind 'My Same', a huge three-tiered birthday cake was wheeled on stage. Her mother was hiding behind it. Adele shouted to the audience that it was her mum as the two embraced. Penny, looking slim and twenty-something, led the audience in a verse of 'Happy Birthday', while a cascade of balloons was launched into the auditorium. 'That was embarrassing,' said Adele, as her mum blew her a kiss and was gone.

The tour ended at the Hollywood Bowl on 28 June. Playing this iconic auditorium is a big deal for any artist. This was the show at which Etta James was due to appear, but, when she withdrew through illness, Chaka Khan was a rousing substitute, playing many of her crowd-pleasing old favourites, including 'I Feel for You' and 'Ain't Nobody'. Adele took to the stage and announced, 'I feel like Beyoncé or something. There's so many of you.' She chatted easily about being sunburned and wearing too much make-up, which made her look like a drag queen. She apologised in advance, as she often does, for messing up some lyrics, and once again nobody cared when she did.

The *Los Angeles Times* made an interesting observation that her charming guilelessness was a highly effective bit of stage-craft: 'Because Adele's just-folks persona prepares you for a just-folks voice, the real thing ends up sounding even more magnificent than it is.'

Adele threw herself into her performance and sang 'gorgeously'. Rick Rubin, who was in the audience, was impressed. He told her afterwards that she needed to introduce that same quality of raw emotion that he had heard in the live performance into her studio recordings.

After one last concert at a Dutch pop festival, she could finally relax and take stock of her life. She went on holiday to Portugal, but wished she hadn't when she succumbed to a nasty heat rash. 'Sunbathing's so boring,' she complained. Now that the tour was over, she felt able to enjoy a drink again, but didn't return to the bad old days.

She decided to get a little dog – a better companion than any man. The 'doglet', as she referred to him, was a smooth red dachshund. He was born on a night she went to see Britney Spears in concert at the O2. She explained, 'I almost called him Britney, even though he was a boy. But it only lasted a few hours until my hangover stopped.' She also toyed with the idea of calling him Aaron after the flying Spurs winger Aaron Lennon, her favourite player.

In the end, he sort of chose his own name by howling as Adele sang along to a Louis Armstrong and Ella Fitzgerald track. She called him Louie, saying that if she ever found him a female companion, then the second dog would be Ella. Sometimes she refers to him as 'sausage' and occasionally 'Louis Armstrong' if he is being particularly naughty.

In pre-Twitter days, Adele used to write an occasional blog and she reported that she and Louie were bonding: 'He is too cute; he is so friendly and loves everyone he's met so far.' She took him everywhere and his little face could invariably be seen poking out the top of one of her large, expensive designer handbags. He was undeniably very sweet, although Team Adele would have to get used to the shout, 'Louis needs a poo, can someone take him?' Interviewers, too, were subjected to his suspicious and penetrating stare as he sat protectively on her lap.

After acquiring her guard dog, the next important break-up decision Adele made was to move. The flat in Notting Hill had some painful memories and she didn't want to be stuck there moping. She found a much larger apartment in a secure block across from Battersea Park. She paid £890,000 for the flat in Prince of Wales Drive and promptly asked her mother to move in. Penny was still living in their old home in West Norwood, so was pleased to accept. The new place was so spacious they would never be under each other's feet. Louie moved in as well, of course. There was a wooden floor in case of any accidents and the park was ideal for walkies. He wasn't too impressed by being bitten on the nose by a Jack Russell Terrier, and subsequently refused to go to that particular area of grass again.

Reports in the papers suggesting that she had 'moved back in with mum' gave entirely the wrong impression of an arrangement that suited both women. Penny was a youthful forty and working with adults with learning difficulties. She had her own social circle and her old haunts were only twenty minutes away.

Adele was happy to be back with her mum. It suited her. She could see her friends and hang out away from the limelight and the cameras of the paparazzi she loathed. She and Penny popped down to see everyone at the BRIT School and watch some of the current intake perform at a concert in the auditorium. For the first half, she had VIP seats, while the students and teachers occupied the standing area in front of the stage. Liz Penney recalls, 'In the interval, we went into the music room with all the VIP people and she said, "Can I come and stand with you in the second half?" So she came down and stood with the rest of the commoners. At the end, we went into the green room where the students were getting changed and she said a few words to them, like you are great and you have to appreciate what you've got when you are here and work hard and it will all work out for you. So that was very nice and generous of her. Afterwards, she came to the Selhurst Arms with Penny and about fifteen of the staff. We were reminiscing and all I remember of that night is Adele swearing and laughing.'

Adele was writing again. The emotions she felt composing the new album were entirely different from those she had expressed as a teenager on *19*. Then she wanted to punch the boy who cheated on her; now she had a more mature approach, acknowledging her own faults, as well as those of her ex-boyfriend.

'This time, nobody did anything wrong,' she admitted, sadly. 'We just fell out of love with one another. I had to deal with the devastation of feeling like a failure because I couldn't make things work.'

Once again it was a creative summer and autumn as she took a more reflective and intelligent approach to songwriting. She stayed in, listening to different types of music, not simply her old favourites. She developed a taste for country music and the blues, an interest that had been sparked by listening to the tapes provided by the tour bus driver in the US.

She understood she was being stubborn to think she could do everything by herself for the follow-up to *19*. She realised she needed to find collaborators to share more of the load this time. By chance, when she was still living in Notting Hill, Jack Peñate, who remained one of her closest friends, phoned to ask if she could sing on his second album.

This time he was working with a producer and songwriter called Paul Epworth, who would become a key figure in Adele's musical story. Paul hailed from the quiet Hertfordshire market town of Bishop's Stortford, the son of an electronics engineer who had an impressive collection of old records. Paul grew up listening to early Dylan, the sophisticated synthesiser music of Yes and the soul music his mother liked. He loved the work of Motown great Smokey Robinson and the anthemic sounds of Phil Spector.

The house was full of musical instruments and Paul turned to the electric guitar in his teenage years, playing in an indie band, Lomax, before deciding he was better suited to mixing, producing and songwriting. He made his name working with guitar-led indie-rock bands Bloc Party and Maxïmo Park before branching out into different music, with songs for Plan B and Kate Nash.

More relevant to Adele, he worked on two tracks for her friend the Australian singer-songwriter Sam Sparro, who opened for her on the UK leg of her tour in 2008. Paul also co-wrote and produced some of the tracks on *Lungs*, the acclaimed debut album of Florence and the Machine. His credentials, as far as Adele was concerned, were impeccable, and he was fun to work with, which was a priority with her.

Paul and Jack wanted Adele for a stunning track called 'Every Glance'. You can't really tell that it's Adele singing backing vocals, but she enjoyed the experience, especially when Paul told her to pretend she was a monkey. The album, *Everything Is New*, came out in the summer of 2009 to good reviews, but Jack hasn't released another.

Adele kept in touch with Paul and invited him to work with her on some of her songs. They collaborated throughout the year, eventually finishing five tracks, three of which would appear on the album. One of them, 'He Won't Go', was their first track together and the first ballad Paul had written. It began as a lament for her lover, originally entitled 'What Is Love', but ended up about the bond shared by a young couple whom she had met through a mutual love of dogs when her tour finished. She had no idea that the man was a heroin addict. Two months after they met, he went into rehab, and the strength of the couple's love helped pull him through. In the lyric, Adele wonders if the man will choose the 'poison' over his relationship and realises that he can't overcome his addiction on his own. She explained, 'It's about undying love. When he was in rehab, I was with her the whole time. So I wrote him a song about it.'

In October 2009, Adele received some deeply upsetting news that her former boyfriend had become engaged a matter of months after they had split. She couldn't believe it. She sat mournfully on the end of her bed and roughed out the idea for a song called 'Someone Like You'. She had arranged a studio session with Paul the following day and went in clutching this deeply emotional ballad.

Sensing her inner rage, he was having none of her melancholy and instead told her to be a bitch about it. He understood she was experiencing some powerful emotions. Instead of a heartbreaking ballad, they wrote the ball-breaking 'Rolling in the Deep' that day. For about two hours, they weren't getting anywhere, while Paul tried to interest her in some random melodies. Finally, she interrupted him and said she had a riff in her head. 'Go on then, what is it?' he encouraged. She closed her eyes and began, 'There's a fire …'

She had roughed out the 'Fuck you!' lyric earlier in the year in a Chinese restaurant, but hadn't been able to get it right with other writers until she sang it to Paul that day. They finished the song in under three hours. She told *SPIN* magazine, 'It's me saying, "Get the fuck out of my house", instead of me begging him to come back.' There may have been regret, but there was absolutely no chance of reconciliation.

Paul knew that they captured something special in her vocal performance that day. He told the *New York Times*, 'She had had her heart broken, and she was in pieces, and you can really hear that, her anger and her sadness. Sometimes I just don't think you can recreate that or fake it.' Looking back on working together, Adele said, 'He helped me finish the songs that were meant to be great but I couldn't make great on my own.'

She didn't want to work with Paul exclusively, however. She stuck to the game plan of collaborating with different leading writers to try to make every song as perfect as possible. She wrote the dramatic power ballad 'Set Fire to the Rain' with Fraser T. Smith, whose impressive list of chart credits included number one hits for Tinchy Stryder and Taio Cruz, as well as album material for Kylie Minogue and Britney Spears. Adele liked the work he had done on 'Broken Strings' for James Morrison and Nelly Furtado. She told him she wanted something rousing.

When she first went to his unassuming studios in Fulham, they had nothing. Adele sat in the kitchen, drinking cups of coffee and scribbling down lyrics, while Fraser worked up a piano riff that he had started humming as he walked in that day. Every so often, Adele would nip outside for a cigarette. Fraser recalled, 'It was a stormy day and the rain had started to lash down and she couldn't light her fag because her lighter was wet.' 'Set Fire to the Rain' was born. She thought of the title as she was using the outside loo. Many of her best ideas, she admits, have come to her when she is having a wee.

She'd brought Louie with her for the day and he was being a nuisance, wandering round the studio, cocking his leg on everything. Fraser told the *Daily Mail*, 'Then I spotted him chewing through the cables and I thought, "I'm in the middle of producing one of the greatest records of my career and this dog is going to blow the studio up."

'Then the dog started crying while Adele was singing, but thankfully, he calmed down and came and sat on her lap.

'Some of the best takes we got were done with a sausage dog perched on her knee.'

Later Adele would explain that the song was similar to 'Chasing Pavements' in that setting fire to the rain was something you couldn't do. The lyric is vague and poetic, but, crucially, open to personal interpretation by anyone listening to it. Time and again Adele fans, particularly women, will say they can relate to a song: in this case, falling in love, being lied to, realising it's over and he's gone for ever but missing him deeply.

Ryan Tedder flew into London to work with Adele and came up with the title 'Turning Tables', simply because he wanted something that had a similar rhythm to 'Chasing Pavements'. It captured the feeling Adele had that she was always losing arguments with her ex-boyfriend even when she was in the right.

They worked on the sound and recorded it with Jim Abbiss producing and Neil Cowley on piano at Adele's local Sphere Studios in Battersea. Later that evening, Ryan was back in his hotel room, laptop on his knee, going over what they had done. He messaged Adele, 'I'm sitting here listening to your song and I'm covered in goosebumps from head to toe.' She was doing the exact same thing and wrote back immediately, 'I am so glad you feel that way because I am sitting in my flat listening to this song and I can't stop crying.'

They both knew it was a special track. Ryan and Adele made an intuitive connection. He enjoyed her company and admired the way she could still be great fun, laugh and crack jokes in the midst of all her heartbreak and turmoil. 'That was pretty ballsy and it was kind of, like, the joke was on him.'

Regretfully, Adele had to leave Louie behind in Penny's care when she set off for Malibu in the early spring of 2010 to work with Rick Rubin at last. He had so many commitments that it had been difficult to find the right window. She hadn't rushed the writing, but now she was armed with some amazing demos, ready for him to weave his production magic on them. The idea, at this stage, was to have a Rubin-produced album.

She didn't much care for the idyllic California coastline or the 80 degree March heat. She complained, 'I can't do the beach. I'm so pale, I just melt.' She didn't much like Malibu either. She was hoping to hang out with new friends in coffee shops and bars and not be stressed by the prospect of paparazzi jumping out from behind a potted palm, but it wasn't like that at all. 'Everyone lives behind a gate, and they're so fucking rich they never have to leave, so I didn't meet anyone.'

She did love working with Rick, although not everything was going smoothly in his Shangri-La Studios – a slightly ironic name considering how far removed from paradise Adele was feeling. She set her heart on including a cover of the INXS hit 'Never Tear Us Apart', one of the first songs she learned to play on the guitar, but she hated her interpretation when she sang it in the recording booth. 'I was devastated because I sounded so unconvincing on it.' She didn't believe a word of what came out of her mouth.

While everyone sat around wondering what to do, one of the session guitarists, Smokey Hormel, suggested 'Lovesong' by The Cure, which immediately brought back childhood memories for Adele. Apparently, Rick had been working on a bossa nova version for Barbra Streisand. That version had never materialised, but his musicians were familiar with it. Adele liked the idea, nailed it on the first take, of course, and then worried about how she was going to tell her mum that she had turned one of her all-time favourite songs into a bossa nova. Penny was mortified until she heard it, and fortunately loved her daughter's version: 'She'd disown me if she didn't like it.' Rick was impressed with Adele's genuineness, observing, 'At no time does it feel like product. So much of pop music feels like product.'

Adele finished other songs on her trip to the West Coast. First, she hooked up again with Ryan Tedder and they wrote 'Rumour Has It' about her friends believing all the gossip they heard about her when she was away on tour. They put it together one day and recorded it the next. Adele's songwriting had a definitive pattern to it: when everything was right, it was all done very quickly.

She still had that pesky ballad burning a hole in her handbag, however. She had already written two songs with the Harvard-educated Dan Wilson, a multi-talented musician and visual artist. They were 'Don't You Remember' and 'One and Only', both produced by Rick Rubin at Shangri-La.

At this stage, the plan was to have 'He Won't Go' as the last track on the album. That was before 'Someone Like You' took shape one afternoon in a studio in West Hollywood. The intention was to record a demo ready for production. Dan envisaged the final version as a big number with strings and angelic choirs, but for the moment they were happy with his sorrowful piano chords. They were both pleased at the end of the first day. Although there were still lyrics to finish, the kernel of the song was there.

Dan didn't realise that Adele, from the outset, saw the song as a life-changer. He had no idea she was going to play it to her manager and her mother that night. The next day, when she told him she had done that, he was a bag of nerves wondering what they had said. 'My manager loves it and me Mum cried,' she replied. She didn't tell him that Penny had also told her that, with this beautiful song, she was fixing hearts after all.

15

ROLLING WITH IT

Adele wasn't entirely happy with the album. She'd flown back from Los Angeles with a niggling worry that overall she had lost something that was present when she had first written and recorded the songs. Perhaps they had become a little too glossy. Perhaps they were a little too immaculate. She decided to revisit some of them with her collaborators in London. XL, which always put the artist and their creativity first, had no problem with her taking a second look. There was time before the planned release of the lead single in November 2011.

Her studio pianist, Neil Cowley, was called in to play at another session on 'Rolling in the Deep'. He arrived at Paul Epworth's and listened to what they had done so far. 'I thought it was a corking tune. I really loved the backing vocals and I said to Paul and Adele, "Who are those girls?" And she said, "It's me!" Paul had made her sing in a different voice. You can almost picture these women, but it's Adele. I loved it. There is some cleverness there.'

They used her original lead vocal, because it best captured her raw emotion. She also went with their original recording of 'I'll Be Waiting', but he told her that Rick Rubin's production of 'He Won't Go' was better, so they stayed with that. She went back to Jim Abbiss for 'Turning Tables' and 'Take It All', while her vocal for 'Rumour Has It' was re-recorded. She stuck with Fraser T. Smith for 'Set Fire to the Rain'. Finally, as autumn approached, she pronounced herself satisfied.

'Rolling in the Deep' was chosen as the first single and released at the end of November, well in time for Christmas stockings. *Rolling Stone* said the song found Adele in 'bluesy gospel mood, sounding powerful but not particularly pop'. The magazine had unwittingly focused on the appeal of the song and one reason for its astonishing commercial success: it was impossible to pin down the song to one genre. Adele described it as a 'dark, bluesy, gospel, disco tune', which just about covered all the bases.

As a result of this style mix, *Billboard* reported that it was the biggest crossover song for a quarter of a century. In the US, it appeared on twelve separate charts, including rock, pop, R&B/hip-hop, dance and, weirdly, Hot Latin. The song received airplay on practically every radio station you'd care to mention. The first chart it debuted on was the Triple A adult alternative chart at number one.

For *19* and 'Chasing Pavements', the release in the UK and US were staggered to allow Adele to try to break both markets. A simultaneous release is impossible, because an artist can't be in two places at once. For 'Rolling in the Deep', however, Adele was an established BRIT and Grammy Award winner and publicity was global. She premiered the song in Holland, sang it on *The Ellen DeGeneres Show* in Los Angeles and then was back in the UK for her first Royal Variety Performance at the London Palladium. She was part of a starry cast that also featured Take That, Kylie Minogue, Susan Boyle and Cheryl Cole. The show has a tame TV audience of eight million, so it was gold-plated publicity. All the artists were ignored in the papers, however, after the official car carrying the Prince of Wales and the Duchess of Cornwall was attacked by a mob of students, who threw paint bombs at their Rolls-Royce.

Surprisingly, perhaps, the song didn't reach number one in the UK. It was denied the top spot by 'Grenade' by Bruno Mars. The critics were generally impressed. Fraser McAlpine in his BBC Online review observed memorably, 'It's clearly the kind of huffy soul strop that matches her no-nonsense personality. Rather than mimsying around town, wondering what to do with herself, she's got some poor soul by the knackers and has lifted him off the ground.'

The video, which would subsequently win an armful of awards, once again continued the low-key, less-is-more approach, with Adele being the sole focus of attention. XL hired the much-sought-after director Sam Brown to devise the film. He had won prestigious MTV Video Music Awards (VMAs) for his work on Jay-Z's 'On to the Next One' and Corinne Bailey Rae's 'Put Your Records On'. He also shot the minimalist video to 'You're Beautiful' by James Blunt, in which the singer sits shirtless, shoeless and very sad in the snow.

Sam's hardest job was to persuade Adele that the video worked best if she did very little and sang while seated the entire time. He thought it was more empowering and allowed the viewer to focus on her emotion. As always, Adele had given great thought to the mood and the image she wanted to create. 'She wanted it to be dark and angry and mysterious,' said Sam.

He placed her in a room in an abandoned house, where the furniture was covered in plastic sheeting. As she sings, we see thousands of glasses covering the floor of an upstairs landing. A drummer starts playing and the glasses begin to vibrate as if some extraordinary powerful energy is being created.

Sam explained that he was trying to express anger: 'I suppose I was thinking of the house as her mind and then the rooms as everything happening inside it.' As a concept, it perfectly depicted the maelstrom of emotions represented in the song and, incidentally, the album as a whole. His efforts were well rewarded when the video won three VMA Awards in 2011 and was nominated for a further four.

The message in the song was clear, although nobody seemed completely sure what the phrase 'Rolling in the Deep' actually meant. It was similar to 'Chasing Pavements' in that respect. Adele said it was a corruption of the street slang 'roll deep', which broadly speaking was to have someone's back, to trust someone enough to save you from any trouble. Since the song came out, the expression is more concerned with the joy and pain of a deep and trusting love.

It was in the top ten for ten weeks, so its success kept everything bubbling along, ready for the release of the album. At one time, *Rolling in the Deep* was even being considered as the title of the album, but was rejected because everyone was concerned the American market wouldn't understand it.

At first, she thought calling her second album *21* was too obvious. 'I kept swerving it,' she recalled. But sometimes the public don't want an artist to be too clever or arty with titles.

21 was straightforward and clearly represented someone who had moved on from her teenage album, if only by a couple of years.

Adele revealed her thinking on her blog: 'It's different from *19*; it's about the same things but in a different light. I deal with things differently now. I'm more patient, more honest, more forgiving and more aware of my own flaws, habits and principles. Something that comes with age, I think. So, fittingly, this record is called *21*.'

The cover was more grown-up as well. She continued her subtle branding as a woman standing alone, with a picture of her pensive face lit against a dark background. 'The image is powerful, contemporary and timeless in monochrome,' commented Alison Jane Reid. 'It is startling and intense and designed to reinforce Adele's status as a major artist.' It may have been too soon to describe Adele as an icon, but here was a cover worthy of that status.

Her image seemed to be everywhere when the album was released on 30 January 2011. It went straight to number one with first week sales of 208,000, then a record. Simultaneously, it was number one in sixteen countries. The day it reached the top in the UK, she flew across the Atlantic for more promotion there prior to a February release. The expectation in the US had become immense.

The critics weren't universally impressed. Andy Gill in the *Independent* liked 'Rolling in the Deep' and 'One and Only', but thought the rest sunk into 'a mire of turgid, characterless piano balladry swamped in routine string arrangements'. He didn't even mention the final track on the album, 'Someone Like You'.

This would be the song that would resonate more than any other with her mainly female fan base. Fiona Shepherd, in the *Scotsman*, acknowledged, 'This is where it all comes together – the simple piano-backing, elegant, fluid pace and heart-wrenching lyrics sung in a voice haunted with regret and the occasional agonising crack.'

Adele planned to showcase the song at the BRIT Awards on 15 February, the first time they would be held at the O2 in Greenwich. It would be the usual razzmatazz, so surely she would make a greater impact if she sang 'Rolling in the Deep'? She was on stage between Take That performing 'Kidz' and sex goddess Rihanna with a supercharged medley from her album *Loud*. She chose to try something completely different: just her and her pianist Miles Robertson alone on the stage, focusing entirely on Adele and her voice. She confessed, 'All day I was thinking, this is going to be a disaster. Shat myself.'

While that may sound like typical Adele, the song is one of the most demanding she performs in concert. Miles explained, 'I play very lightly on the song. We do it completely live with no backing tracks. It is the most exposed and puts the most pressure on me to execute my parts well, but it helps to think about giving Adele a great foundation without being intrusive.'

Miles had accompanied Adele since 2008, so he understood the qualities she brought to the table. 'Both her first album and the new one are just reflections of who she is and what she is feeling – not every artist can express themselves like that, and it's very cool to work with someone who can.' The classically trained pianist, whose parents were respected musicians in Barbados, knows he has done a good job if nobody notices he is there. He observed, 'I am just a bed for the singer to lie in.' On the night at the BRITs, he was at his most unobtrusive, even though only he and Adele were on stage. You couldn't take your eyes off her.

James Corden, who was host for the night, gave an introduction that encapsulated her appeal: 'There's nothing quite like the feeling when you're listening to a song written by someone you don't know, who you've never met, who somehow manages to describe how you felt at a particular moment in your life.' He continued the build-up as Adele and Miles waited patiently on stage. 'The next artist is able to do that time after time. It's for that reason that she's currently number one in an astonishing seventeen countries. If you've ever had a broken heart, you're about to remember it now. Here, performing "Someone Like You", it's the beautiful Adele.'

Adele was to the side of the stage with a single spotlight framing her vintage dress and making her diamond earrings sparkle in the gloom. Like her videos, it was minimal and monochrome. She was the soul of vulnerability, except for the power and clarity of her voice, which filled every corner of the auditorium. Never have the opening words 'I heard that you'd settled down' been filled with such melancholy.

The BBC Arts Editor, Will Gompertz, described her as being 'alone and exposed like a Brontë heroine in the landscape'. The 16,000 audience were hushed and spellbound. Kylie and Robbie Williams came to the side to watch. Backstage you could literally hear a pin drop. Broadcaster Paul Gambaccini observed, 'The BRITs audience is one of the rudest and loudest and drunkest crowds in show business and if they shut up it is because they have all felt the same thing at the same time. She is stealing the BRITs.'

Towards the end, you could sense the tears were close to the surface as she sang on. When she had finished, she turned to the side and bit her thumb, as if she were the nervous girl in class made to read Shakespeare and not knowing how she did until the teacher spoke. The audience gave her the answer. The DJ and broadcaster Goldierocks memorably described it as 'the roar of a thousand lions'.

Adele began the song a star. She ended it a superstar.

Afterwards she explained why she had become tearful: 'I was really emotional by the end because I'm quite over-whelmed by everything anyway, and then I had a vision of my ex, of him watching me at home and he's going to be laugh-ing at me because he knows I'm crying because of him, with him thinking, "Yep, she's still wrapped around my finger." Then everyone stood up, so I was overwhelmed.'

At the time, she was putting problems with her voice out of her mind. It wasn't something widely known. She told the *Guardian* journalist Tom Lamont a few days afterwards: 'My voice went recently, never before, off like a tap.' She was told in no uncertain terms to take a break from caffeine, cigarettes and copious amounts of alcohol. She observed, 'I had to sit in silence for nine days, chalkboard around my neck. Like an old school mime. Like a kid in the naughty corner. Like a Victorian mute.' It was a warning that no one took too seri-ously … yet.

Within days, many thousands had downloaded a live record-ing of the track and the performance was watched more than five million times on YouTube. Lady Gaga had been expected to hit number one that week with her song 'Born This Way'. Midweek, it had been 20,000 copies ahead. By the end of the week, she trailed Adele by 30,000 copies. 'Someone Like You' had become Adele's first British number one single. That week she was the first female artist to have two albums in the top five and two singles at the same time. Both *19* and 'Rolling in the Deep' were going back up the charts.

She had no time to enjoy that achievement, because she was flying to New York for another appearance on *Late Night with Letterman*. The man himself thought Adele was 'fantastic'. She sang 'Rolling in the Deep', which had Jonathan Dickins biting his nails, because the lyrics contain the word 'shit'. Fortunately, she remembered to change that to 'ship' on the night. The album was about to launch in the US and now was not the time to upset the moral majority.

Her world tour, *Adele Live*, was due to begin in Oslo towards the end of March and nothing, it seemed, could interrupt what had so far been a serene year of success. She was concerned, however, to hear that tabloid journalists had been knocking on Nana's door in Penarth. She learned that they had also been hassling her father, Marc, and brother, Cameron.

Her worries gave way to fury when she caught sight of a front-page story in the *Sun* with the headline, 'I was an alcoholic and rotten dad to Adele. It tears me up inside.' Marc had sold his story and it made grim reading, as he recounted his battle with alcoholism, which involved a bottle of vodka and many pints of lager a day.

Alongside a number of pictures of Adele as a child, he was quoted as saying: 'I was deeply ashamed of what I'd become and I knew the kindest thing I could do for Adele was to make sure she never saw me in that state.' The years hadn't been kind to him. He had lost his hair after a bout of alopecia, although he was still a tough-looking, burly character with a twinkle in his eye.

Marc maintains that he was never drinking to the excess claimed in the newspaper and that his demise into an alcoholic black hole was greatly exaggerated. His version of events leading up to the revelations in the *Sun* was that he felt isolated when he was approached.

He says he spoke to Adele about the problems they were having with reporters and that he was being hounded for an interview. She said, 'Don't worry, Dad, we'll do it together.' Marc told the journalist concerned that he could speak to them both, which met with a delighted response, understandably. Twenty-four hours later, Adele rang and said she couldn't do it. 'I have to go to America,' she told him. 'I asked her what I should do. And she said, "Just go along, Dad, and give them something and then they will leave you alone."'

A reporter and photographer duly interviewed him, took pictures of him and collected shots of Adele as a girl – the ones that appeared in the article. Still unsure if he was doing the right thing, he tried to contact Adele through her management, but got nowhere. Penny was apparently on holiday in Spain, pursuing her new interest of paragliding, so, in the end, he went along with things. Team Adele unsuccessfully tried to persuade the newspaper not to publish.

Adele has never commented about any conversation she may have had with Marc. He says he spoke one last time to her after publication to try to explain that it wasn't his world and someone should have been there to give him advice, but the conversation went badly and they fell out irrevocably. She hasn't spoken to him since.

To make family matters worse, her grandmother Doreen was waylaid in Tottenham and allegedly gave a few quotes about Penny that were blown out of all proportion. Clearly Adele's family, unused to such attention, did need some advice, and Penny was called on to impress on them the dangers of doorstep conversations.

Questions about Marc are off limits in interviews with Adele. She did talk about him once in *Vogue* a year later. Time hadn't softened her attitude and she was clear: 'He's fucking blown it.' She was particularly upset at the implication that her problem with men was down to him. 'It's like, Fuck off! How dare you comment on my life? It makes my blood boil. It makes my family feel awkward, it makes my friends feel awkward around me, it makes me act awkward, it makes me sad.'

Her final words on the matter were, unforgivingly: 'If I ever see him, I will spit in his face.'

16

VOCAL DISCORD

The warning signs were there throughout the American dates of *Adele Live*. In May, she had to cancel her concert at the First Avenue music club in downtown Minneapolis at the last minute after her late afternoon sound check. Stage manager Conrad Sverkerson was there: 'She sang two notes and she knew. Her voice was gone. It was sincere. We sent her right to the doctor.'

She battled on in Denver two days later, but admitted to the audience that she wasn't feeling well. They didn't notice anything different about her rich vocals. Ryan Tedder, who was in the audience and knew her voice so well, could hear something was wrong as soon as she started singing. He turned to his wife, Genevieve, and said, 'She has laryngitis. Something is wrong right now!'

Adele carried on, but she wasn't doing herself any favours. The audience, nevertheless, loved her usual mix of bawdy banter and glorious singing. She introduced her cover of 'If It Hadn't Been for Love' with a no-nonsense 'This fucking boy has no fucking idea what a good fucking thing he's lost'. She first heard the bluegrass song by The SteelDrivers when her bus driver played it for her on the previous tour and liked it so much she made a mental note to try singing her own version at a later date.

The crowd was unaware of the damage she was doing, but then she had to cancel the following night in Salt Lake City, again at the last minute, when her throat felt worse. She was told she needed immediate rest and not to start the concerts again for another week.

Adele had been putting pressure on her natural gift for ten years, ever since she started smoking rollies and drinking cider. Her dressing room and catering rider gave a glimpse of her diet and lifestyle on the road in the US. In her dressing room, she required chewing gum, a pack of Marlboro Lights with disposable lighter and a bottle of the 'very best' quality red wine – Italian, French or Spanish. After the show, she required more supplies for her tour bus – the band and crew travelled separately – including a selection of bite-size Twix, Aero, Milky Way and Mars bars and some bottles of best-quality European lagers, i.e. Beck's, Stella Artois and Peroni. The requirements stipulated in italics that '*North American beer is NOT acceptable*'. Red wine was again on the menu, although, to be fair, she did ask for juice and organic muesli for breakfast.

Five dates were cancelled, but she showed no sign of improvement. After consulting a specialist, the remaining nine dates of the sold-out tour were scrapped as well. Adele told fans, 'I'm really frustrated. I was hoping with a week's rest I'd be better to sing again straight away. However, there is absolutely nothing I can do but take the doctor's advice and rest some more. I'm so sorry.'

She did as she was told and took things easy until she was given the all-clear. She explained what had happened: 'It's basically a hole in your vocal cord, but I sang through it so that's why it popped. I'm better now. It's fine.'

Adele started her tour again, this time with an iTunes festival gig at the Roundhouse in London in July. All seemed well and she chatted away about watching Beyoncé on television performing at Glastonbury. She talks a lot about the American star, but they do share a publicist in both the UK and the US. She also moaned about her high heels and took them off.

Two weeks later came the devastating news that Amy Winehouse had died from alcohol poisoning at her London home. It was one of the saddest and most upsetting events in modern music. Much of Amy's life and career, superficially at least, was mirrored by Adele's, with a vital difference: one, it seemed, could handle the pressures of fame, the sometimes mean criticisms of her physical appearance and the temptations that came with great wealth; the other could not.

Adele paid tribute on her blog to the star who, she said, had revitalised the UK music scene with the album *Back to Black*: 'Amy paved the way for artists like me and made people excited about British music again, whilst being fearlessly hilarious and blasé about the whole thing. I don't think she ever realised just how brilliant she was and how important she is, but that just makes her even more charming.'

She hit exactly the right note of unsentimental appreciation of a great talent and did not wallow in the post-Diana fashion of nationwide, over-the-top grief when a famous person dies. She ended movingly, 'Although I'm incredibly sad about Amy passing, I'm also reminded of how immensely proud of her I am as well, and grateful to be inspired by her. Amy flies in paradise.'

When she relaunched her North American tour in Vancouver the following month, she dedicated a song to Amy, telling the audience, 'She was a big part of my life in so many ways.' Then she sang 'Make You Feel My Love'. At the Hollywood Palladium, she told the audience to hold up their mobile phones in homage to the singer.

Her voice seemed to be surviving, despite the punishing schedule. One reviewer at the Greek Theater in Los Angeles noticed that her voice broke during 'One and Only', but, as before, nobody in the hall seemed to notice. The concerts lasted nearly ninety minutes, so she needed her favourite tea and honey drinks, the brewing of which was the job of a particular member of the touring party who could make it as she liked it.

Ironically, most of the reviews praised her voice enthusiastically. Pam Kragen, of the *North County Times* in San Diego, elegantly captured the appeal: 'It's not overstating to say Adele's got a voice for the ages, a warm-hued, flexible and fluid instrument that channels sadness, regret and (occasionally) joy direct from the soul.'

She obviously was trying to make an effort and follow medical advice. Her artist rider for the renewed tour stipulated in block capitals 'NO CITRUS FRUIT', because she had been advised that oranges and grapefruit were particularly harmful to the voice and were banned.

One extra and very serious demand went out to all the promoters of the tour. There were to be no freebie tickets.

Every guest was required to make a minimum donation to charity of twenty dollars in cash when they collected their tickets. 'There will be no exception to this rule,' said the tour manager, David 'Zop' Yard, who collected the money at each venue. Adele had personally requested that all the money raised in this way went to Sands, the UK-based stillborn and neo-natal death charity that supports parents who have lost a baby. By making this charge, nearly £10,000 was collected on the European leg of the 2011 tour alone.

Sands was founded in 1978 by a small group of bereaved parents, devastated by the death of their babies, and by the total lack of acknowledgment and understanding of the significance and impact of their loss. Over the years, their dedicated lobbying has resulted in many improvements to guidelines, including a 'Seeing and Holding' campaign in 2010 to ensure that parents always be offered a choice about whether or not they wanted to see and hold their baby.

Adele has never indicated if she has a personal reason connected with friends or family for promoting this cause. She is not a fair-weather supporter, however, and again insisted on the fundraising rule for her most recent 2016 tour.

A bad year for cancellations continued when she had to call off the first gigs of her next UK tour in September due to a severe cold and chest infection. 'I've had a rotten cold since I got home,' she admitted. 'I can't hold any notes when I sing and I don't sound like myself. I'd rather not do a show than not do a good one.' Apparently, she had been ill for a week after the MTV Video Music Awards, when she received another standing ovation for 'Someone Like You' and almost stole the show from Beyoncé's baby bump.

In all, she cancelled six gigs before resuming a couple of weeks later and joking with audiences about her illness. She sang at the Royal Albert Hall and film of the concert subsequently became a bestselling DVD around the world. It was a false dawn. She pulled out of her entire US tour. She explained that the problems all stemmed from that day in Minneapolis when her voice suddenly 'switched off like a light'. She told her fans, 'It was literally as if someone pulled a curtain over my throat.'

The laryngitis, it turned out, had been a vocal cord haemorrhage and was extremely serious. Adele described it as a black eye on her vocal cords. She was very upset and wrote on her website that she was heartbroken and worried and that she had been following all the advice to the 'best of my ability but it seems to simply not be enough'.

Singers were at greater risk from the condition because of the frequency of using their voice and the loudness with which they did so. Rest and quiet would generally improve things, unless there was an underlying vocal malfunction, like a polyp or dilated blood vessels. Adele had a non-cancerous polyp and she would need surgery to stop the recurrent bleeding in her throat or risk losing her precious voice altogether. As things stood, she could barely whisper. While there was no evidence that her thirty-a-day smoking habit or the glass of red wine that turned into a bottle were direct causes of her problem, they would have to be given up to treat her voice more kindly.

She flew to Boston's Massachusetts General Hospital to be operated on by the renowned throat surgeon Dr Steven Zeitels. He had treated other famous singers in the past, including Cher, Lionel Richie and Roger Daltrey of The Who. He had also done his best to help restore the voice of Julie Andrews after a routine operation by another surgeon went wrong in 1997. Sadly, despite four operations, he couldn't repair Julie's singing voice completely and her career as one of the great musical stars was over. Her plight would always be on the mind of any singer who developed problems with their voice.

Dr Zeitels used the latest laser technology to remove Adele's polyp, but he had to impress on her that she needed to stop talking for two months so that everything could heal properly. 'It was really hard to get my point across,' he said.

Adele was despondent at the prospect of a silent Christmas and New Year and stayed home watching films most of the time. She observed, with considerable understatement, 'It was a bit traumatic.' Everything went well, however, and after six weeks she was able to resume some light humming.

She flew back to Boston in January 2012, still unsure if the operation had been a success. Would she be able to sing again or was her career over at twenty-three?

Dr Zeitels examined her throat using a laryngoscope and saw that she seemed to have healed properly, but then needed to hear how her singing voice was faring. 'I asked her to test her singing voice and she sang "Rolling in the Deep" beautifully. If anything, her voice sounded cleaner and clearer than before. Of course, I was overjoyed. It was a wonderful moment for both of us and one of the most memorable in my career.' He described his feelings after this private concert, 'There was an overwhelming epiphany that I had restored this beloved voice that would bring joy and inspire millions of people.'

While she had been suffering in silence, the juggernaut that was *21* rolled on throughout the year and the next. In 2011 and 2012, it was the biggest-selling album in the world. The first three singles, 'Rolling in the Deep', 'Someone Like You' and 'Set Fire to the Rain', all reached number one in the US *Billboard* Hot 100. In the UK, *21* stayed at the top of the charts for ten weeks in a row, which beat Madonna's record for a solo female artist. Around the globe, it was a rarity when it did not top the charts. They loved it in Austria and Argentina, in Slovenia and South Africa. Soon, it was the biggest-selling album of the new millennium.

She had been nominated for six Grammys at the 2012 ceremony in Los Angeles on 12 February. It would be the chance for the world to see that she was well and could actually sing again. She was expected to be a winner. Predicting her success a few months before, Elton John had joked, 'Next year a large woman will win everything and it won't be me.'

The year began with the sad news from California that Adele's biggest influence, Etta James, had died at the age of seventy-three from leukaemia. She had also been struggling with Alzheimer's disease for several years. Adele paid a touching tribute on her website: 'What a lady Etta James was. She was the ultimate original. Her voice was breathtaking and her songs are reflections we all recognise in some way or another. It's an honour every time I hear her voice … Thank you to Etta James.'

The awards night was overshadowed by another death. A few hours earlier, Whitney Houston had been found dead in her hotel bathtub. The host, LL Cool J, strolled on in black and announced, 'We've had a death in our family,' and then led the audience in prayers. Stevie Wonder and Bruno Mars were among the stars paying tribute, while Jennifer Hudson sang 'I Will Always Love You'.

Despite the cloud hanging over the Staples Center, it was a joyous night for Adele, as she won every award for which she was nominated. Her acceptance speeches always come across as perfectly natural, unscripted and slightly shambolic. She did, however, remember to thank Dr Zeitels when she collected the award for Best Pop Solo Performance. She declared, 'Seeing as it's a vocal performance, I need to thank my doctors, I suppose, who brought my voice back.'

The doctor had given her voice the all-clear, but she still had to show the millions watching on the night that nothing had changed. Four awards were already claimed when she was introduced by Gwyneth Paltrow, who said 'the singular voice of hers' was back. For once, she began 'Rolling in the Deep' a cappella, belting out the chorus to prove all was well. She looked impeccably glamorous in a black Armani design, exquisite De Beers earrings and a large Harry Winston diamond ring.

Fortunately, her performance matched the build-up and she was given a standing ovation. In the front row, Paul McCartney caught her eye and nodded his approval. She had come a long way from the time when their paths first crossed at the *Fame Academy* awards and subsequently in the studio for *Later … with Jools Holland*.

The final award of the night is the big one: Album of the Year. After Diana Ross had announced *21* as the winner, Adele trooped on stage with her posse of producers and executives and shouted, 'Mum, girl done good!' As she wiped her sniffly nose, she remarked, 'Bit of snot.' She was the only performer in the room who could have included snot in the acceptance speech for the most prestigious award in world music and raised an approving laugh. As she left the stage, she said, 'Oh my God!'

On a sombre night, she had cheered everyone up. In London, her family stayed up late in Tottenham and Enfield to share the excitement of their most famous relative's triumph. Her aunts sent their congratulations on Facebook. Nita messaged: 'Well done to Adele, wow, so proud of you, love, love, love you xxx Auntie Nita, Uncle Dave & all the gang xxxx.' She also remembered Penny, who hadn't travelled to Los Angeles: 'You are so proud we know, amazing mum and sister. Adele is as proud of you as you are of her, luv you loads. xxxxx.'

It was a rare glimpse of how close the family remained. They quietly got on with their lives while Adele was becoming a superstar. Nita, for instance, has run a charity shop for the North London Hospice for eighteen years. Her grandparents have lived in the same modest terraced house for thirty years, and Doreen, her grandmother, carries a picture of Adele in a wallet with her bus pass. 'She's just a girl from London who is making it huge in America,' said Doreen when ambushed by a reporter.

Adele was home in London for the BRITs nine days later. Something more important had happened in the meantime. She was given the news that Rose, her nana in South Wales, had collapsed while shopping in a local supermarket in Penarth and was rushed to hospital. She had suffered a heart attack.

Adele dropped everything and hurried to her bedside at the Heath Hospital in Cardiff. Her father Marc, whom she avoided seeing, recalled, 'We thought Mum was going to peg it. The doctor said to us she was very lucky that she was in a public place. If she'd had it in the middle of the night, she wouldn't have been able to make a phone call and we would have lost her.'

Rose had two stents put in during an operation and doctors reassured Adele all was well. 'It would have broken her heart to have lost her,' said a friend. She was able to honour her commitments to the BRITs, when she again performed 'Rolling in the Deep' and received two awards, one for Best British Female Solo Artist and the other for MasterCard British Album of the Year. As she was presented with the former by the very petite Kylie Minogue, she joked, 'I feel like a drag queen next to you.'

Adele was the big news of the night, but not because of her success. For once, she was more composed in her acceptance speech for what was the last award of the night. 'Nothing beats coming home with six Grammys and then coming to the BRITs and winning Album of the Year. I'm so proud to be flying the British flag for all of you.'

At this point, an embarrassed James Corden interrupted her speech. The programme on ITV was overrunning and they needed to meet a tight schedule, so they had to usher Adele off in order for Blur to finish the night with a medley of hits as part of their Outstanding Contribution to Music Award. Coincidentally, it had been Damon Albarn's rambling speech when he collected the actual award earlier in the evening that had caused the programme to overrun.

Adele was unimpressed. She asked Corden, who was only following instructions in his earpiece, 'Are you about to cut me off? Can I just say, then, goodbye and I'll see you next time.' As she turned to leave, obviously furious, she flipped her middle finger towards a table of executives. It was classic Adele.

She made it clear afterwards that her playground rude gesture wasn't aimed at her fans: 'I'm sorry if I offended anyone, but it was the suits that offended me.' ITV and the ceremony's organisers both apologised to her. James Corden dashed to her dressing room without even staying to hear Blur. He revealed, 'She was fine with me, but really upset. She had a speech and a list of people she wanted to thank. I was so upset myself and I can understand why she was.'

There was only one talking point afterwards. Social media was awash with people unable to believe that they had cut off Adele. Jamie Oliver spoke for the nation when he wrote, 'Why did you cut off Adele! Bloody rude!'

17

A PREGNANT PAUSE

Inevitably, there was some speculation about Mister 21. All the awards the album received kept the interest going. Adele didn't say who it was and it never became a big guessing game like the identity of the killer in *Broadchurch* or who shot JR in *Dallas*. She was forthright in her refusal to reveal anything more and told the *Guardian*, 'Who cares? Nobody famous, just old boyfriends. I don't date celebrities. I ain't fucking Taylor Swift ...'

Heat magazine claimed he was a photographer called Alex Sturrock, who was in his early thirties and had worked for both *Vice* magazine and the *Guardian*. He wasn't named until April 2012, long after *21* was the biggest-selling album in the world.

If anyone had wanted to, they could have come up with him when the album was released. *The Sunday Times* said the songs from the album only flowed when she was breaking up with her 'photographer boyfriend'. He was, according to *heat*, with her for most of the *An Evening with Adele* American tour, when she handed him the job as her official tour photographer.

And, of course, she nearly gave it away when she thanked 'Alex' by name at the Grammys.

The magazine claimed they dated between the summer of 2008 and the spring of 2009. It unearthed a friend who said the couple had hit it off straight away: 'He shot her a few times and that was it. They spent all their time together – and when they weren't together, they would ring each other constantly.'

According to the source, he was her best friend, as well as her boyfriend, and he was very protective of her: 'He's a very normal guy and they'd laugh a lot together, eat junk food and ignore the fact that her career was about to go stratospheric. It was an intense period for them.'

One particularly upsetting aspect of the relationship for Adele was that he never properly acknowledged her as his girlfriend, even though the magazine said they shared the same hotel rooms and he was living with her in London.

His official pictures of Adele featured on the *Guardian*'s website and included photographs of her in the New York offices of *Vogue*, hanging out backstage with the guitarist Slash, chomping on an In-N-Out burger and drinking lemonade in an Omaha diner.

More interesting, however, were the candid and intimate shots of Adele on his website. She is shown smoking in bed, clutching an 'I Love You' balloon, reading a Spiderman comic, making funny faces snuggled into her white duvet, and laughing with a face mask on and her hair in curlers. She is clearly very much at ease with the photographer.

The pictures remained on his website, even after the stories first appeared that he was Mister 21. Coincidentally, on the *Vice* website, under a feature entitled R.I.P. Love in May 2008,

Alex includes a picture of a former girlfriend called Emily, also snuggled under a white duvet clutching a cuddly toy. Next to it he has written, 'We went out for a couple years, and we broke up just before she left to go to university. Somehow things got ridiculously overcomplicated. Right now we are on good terms and I still believe she is God's cutest creature. Whenever I was with her, I literally wanted to bake her in a cake and eat her.'

Neither Alex nor Adele has ever uttered a word about their alleged relationship. For him, it would be professional suicide. In any case, the stories may or may not be true. Adele very rarely denies anything, although she did have something to say about reports linking her with Slinky Sunbeam. Alex's photos of her have been easily viewable online for several years now and he continues to thrive through his acclaimed street photography of London.

After a flurry of stories that he might be the man, the media lost interest. In any case, by that time, Adele had a new, very serious boyfriend and she was pregnant.

If the world had been paying better attention, it would have noticed a curious tweet that Adele posted out of the blue in December 2011. She wrote, 'Right! It's me! I will start tweeting if 10K of u start following @dropfordrop and their trip to India this wk. It's a wonderful charity. Go! A xxx.' It took less than twenty-four hours to achieve that goal.

Nobody knew yet that Adele had met and fallen for the founder of drop4drop at a charity function earlier in the year and the two were having a serious relationship that would soon lead to them having a child together. His name was

Simon Konecki. He was fourteen years her senior, an old Etonian and former investment banker and, superficially at least, not at all the person you might have expected to become romantically involved with Adele and her left-wing tendencies.

Adele subtly prepared the way for them to be recognised in public as a couple. As long ago as the previous August, she admitted, 'I like all sizes, it doesn't matter – if they make me laugh I am on it. I also like a man who can cook and someone who can be passionate for life. I like someone who really inspires me and I admire.' She also said that when it came to husband material, her taste ranged from Leonardo DiCaprio to Zach Galifianakis, the bearded American actor and comic who starred in *The Hangover*.

A week after her December tweet she said, 'I haven't been ready to be in love again since summer 2009 ... until now.' The couple were seen together in public for the first time at The Ginger Fox, a picturesque thatched-roof country pub near Hassocks in Sussex, about seven miles from Brighton, where Simon's charity is based. Fortunately, there were no photographers present when, according to an eyewitness, the couple held hands sweetly. Adele was still under instructions to save her voice, so Simon had to do all the talking, presumably making her laugh frequently. He also paid the bill.

Just after New Year 2012, the tabloid papers had spotted them on holiday in Florida. They were seen enjoying a trip to the Everglades National Park. According to the *Sun*, they strolled along a beach before embracing and later took a ride on an airboat to go alligator spotting together. Simon certainly bore a resemblance to Galifianakis and was charmingly unglamorous and natural in a pink hoodie, knee-length shorts and white trainers. He seemed laid-back and the two embraced quite naturally.

This was the very first time – and probably the last – that Adele had been photographed in such circumstances. It was as if she had decided to let the world know she was happy and in a relationship so that they wouldn't be hounded. The Grammys were coming up and she wanted Simon to be with her. In the real world, if she had seen a photographer while on her holidays, she would have bopped him on the nose.

The media didn't realise that Simon's parents had a million-dollar waterfront holiday home an hour and a half away in Boca Raton and this was actually part of a Happy Families sunshine vacation to celebrate New Year. For most of the time, his mother and father, Rosemary and Andrew, live in Vevey, a town on Lake Geneva in Switzerland much favoured by celebrities who want a quiet life and lower taxes. David Bowie once lived nearby and Phil Collins had a villa the other side of Lausanne.

Simon has Polish ancestry. His grandfather, Leonard Konecki, was born during the First World War in Białystok, the largest city in north-east Poland, close to the border with Belarus. He worked as a wireless operator aboard cargo ships before settling, with his wife Dora, first in south-east London and then in Chislehurst, Kent, where Simon's father was raised.

Andrew was working in the City as an international money broker when Simon was born, on 17 April 1974, in Farnborough Hospital. His birth was announced in *The Times*. He is the middle child, between two sisters, Alex and Vicki. The family moved for ten years to New York, where Andrew's career flourished, before coming back to the UK to settle in a spacious house in Brighton.

Simon was sent to Eton, while his two sisters went to Roedean, the leading girls' public school. At the famous Berkshire college, he was briefly a contemporary of the TV adventurer Bear Grylls and the Duchess of Cornwall's son, Tom Parker Bowles. He was in DAE, the house of the popular history teacher David Evans, which had a reputation as the most badly behaved in the school.

Even at Eton, Simon was a larger-than-life character. According to the *Evening Standard*, Evans would use Simon as an example of bad behaviour. A former pupil recalled, 'Our headmaster used to refer to him as the naughtiest boy he ever had in the house. "Don't misbehave or you will end up like him," he would say.'

Another boy, who was in his year at school, recalled, 'He had a terrible Eighties mullet and awful acne.' He used to be part of a smoking gang that enjoyed Marlboro Lights behind the rackets courts, before he left unexpectedly in 1989, aged fifteen, in unexplained circumstances. He may have simply hated it because of his emerging left-wing views, didn't fit in with the other pupils or have left under a cloud for some reason.

If you leave Eton with an unblemished record, you automatically become a member of the OEA (Old Etonian Association) and are listed in its handbook. Simon is not included in either the 2000 or the 2006 editions, but does pop up again in 2008, nearly twenty years after he left. He would probably have had to request his inclusion.

He provided an insight into his character when he was asked by the *Financial Times* if he could remember his first donation to charity. It was at Christmas, he recalled, when he was thirteen. He had £10 to spend and was walking through Brighton: 'I saw a hobo. He was in a bad way, so I gave him the tenner. When I got home my dad said, "You're crazy. He's just going to spend it on drugs." But I think he needed it more than I did that day.'

At seventeen, he followed his father to the City and started his first job as a trainee foreign exchange broker. He recalled that he wore a pin-striped suit with red braces to the interview, a look inspired by the Charlie Sheen character Bud Fox in the film *Wall Street*. He said, 'They took me to the pub and proceeded to take the mickey out of me for hours. But I got the job.'

He added, with the deprecating sense of humour that Adele likes, 'They used to call me Swampy, after the kid who tunnelled under Manchester Airport runway – probably due to my long hair and lefty views.'

Those socialist leanings took a back seat while he flourished. There were stints as a senior trader at Lehman Brothers and EBS, Electronic Broking Services Ltd, where he was made a director in 2004, a couple of weeks before his thirtieth birthday. This is a very substantial company, owned by various banks and used by them as a foreign exchange trading platform. Simon wasn't a shareholder, but as a director he would have earned a substantial salary and one of those high bonuses that always receive so much bad publicity.

That same year he had fallen in love with and married a willowy stylist from Swindon called Clary Fisher. They first set up home off The Highway in Tower Hamlets, East London, before moving to trendy Hampstead, where they became part of a vibrant social scene. Simon's friends included *EastEnders* actor Sid Owen, whom he had met when they used to frequent the same London nightclubs, Ronnie Wood's son Jamie and playboy Lucas White, who inherited £70 million when his father, the financier Sir Gordon White, died in 1995.

A year after becoming a director at EBS, Simon had fallen out of love with the financial arena: 'I was doing well and earning a lot of money, but I got sick of that greedy and corrupted world.' He wanted to do more with his life than put on a suit every day and look at pound signs. He hit upon the smart idea of linking business with charity in a way that appealed to his philanthropic nature.

He set up a company called LifeWater, with the aim of providing an ethical alternative to the bottled water market. Life is bottled at an organic source in Pembrokeshire and the proud boast is that every one litre bottle sold funds up to 1,000 litres of clean drinking water to communities in the developing world through the drop4drop charity he established at the same time.

Looking to change lifestyle completely, he and Clary moved to Brighton, near his parents, with their baby daughter Georgie. He set up the headquarters of his new enterprise in the fashionable seaside city. He was a popular and easy-going figure, riding to business meetings on his black Vespa scooter.

Simon is not independently wealthy and, sadly, the pressure of building a new business from scratch and the time he spent away from home seeking endorsements and new contacts put a strain on the marriage. By 2009, he and Clary had split up. His efforts hadn't led to immediate success. Accounts filed at the end of 2011 revealed a pre-tax loss of £82,000.

Prospects improved when he signed a deal with Waitrose to stock his product. He gained enormous satisfaction from his trips to India and Africa to see his initiatives put into practice. He loved to see the smile on children's faces when they tried clean water for the first time.

Adele's involvement improved the public profile of the charity. Simon was proud to declare, a short time after they were seen in public, that drop4drop had given 200,000 people clean drinking water so far. 'I'll get excited when we get to just a few people left without water,' he added.

The pictures of Adele and Simon in Florida prompted an immediate flurry of unwelcome stories that Simon was not yet divorced and Adele was, in fact, dating a married father of one. She was furious and immediately issued a strong denial on her website: 'This is the first and last time I will comment on the details of my relationship with Simon. Contrary to reports and headlines in the press today, Simon is divorced and has been for four years.

'Everyone in our lives separately and together wish us nothing but the best, and vice versa. These are the facts.'

Their friends were discreet. Jamie Wood said simply, 'They are a wonderful couple.'

As if to confirm that their relationship would not be played out in public, Adele avoided the hoopla of the nominations launch party for the BRITs, leaving the red carpet to the likes of Jessie J and Emeli Sandé, while she and Simon slipped away to the Asian restaurant Gilgamesh in Camden to help Sid Owen celebrate his birthday.

Quietly, she bought a £2 million house in a prime location on the beach in Brighton, where neighbours included Zoe

Ball and Nick Berry. It was convenient for Simon's business and, more importantly, near his daughter Georgie, who was only five. At twenty-three, Adele was effectively a stepmother. Clary had moved on as well, dating the author and illustrator Paul Collicutt, who works from a studio in the city.

Simon was sitting next to Adele at the Staples Center when she received her Grammys and embraced her affectionately when she won. At the end of her speech, she thanked him – as she had done with Alex when she had first won awards in 2008. This time there was no hiding any relationship. The whole world knew that the bear-like, slovenly-looking gentle guy with a beard and glasses, who had the air of a Hollywood director, was her 'man'.

She was happy to talk about him in glowing terms, telling *Vogue* that he was wonderful and that she planned to take four or five years off. She told *60 Minutes* that she couldn't write another break-up record: 'I'm madly in love and I don't want to be like, "Babe, I'm sorry, we've got to break up. I've got a new album to deliver."'

Simon was also with her at the BRITs, on a table that included Sid Owen, his fiancée Polly Parsons and the comedian and chat-show host Alan Carr, who had become a good friend.

In March, there were reports that Adele was keen to start a family and was feeling broody – stories that could readily be dismissed at the time as fluff, but which turned out basically to be true. It was actually the perfect time for her to be pregnant: she wasn't supposed to smoke or drink and there was nothing in the diary.

She told her friends and family the happy news first, warning them to keep it a secret until an official announcement was made. She called her nana in Penarth to tell her, but didn't contact her father. Instead, Rose rang Marc and said she had some important news for him. 'Adele is expecting a child,' she said, adding that his daughter was hoping for a boy. His happiness at the prospect of becoming a grandfather turned to gloom when he realised that Adele hadn't wanted to tell him personally. He tried to contact her to offer his congratulations, but got nowhere and realised he was completely out of the picture. He hadn't met Simon, of course, but Rose told him he was a lovely chap, which was reassuring. Both her grandmothers like him. Doreen, back in Tottenham, said that the whole family was so pleased for Adele.

She revealed her pregnancy to the rest of the world on her website, on 29 June, in a brief message that read as if it had been written by a PR person: 'I'm delighted to announce that Simon and I are expecting our first child together. I wanted you to hear the news direct from me, obviously we're over the moon and very excited but please respect our privacy at this precious time. Yours always, Adele xx.'

18

SKYFALL

During the early months of her pregnancy, she and Simon were living in a palatial ten-room mansion in the village of Partridge Green, near Horsham in West Sussex, about half an hour from Brighton. She was waiting for work to be completed on their new home by the sea, so this was only temporary. She had originally chosen Lock House because she was concerned about the effect pollution in London might have on her voice and thought the country air would be better. Renting the house, complete with swimming pools and helipad, cost £19,000 a month, but Adele could afford it. *The Sunday Times* Rich List placed her first among most wealthy young musicians, with an estimated fortune of £20 million.

She showed a film crew, led by the Emmy Award-winning American broadcaster Anderson Cooper, around her new surroundings – something she would never do if it were her own family home. It would have been the perfect setting for a murder mystery weekend. There were ten bedrooms, which made Adele laugh, because she would be using only one of them.

The interview was very jolly, with Adele baking cupcakes in the luxurious open-plan kitchen. You could have fitted the whole of the first floor flat in Shelbourne Road, Tottenham, into the space. She showed Anderson the two pools — one indoor, one outdoor, the tennis court, some of the 25-acre grounds, the music room and the area reserved for her wig and hairpiece collection. She confided that she had a different name for each of them, including a Joan Collins and a June Carter, after the wife of Johnny Cash. It was all great fun, if a little surreal to see her in such a place.

Adele didn't stop work completely. She was asked to write the theme tune for the new Bond film, *Skyfall*, and, on her usual default setting, said no. She was asked to do so many things that it was often easier to say no. She desperately wanted to do it, though, and was 'dying inside' after turning it down. Fortunately, the producers, Barbara Broccoli and Michael Wilson, asked again and so, encouraged by Simon, she had the chance to accept a dream project.

Her initial apprehension was understandable. The music for the iconic series was a vital promotional tool and always much anticipated. Inevitably, her song would be compared to previous offerings. Would she measure up to Shirley Bassey's unforgettable 'Goldfinger' and 'Diamonds Are Forever' or would she come across as too cheesy?

The first thing she did was read the script from beginning to end, so she could get a feel for what turned out to be the most emotional of all Bond stories. She was used to writing about the drama in her life, so she needed to be immersed in 007's. Her involvement was meant to be a secret, but it seemed common knowledge for the six months that she was doing it.

She sought advice from the director Sam Mendes, who told her to make it personal. He pointed out that 'Nobody Does It Better', the Carly Simon theme from *The Spy Who Loved Me*, was an 'incredibly personal song'. He didn't expect her to write one that followed the narrative, in particular the opening sequence in which Sam showed Bond plummeting into the water and down into the underworld. He observed, 'She just got it.'

Adele took a serious and intelligent approach to the brief from Sam for a dramatic ballad, which was, after all, her speciality. She asked Paul Epworth to be her collaborator on the song and he adopted a forensic method to getting the sound right. His professional star couldn't have shone brighter after his success at the 2012 Grammys, when he was named Producer of the Year for his work on *21* and, in particular, 'Rolling in the Deep'.

Adele and Paul wanted something that reflected the dark sense of finality in the film but also turned into something that suggested a rebirth. They looked back through all thirteen Bond films, searching for the common factor that gave the music the mood and 'that kind of Sixties jazzy quality' they possessed. Paul tried to identify any chord that linked the theme songs, until one day it all came together and he had a moment of inspiration: 'Literally, these chords fell into my head and they were like nothing I've ever played before, and it was a bit of a "Eureka!" moment, really. It wasn't meant to mimic, it was meant to be what it was, and be respectful to those classic things.'

He had deciphered the musical equivalent of the Enigma code: the songs relied on a 'minor ninth as the harmonic code'. Paul lost no time in writing some music to encapsulate what he had discovered, which perhaps explains why 'Skyfall' sounds like every Bond song but better.

He invited Adele over to the studio, little realising that she had been working hard on the lyric and where the song needed to go. He told *Hollywood.com*, 'I rang her up and said it might be too dark but she said she loved it.' When Adele arrived, it was all in her head and they sped through the first rough draft in ten minutes: 'It was the most absurd thing. She's fast, but it was really quite phenomenal.'

He intended it as a compliment, but taken out of context it smacked of arrogance that she could record such a wonderful song in ten minutes. He took to Twitter to explain that he only meant the first draft of the verse and chorus. He had been impressed by her vocal control: 'She had great finesse and skill. She's not just a powerhouse – it's a lot of careful technique.'

The final, full-blown version of the song was recorded at Abbey Road Studios, using a seventy-seven-piece orchestra conducted by the renowned composer J. A. C. Redford. Daniel Craig cried when he heard it, which didn't sound like a typical James Bond response. He explained, 'From the opening bars I knew immediately, then the voice kicked in and it was exactly what I wanted. It just got better and better because it fitted the movie.'

The finished track was launched first of all with a ninety-second clip on Adele's website on 5 October 2012, Global James Bond Day, which coincided with the fiftieth anniversary of the release of the first Bond movie, *Dr. No*. The critics rushed to review it, even though they only had a minute and a half to go on. Jude Rogers remarked in the *Guardian*, 'Her delivery reveals the best of Adele: the sound of an ordinary girl capable of extraordinary feeling.'

Surprisingly, the song failed to reach number one, despite all the hype and anticipation, kept off the top by Rihanna's 'Diamonds'. The song, though, was everywhere in the run-up to the royal premiere of the film attended by Prince Charles and Camilla at the Royal Albert Hall in London. The stars were all there – Daniel, Javier Bardem, the villain, and Dame Judi Dench among them – but not Adele. She had been a mum for four days.

There was no announcement in *The Times*, or even on her website, acknowledging the birth. 'We are not releasing a statement at this time,' said a spokesman at Purple PR, and that was that. Regrettably, it didn't stop the Internet trolls from making some nasty comments on social media. Even the late comedienne Joan Rivers posted an ill-judged joke: 'Congratulations to Adele on the birth of her 68 pound 8 ounces bouncing baby boy.'

Simon was so thrilled to be a father for the second time that he bought Adele a £3,000 gold pendant designed by his aristocratic friend, the artist and sculptor Lady Marina Cowdray, who lives in a stately home in West Sussex. The striking piece was based on a sculpture she had crafted called 'The Meditator', which resembled a Buddha. It was her interpretation of the quality of wisdom, knowledge, compassion and human perfection – a perfect gift for the start of a new life. He purchased an identical one in solid silver with a leather cord, so they would have a memento each. Lady Marina said, 'He wanted to get a matching one for himself, which was sweet.'

The redesign and renovation of the house in Brighton, reportedly at a cost of £500,000, was not yet complete, but Adele had discreetly bought a mews house in Kensington for £5.65 million. Her property empire was beginning to grow substantially, although she transferred ownership of her first flat in Notting Hill to her mother.

Adele preferred not to leave London unless she had to and wanted to enjoy the first few months quietly with her baby. She decided they would have more chance of being left alone by the paparazzi if they spent some time in Los Angeles. Adele looks very different without her star make-up and was unlikely to be recognised. In any case, they could rent in a gated community, which would guarantee their privacy.

They flew into Los Angeles International Airport (LAX) with a weary Adele, flanked by bodyguards, clutching her six-week-old baby, who had a blanket hiding his face from any prying paparazzi lens. Adele had not much enjoyed previous visits to California, finding it too hot and impersonal, but on this occasion she really enjoyed it – mainly due to a blossoming friendship with the actress Ayda Field, wife of Robbie Williams, who had given birth to their daughter, Teddy, a month before Adele.

Ayda invited her round to their Beverly Hills mansion for some tea. Robbie doesn't drink alcohol, so his wife had become an expert in making a brew, which met with Adele's approval. It was comforting to talk to another young mum who was going through the same feelings of exhaustion and elation and the two women bonded. They joked that it was never too soon to matchmake and, growing up, their babies would be pop royalty.

Robbie and Ayda joined her and Simon for the Golden Globes ceremony at the Beverly Hilton hotel, the big opening night of awards season in LA and the first time Adele had been seen out in public for months. The ghastly walk through the airport didn't count as an event.

Adele's appearance was such a talking point, she almost stole the limelight from Daniel Craig, who posed on the red carpet in secret agent shades. She looked Hollywood fabulous in a black Burberry gown and blonde beehive. She told an interviewer that it was too soon to reveal the name of her son. 'I'm not ready,' she explained. 'It's too personal and intimate. I'm enjoying him on my own at the moment' – forgetting that Simon was there with her.

As usual, her London accent was mistakenly referred to as cockney when she took to the stage to accept her award for Best Original Song from Jennifer Lopez. 'Oh my God, Oh my God, Oh my God,' she began. 'Honestly, I came for a night out with my friend Ayda. We're new mums. I was not expecting this, thank you so much. It's very strange to be here. Thanks so much for letting me be part of your world for a night. We've been pissing ourselves laughing at all of this.'

She thanked Daniel Craig for being a wonderful Bond. He looked delighted for her. He had taken a liking to Adele, who is refreshingly unstarry. He'd given her some designer baby grows and a miniature James Bond Aston Martin when her son was born. Celebrities often give each other presents. Rihanna also sent round some baby grows bearing the logo 'Just Done Nine Months Inside'.

Adele finished her acceptance speech by dedicating the award to 'my boyfriend Simon who convinced me to do it, and my lovely son.' She frequently mentions crying when she's chatting away, but she really looked as if she was going to have a big sob when she mentioned her baby. As she came off stage, she reached for someone's hand to help her and it was only 'George Fucking Clooney's'.

One amusing sidebar to Adele's triumph came when the cameras focused on Taylor Swift, a losing nominee, who appeared less than delighted. For once, someone who didn't win wasn't sporting a delighted showbiz grin when they missed out.

Adele's son's anonymity didn't last long. She was seen leaving a Hollywood store wearing a gold necklace bearing the word 'Angelo' and he was soon revealed to be Angelo James Konecki. Adele preferred to call him Peanut.

The Golden Globes was the start of a magnificent four. Next, she won the Best Pop Solo Performance Grammy for her live performance of 'Set Fire to the Rain' at the Royal Albert Hall, which was all the more commendable because the concert took place at a time when she was beset by her vocal problems. She wore vibrant red instead of her usual black, but the Valentino dress, while it looked exquisite close-up, wasn't a hit with the fashion critics, who likened it to a pair of embellished curtains.

She chose not to fly back to London for the BRITs, which was probably just as well after the debacle of the previous year. She accepted the award for 'Skyfall' as Best British Single by video link, saying she wasn't there because she was rehearsing for the Oscars. She couldn't resist a gentle barb: 'I won't keep you too long, because I don't want to interrupt the Best Album speech at the end of the night.'

Adele had already won upwards of a hundred awards, but the Oscars have a special significance. They represent an old-fashioned unobtainable glamour, a world she had watched on television as a child and could only dream about. And now, here she was, aiming for a clean sweep of all the major award ceremonies. She was to sing live for the first time in a year, performing 'Skyfall' in a dramatic fashion in front of an orchestra as part of a special Bond presentation that also featured Shirley Bassey.

Beforehand, Adele had confided to Ayda about her stage fright and the actress recommended Qigong, a Chinese breathing therapy that Robbie, another sufferer, uses to calm his nerves before performing. Adele has a very specific form of stage fright. She worries that she will walk on, open her mouth to sing and nothing will come out. It never happens, thankfully.

She was genuinely almost lost for words when 'Skyfall' was announced the winner by Richard Gere and Renée Zellweger. She only just managed to avoid tears once again as she thanked Paul Epworth for believing in her all the time. She remembered to thank Simon – 'My man, I love you, baby.' It was left to Paul, looking very dapper, to give a more considered speech, which he ended by thanking Adele, who, he said, is 'the best person I have ever worked with'.

In Los Angeles, Adele didn't feel as much a hostage to fame as she did at home in London. She was absolutely determined that her son wasn't going to become public property. She understood that she was a celebrity, but didn't want to be snapped pushing a buggy in the frozen food aisle of Waitrose.

She was furious, therefore, when she was photographed by a paparazzo taking eight-month-old Angelo for a day out at

Central Park's Tisch Children's Zoo in June 2013. He was wearing a little sky-blue bib and a white sunhat and she held him securely in her arms. They were sweet pictures, but that wasn't the point: this was a private family outing.

When further pictures taken at Chelsea Farmers' Market appeared a few months later, she decided to put a stop to it and instructed her lawyers to act. In Angelo's name, she and Simon took action against the picture agency involved. When the case came to the High Court in July 2014, their solicitor, Jenny Afia, of Schillings law firm, said, 'It is a matter of profound sadness that many of his milestone moments, such as his first family outing and his first trip to playgroup, were photographed and published worldwide expressly against his family's wishes.'

Angelo accepted a five-figure sum in damages, legal costs and an undertaking from Corbis Images UK not to use the pictures again. The financial details aren't important; Adele had successfully made a point. Ms Afia explained that Adele and Simon, who were pleased the matter had been resolved, would hold the damages on trust on behalf of their son, the claimant. She concluded, 'The children of famous parents are not celebrities. The law can, will and should protect them.'

On a happier note, Adele had a capital letter A tattooed just behind her right ear. When she had it done, she was still keeping Angelo's name a secret. In the summer, during the visit to New York when they were papped, she visited the famous tattooist Bang Bang at his Manhattan studio.

Bang Bang was thrilled, especially when she volunteered to swap roles and ink the number 21 on his leg. He observed graciously, 'I tattoo a ton of amazing, talented people, but not often do I tattoo someone you can say makes timeless art. Obviously, I meet so many pop icons and they're making music for now and they're great at it – of course, I'm not knocking anybody – but Adele … I just felt like, Oh my gosh I'm tattooing, like, the modern-day Frank Sinatra. It was really cool.'

She had decided on three tattoos and knew exactly what she wanted. She and Bang Bang sat down at his computer to work out the right font and shade. First, she had the number 5 put on the inside of her ring finger. She has never explained that one. Then she had the word Paradise inked on the edge of her left hand and Angelo matching it on her right because, as she said, 'Angelo is my Paradise.'

19

HELLO AGAIN

It must be the way the Prince of Wales tells them. Adele had a fit of the giggles when he pinned her MBE to her dress. They chatted easily for several minutes at the ceremony in Buckingham Palace just before Christmas 2013. She strode off, guffawing merrily, to have her picture taken with her award. She managed to tone down her trademark laugh or they would have heard her in Trafalgar Square.

Afterwards, she played it safe, issuing a statement rather than chatting to the press directly, when she might have said something untoward: 'It was an honour to be recognised and a very proud moment to be awarded alongside such wonderful and inspirational people. Very posh indeed.' There's a time and a place to be the potty-mouthed girl from Tottenham and one to be reserved and respectful. This was definitely the latter.

She certainly looked the part. She had her nails done specially for her trip to the Palace. They were painted royal blue and on the ring fingers of each hand they featured tiny silver-coloured crowns decorated with red stones. She wore a

Stella McCartney midnight blue prom dress that cost close to £1,000 and sported a Philip Treacy fascinator over her beehive hairdo. She looked glamorous and fashionable but not overdressed.

Simon was there, supporting her, but leaving the limelight discreetly to the mother of his child. The boy himself couldn't be there, sadly. He had to stay behind with his nanny. Afterwards, Adele put her award in a frame and placed it in the toilet. She doesn't have too much homage to herself round and about, although her Oscar is on display in a glass cabinet in her dressing room, alongside the Burberry dress she wore – an idea she had when she learned that Barbra Streisand had done something similar.

For the most part, Adele spent three years being a mum and worrying about her next album. She gave no interviews and, after her flurry of awards, wasn't seen on red carpet duty. She has always pointed out that she wasn't a recluse during Angelo's earliest years. She went out. The young woman in a baggy black jumper, leggings and Converse trainers didn't look like the superstar Adele, so few noticed her.

She might have been the person next to you rummaging through the buy one get one free offers in a local children's clothes store, but you didn't pay her much attention. Even her driving instructor didn't know who she was when she started having lessons. Noel Gaughan has taught some well-known celebrities to drive, including Niall Horan of One Direction and actor James McAvoy, but he didn't recognise Adele, even when she started singing to him. He recalled, 'She would sing some beautiful songs and say, "You must know this one".' He didn't.

Adele impressed Noel by working hard and learning quickly. She passed her test the first time, which she was particularly pleased about, because it meant she could drive her son around. She couldn't wait to do that. She already had her first car on order: a top-of-the-range black Porsche Cayenne, which is not a sports car but a £100,000 SUV, perfect for a fashionable young mum ferrying her child around London. She also purchased a less ostentatious Mini.

The problem with being happy, as she was discovering, was that she had nothing to write about. There was little emotional feeling attached to a trip to Waitrose or the organic food shop she favoured in Chelsea. She couldn't sit in a darkened room being miserable when she was required to sing another chorus of a nursery rhyme in the playroom. She observed, 'It's nice. I haven't been as stressed out.'

She tries not to be ostentatious with money where Angelo is concerned, although she did buy him a Victorian-style play-house, complete with turrets, a wicker fence and a veranda, which apparently cost £15,000. She is careful not to be too flash for fear of alienating the millions who relate to her through her music and everywoman persona.

Her lifestyle had changed dramatically since the birth of Angelo. She was close to being a chain-smoker and needed to give up for the sake of her voice, as well as the welfare of her son. She found it very hard. Smoking had been so much of her lifestyle and she enjoyed it. She went to see Harley Street hypnotist Susan Hepburn in 2014 and that worked for a while, but she relapsed.

Adele understood that she risked causing long-term damage to her health if she continued, so she tried again. This time she attended the renowned Knightsbridge clinic of Max Kirsten, where she paid £480 for a three-hour session. He helped the actor Ewan McGregor quit and is also rumoured to have treated David Cameron. So far, she hasn't smoked again.

Drinking hasn't been such a problem for her. She hasn't drunk to excess since she was first diagnosed with voice problems. When she pops round to watch TV at Alan Carr's – they like *Come Dine with Me* – she ignores his suggestion of a nice glass of red wine in favour of a nice cuppa and a Hobnob. He joked, 'It's like having Sister Wendy round.'

She is particularly worried about picking up infections, coughs and colds from her little boy, because she can't sing at all when she is ill. And if she ever finished the new album, she would need to be singing often and at full power.

After *21* and before the welcome distraction of Angelo, Adele said, 'I'll disappear and come back with a record when it's good enough.' That sounded fine in 2011, but nobody expected it to be this long. Her fans thought it would come at the end of 2014, especially after she tweeted on her twenty-sixth birthday, 'Bye bye 25 … See you again later in the year', but nothing happened, despite her best efforts.

Once again, she looked to associate with new writers and renew collaborations with some she had worked with successfully before. She had a long list. She met up again with Ryan Tedder on her first visit to New York with Angelo. They came up with the song 'Remedy', which was an encouraging start and, for a moment, she thought she was on a roll. That proved not to be the case. She was writing songs, but they didn't sound right.

She was impatient, however, and asked Rick Rubin to fly over to hear what she had so far for *25*. He wasn't impressed. 'I don't believe you,' he said, recognising, as ever, that it was a requirement of every Adele song to be genuinely felt so that it could make a connection with the listener. He believed the new songs sounded as if they could feature on any pop artist's album. They were professional and well made, but perhaps lacked enough of her own stamp. 'It's not just her voice singing any song that makes it special,' he said.

Jonathan Dickins was equally unenthusiastic about the new material, telling her, 'It's just not good enough.' His long partnership with Adele is based on mutual respect. She trusts his judgement. He doesn't roll over and tell her she's wonderful every day. During one interview on a video shoot, she was perched atop a high director's chair, when she dropped her cigarette. 'Get that for me,' she casually said to her manager. 'Get it your fucking self' was the response. So she had to climb down, fetch her ciggie and then hoist herself back up again.

When she presented him with Manager of the Year at the *Music Week* Awards, she thanked God that she had chosen him as her manager, because he had 'fucking smashed it'. He could not write her new album for her, however. She needed fresh inspiration. The songs about Angelo, a natural topic for her, failed to excite – even Simon thought the material boring.

Some collaborations worked better than others. Greg Kurstin proved to be a great success, and working with him on a track called 'Hello' breathed new life into the album. He was another multi-talented musician, producer and composer who could play practically any instrument and transform a humdrum song into potentially a great one. In the business he

– and others like Paul Epworth and Fraser T. Smith – are called artist whisperers, a play on the expression 'horse whisperer'.

He won three prestigious Ivor Novello Awards for his work with Lily Allen on her number one album *It's Not Me, It's You*, co-wrote and produced 'Stronger (What Doesn't Kill You)' for Kelly Clarkson and 'Burn' with Ellie Goulding, which topped the UK charts in 2013. 'Burn' was originally written by Ryan Tedder, who was able to recommend Greg to Adele. Greg also had a long-standing association with the innovative artist Sia and co-wrote or produced much of her 2014 American number one album *1000 Forms of Fear*, which included the unforgettable dance hit 'Chandelier'. His credentials, therefore, were impeccable. He was thrilled to be asked to work on an Adele album – the equivalent of winning the lottery in the music world.

They met up at the Metropolis Studios on the Chiswick High Road. This was strictly business and Angelo was left behind so as not to distract Mum. She had blocked off a week in her diary to see if they could come up with anything. Adele had a pristine new lyric book. Greg sat at the piano – an old-school approach – and they kicked around ideas and played with chords.

Greg was another musician who liked to work fast and that always suits Adele's agile mind. When they had an idea, Adele would start scribbling lyrics, while he recorded himself on drums, keyboard and guitar, so they would have the foundations of a good demo there and then. Greg liked to play all the instruments for the simple reason that he knew what he wanted in his head and it was faster if he did it himself. He expected to finish a song in a day.

That didn't work with 'Hello'. They wrote most of it not long after he got off the plane from LA, but couldn't finish it. He recalled, 'We tried different choruses, but we didn't quite nail it. I didn't know if we ever would. I thought maybe this one was going to end up on the shelf.'

Their first week-long session wasn't entirely wasted. He found Adele great company. She was funny and down to earth and he felt comfortable around her. They managed to finish a track called 'Water Under the Bridge', which Adele wrote about her relationship with Simon. On first listening, it sounds as if it's a break-up song but, as she later explained, it's more to do with her waiting for him to be horrible and what would happen if he was. She was quick to tell radio DJ Zane Lowe she didn't expect that to happen and that Simon was the man for her. For a while, there were media rumours that all was not well with them, but these were never substantiated and he was by her side when she re-emerged into the public eye.

By the time she asked Greg to return for another week, six months had passed, and she finally had a better approach for the album. It was about looking back on her life so far: the past that made her, friends and family, and the surroundings that had shaped her character and provided the memories she kept with her. It was a nostalgic clear-out of emotions. She told *i-D* magazine, 'It's about missing things you had no idea were precious. It's about what was, what is, what might have been.'

'Hello', for instance, is about reaching out to those whom she has hurt in her life and apologising for it. She is also saying sorry to herself. She explained, 'It's about hurting someone's feelings, but it's also about trying to stay in touch with myself, which sometimes can be a little bit hard to do. When I'm away, I really, really miss my life at home.'

They moved forward quickly with 'Hello', especially once Greg lowered the key. He knew they had it when Adele sang the chorus for the first time. He enthused, 'When Adele gets on the mic, she blows your mind. I was moved when I first heard her sing "Hello" and I'm still moved every time I hear it.'

The major problem for Greg, when he jetted back to California, was that he had to keep his mouth shut about the recording. He had to be discreet for a whole year: 'It's not easy to hold that information in for that long. You kind of want to shout it out, run around in the street, yelling to random strangers what you've just done.'

He had to keep silent because there was still much work to do. Not all of her collaborations were as successful as theirs. Phil Collins worked on several songs but none of them made the final cut. He didn't take it personally. 'She's a slippery little fish is Adele,' he commented cheerfully. Likewise, none of the songs she composed with the queen of songwriting, Diane Warren, made it onto *25*. Adele teamed up with Sia on a track called 'Alive', which featured on her co-writer's own album, *This Is Acting*.

Sam Dixon had been Adele's bass guitarist on the *Adele Live* tour and had previously forged successful partnerships both with Sia and Greg, so, in the small musical world Adele inhabits, he seemed a good bet. They wrote 'Love in the Dark' together, one of the saddest songs on the album.

It didn't seem to matter how famous the collaborator was: nobody was treated differently and it was all about the song.

Pharrell Williams, who wrote and performed the huge-selling number one 'Happy' and was one of the hottest names in the music business, gave a fascinating insight into working with Adele when he spoke to an audience at the Cannes Lions International Festival of Creativity: you don't get much time with her. 'She's kinda like, "OK, guys, I'm gonna open my diary for twenty minutes." ... Then she gives it to you and closes it up and disappears, and she's off with her beautiful boy and that's what it's all about.' He did add that he thought Adele was a 'masterful writer'.

By far the least successful collaboration was with Damon Albarn and it developed into a full-blown spat between the two. It was all the more surprising because the lead singer of Blur is the best friend of the boss of XL Records, Richard Russell. Damon and Adele didn't get on at all and failed to finish even one song.

Reading between the lines, Adele couldn't bear him, declaring that it was definitely one of those 'don't meet your idol' moments. Instead of keeping his own counsel about it, Damon was quoted as saying that he found Adele insecure, which enraged her. He apparently said, 'The thing is she's very insecure. And she doesn't need to be, she's still so young.'

Adele didn't laugh it off. Her response to *Rolling Stone*, one of the few magazines she has talked to throughout her career, was that she was asking his advice about returning to work with a young child. She fumed, 'He called me insecure, when I am the least insecure person I know.'

Jonathan Dickins reportedly saw Damon at the Ivor Novello Awards and tried to smooth things over, but was rebuffed. Damon was there to pick up a Lifetime Achievement Award.

Adele won Songwriter of the Year, but did not attend, which was probably a good thing if relations between the two are really as frosty as media reports suggested. The feud is unusual for Adele, who generally likes everyone when asked about other stars in interviews. Taking strong offence at Damon's remarks was uncharacteristic.

Much more satisfying were her trips to Los Angeles to work with Bruno Mars and Tobias Jesso Jr. Bruno is obviously one of the biggest stars in the world, so they made a dream team. They intended to write something upbeat and danceable, but ended up with the maudlin 'All I Ask', with a dramatic key change that could literally bring tears to your eyes.

Engagingly, Canadian-born singer-songwriter Tobias was a real fan of Adele, not a showbiz type who gushes about whomever they are working with next, but someone in genuine awe of a favourite artist. It was his first professional collaboration. He posted a blog in which he said, 'I was as nervous as shit.' He needn't have been. They got along famously and spent two days working together at his house. They wrote a lot during that time – not in a studio, but with the two of them sitting around a piano, which he had inherited and used to belong to the renowned composer Philip Glass, a friend of his grandparents.

Tobias was impressed with Adele: 'I can tell from the bottom of my heart she means what she says and the words she puts into her music. Every lyric and every line comes from a place she feels. She doesn't settle.' One of the tracks from that session, 'When We Were Young', a power ballad of nostalgia, with one of the great money notes at the end, made it onto the album and is Adele's favourite. The track should come with a warning that it is not to be sung in karaoke.

She was having lunch with Ryan Tedder in New York when the Taylor Swift hit 'I Knew You Were Trouble' came on the sound system. Adele was impressed with a record that didn't seem to be a typical Taylor track. She wanted to know who was responsible. Ryan told her it was a Max Martin song and, legend has it, Adele had never heard of one of the most famous names in pop. The Swedish-born songwriter and producer has been responsible for some of the best-known songs of the past twenty years. He wrote '… Baby One More Time', the breakthrough hit for Britney Spears, as well as major chart-toppers for Backstreet Boys, 'N Sync, Jessie J and Katy Perry. Only Paul McCartney and John Lennon have written more number ones in the *Billboard* Hot 100 than Max.

The Hit Factory, based in Stockholm, was the dominant force in uncomplicated pop music. Max and his crew flew to London to meet with Adele after Jonathan had contacted them. She took her guitar along to a session at Eastcote Studios in West London and played them the basic melody to a song. They recorded it, added a beat to it and 'Send My Love to Your New Lover' was born. She had written the basic idea of the song aged thirteen and was dusting it off all these years later. The final version is arguably the most unusual track on the album. Refreshingly, it doesn't sound like an Adele song at all.

At last, the long-delayed album was taking proper shape. Greg Kurstin flew back to London and they wrote the most blatantly nostalgic of all the tracks on *25*, 'Million Years Ago', a song of regret for time passing, written after she had driven past her old haunts in South London.

She went back to Paul Epworth at the iconic Church Studios in Crouch End for two tracks. First, they wrote 'I Miss

You', a song that came to her in bed one night. It is obviously about sex but, according to Adele, is also about intimacy on all sorts of levels, even drunken arguing, when a 'drunk tongue is an honest one'. One of the things she no longer liked about drinking was the panic she felt the next morning, trying to remember what was said. Because of its deeply personal nature, she spoke to Simon about it, but he was unfazed, believing her writing was nothing to do with him and he had no wish to interfere.

The second track was 'Sweetest Devotion', a love letter to her beloved son. He is heard at the beginning and end of the song saying, 'I want to sit next to my mummy.' She was telling the world of the fulfilment she had found in her child – the 'light in her darkness'. The song was placed at the end of the album, a sign of her optimism going forward. She observed, 'I love it that my life is about someone else.' Being a mum is now her number one priority.

It was decided that 'Hello' would be the lead single from the album, which would be released in time for Christmas 2015 in both the UK and the US markets. It had the perfect title for what was, in effect, a comeback record. She flew to Canada to shoot the video in the countryside around Montreal. She had approached one of the bright young things of cinema, the indie film-maker Xavier Dolan, to direct it and he decided to shoot the film in IMAX to stunning effect. He is renowned for his attention to detail, even down to designing the coat Adele wears. She is pictured – not for the first time – in an abandoned house, making a phone call to a departed lover, played by Tristan Wilds from *The Wire*.

Her acting, full of anguish, was a considerable improvement from the wooden days of *Ugly Betty*. After that forgettable experience, she declared that she would never act, but discovered she really enjoyed making the video, even when she had to cry to order. She said she would act in a film if Xavier asked her.

Finally, everything was in place for an Adele blitz. It began without warning during an ad break in *The X Factor* on 17 October 2015. Against a black screen, her voice sang, 'Hello, it's me.' We heard thirty seconds without explanation, just the words of a new song flashing on the screen and her unmistakable tones. It was a brilliant tease for the new album. Adele, it seemed, was back.

20

THE BIGGEST STAR
ON THE PLANET

When Adele eventually emerged into the spotlight once again, she looked like a film star, more elegant and grown-up than ever before. The first sighting was when Xavier Dolan's video was available to watch online a week after the television teaser. Everyone wanted to see her. In five days, it had received 100 million views. Within three months, that figure had risen to one billion.

Most noticeably, her hair was different. She had left her hairpieces behind in favour of a new, more sophisticated blunt-cut elfin bob that blew around her face naturally in the wind. Her signature eye make-up had changed too. She had ditched the Dusty Springfield retro appearance for a more wide-eyed feline style.

It takes her team of make-up artists and stylists, armed with every conceivable size and shape of contour and eyeliner brush, two and a half hours to prepare Adele for the world. That's longer than Kim Kardashian takes to put her face on. In the past, she used to enjoy it, but these days she invariably has plans for Angelo and chivvies her team along. At least her new hairstyle has considerably cut down the length of time they have to fiddle around with her hair.

Adele's styling team has remained quite constant in recent years. Her chief stylist is Gaelle Paul, former fashion writer with the *Observer* and the go-to person for Sony when they are developing a new artist. Although now living a glamorous life in Los Angeles, Gaelle is originally from Barking and was brought up a few doors down from Bobby Moore's mum and dad.

She changed direction when she started to style models for fashion shoots before moving on to work with celebrities. With models, her work is quite straightforward, because it's all about the clothes. Celebrities, however, come with publicists and image consultants – they are more challenging.

Her association with Adele changed things again. She explained, 'With her, I do everything – every day she works basically. For events, I have to figure out how many outfits she'll need, and then I reach out to designers with a brief, show Adele and see what she thinks. She'll get the final say.' Adele likes to have the final say in every aspect of her career. Only Angelo's wishes carry more weight than her own opinion.

Designers are falling over themselves to dress Adele. Not every suggestion is welcomed. One designer wanted her to wear a figure-hugging mesh mermaid dress, tight to the ankles with a little slit at the base. Gaelle was horrified. For starters, how on earth was Adele meant to go to the loo? She has always said that the toilet is the very first thing she looks for when she arrives at a venue. Everything she wears at public events has been designed especially for her. Gaelle styled her for the Oscars, the Grammys, the BRITs, her MBE at the Palace – all the momentous occasions. She is particularly pleased with the dark-blue Burberry dress Adele wore when she won six Grammys in 2012 and was photographed afterwards, clutching them all triumphantly.

They don't see much of one another, usually working online or over the phone, but Gaelle is with her the whole time at events, helping her change outfits and making sure everything is perfect. She only leaves Adele as she steps on to the red carpet. Gaelle is like the caddie helping a golfer line up a putt before stepping aside to let the boss get on with it. These days if there is so much as a hair out of place, some writer is going to give the outfit only one star.

Adele wears Spanx on the red carpet because 'it smoothes you out', according to Gaelle, but she is not plagued by the insecurities that beset so many actresses under the cruel glare of the camera lens. 'Adele is really OK with how she looks. I don't think she ever lacked confidence.'

While Gaelle is responsible for overall style, Adele's hair and make-up for these events has been looked after by New Zealand-born Michael Ashton since 2007, even before *19* had been released. They were introduced by a mutual friend. He popped over to West Norwood to trim her fringe and she asked if he could do a quick bit of eyeliner before she went out to meet friends. Adele has never been that good at doing her own make-up, so Michael was a great find for her. He is complimentary about her: 'Adele has beautiful almond-shaped eyes and fantastic natural bone structure, which is the perfect canvas to work with, so at the beginning it was always about making the eyes a focus.'

While her eyes remain her signature feature, she had clearly lost a lot of weight, which was apparent when she was interviewed by Graham Norton for *Adele at the BBC*. According to Alan Carr, it was simply because she had stopped drinking alcohol. She preferred to attribute the weight loss to two important changes to her diet: strictly no curries and giving up the two sugars in the ten cups of tea she drank every day.

The renowned fashion guru Karl Lagerfeld will never live down his comment from 2012, when he said: 'She is a little too fat, but she has a beautiful face and a divine voice.' His remark went round the world and he was vilified for such insensitivity. It was as if he had savaged the Queen or, even worse, a puppy. Adele is a hero to so many women who identify with her and her shape. They nodded approvingly when she declared, 'I don't want to eat a Caesar salad with no dressing, why would I do that?'

Her chat with Graham Norton was comfy and reassuring on two levels. First, she looked spectacular in a forest-green calf-length dress designed by Jenny Packham, who is best known for her association with the Duchess of Cambridge. The outfit was covered in silver beads, sequins and crystals, the sort of intricate detail that Adele has always liked. Jenny, who dresses, arguably, the two most popular young women in the world, observed, 'Adele is very passionate about clothing. She is very aware of how she wants to look, and knows what she wants.'

Secondly, she still sounded like the old Adele, full of banter and life, although she was on her best behaviour as far as the F-word was concerned. She revealed a comedic touch when, complete with prosthetic nose and chin, she took part in a

filmed sketch in which she pretended to be an Adele imper-
sonator at an audition. It was funny and strangely moving
when she began to sing 'Make You Feel My Love' and the
other singers gradually realised she was the real thing and
promptly burst into tears. The clip went viral on the BBC's
YouTube channel and quickly became its most watched video
ever, with 38 million views.

On the show itself, she sang a mixture of old and new,
including 'Hello', 'When We Were Young' and 'Hometown
Glory', in which she managed to avoid saying 'shit', just leaving a space where the word should have been in the lyric. She
conveyed the emotion of her songs as much as ever. Backstage
she had been careful to preserve her voice and refused to
speak, communicating using a notepad. Rumours that it was
touch and go whether she would sing at all were strongly
denied.

By the time the show was broadcast at the end of November,
'Hello' was a worldwide number one, claiming the top spot
on the iTunes chart in eighty-five countries within twelve
hours of release. Adele breaks so many records that after a
while they lose their significance and become boring, but *25*
was number one in seventy-seven countries on pre-orders
alone, one month before it was officially available.

Not every critic liked it – *Time Out* thought it was 'a bit
dull' – but mostly it was handed five-star reviews. The *Daily
Telegraph* observed, 'What it sacrifices in youthful rawness, it
makes up in maturity and sheer class.' The *Washington Post*
made the observation that the underplayed production left
her voice exposed in a way that suggested vulnerability 'but
actually allows for fantastic displays of power'.

The financial magazine *Fortune* carried a banner headline that boasted 'Adele is here to save the music industry'. The article suggested a mere handful of artists could persuade the public to part with hard cash in the age of YouTube, Spotify and Apple Music by buying physical copies or digital downloads. Only five could do it and they were all women: Taylor Swift, Beyoncé, Katy Perry, Rihanna and, first on the list, Adele.

The campaign to promote *25* was brilliantly orchestrated. Taking part in her friend James Corden's 'Carpool Karaoke' for his US chat show was a masterstroke. So far the clip has been viewed more than 100 million times – priceless publicity. The segment had an unmistakable feel-good factor, as the two of them sang along to the Spice Girls and Nicki Minaj while driving through London traffic. James Corden had a surprisingly good voice as he coped with 'Hello' and 'All I Ask'. When they chatted, Adele revealed that she hadn't had a drink for eight months, but had fallen off the wagon temporarily the weekend before, when she had been drunk three days in a row.

It's all about building hype and anticipation. She has a few favourite publications, including *Rolling Stone*, the *Guardian*, *i-D* and, of course, *Vogue*, and she gives them a great deal of access so they can write in-depth comprehensive pieces about her. Just about every other publication in the world, particularly online, will find something in the articles to interest them and repeat. Adele, therefore, receives a blizzard of publicity from one interview. It's a very smart operation.

Her association with *Vogue* has been a happy one over the years. A combination of great pictures and proper insight have made her a success story for the magazine, which might have seemed unlikely when she represented 'curvy' many years before.

She reached new heights, however, when she was photographed by Annie Leibovitz for a second time – not for one picture but a whole series that depicted her as a Jane Austen heroine. Her look was reminiscent of a young Kate Winslet in *Sense and Sensibility*. We see her writing in her diary and at home in her stately home, wearing a succession of couture gowns and embellished day dresses by leading designers, including Gucci, Erdem, Giambattista Valli, Salvatore Ferragamo and Burberry, her favourite. In fashion terms, it was an A-list moment for Adele.

To her great surprise, she has become a fashion icon and a role model for ordinary women in an age when fashion has been overly sexualised. Alison Jane Reid observes, 'Gone is the slightly awkward big girl who used to live in grungy smock dresses, jeans and ballet pumps and an overdose of eyeliner. In her place is a grown-up, sophisticated swan with chiselled cheekbones, full bee-stung lips, a halo of pale golden hair and a stellar allure.

'You get the sense she is finally embracing the idea of being a fashion icon and having some fun, instead of retreating to an endless roll call of black dresses. She is proof that voluptuous is beautiful and powerful and that you don't have to be dangerously thin to be hugely successful.'

In general, Adele interviews tell us much about the music but not much about Adele herself. She is careful not to mention money or how she spends it. She did not, for instance, chat about buying the house next door to her home in

London for £5.38 million. The combined value of the two houses is more than £11 million, but that figure might be even higher if she knocks them through in order to create extra space. The seafront house in Hove was put on the market for £3 million, giving substance to the reports that she had purchased a property in Los Angeles and would alternate between there and London. The house in Beverly Hills cost £7 million, has four bedrooms, six bathrooms and a pool. Apparently, it came with an outdoor train set and a treehouse for Angelo.

She has a full-time personal assistant, a nanny and a body-guard who used to work for Lady Gaga. Most of the time he helps her with her shopping bags, but she is very careful about her personal security and especially that of her young son. None of this comes cheap. Her wages bill must be well into six figures and that's before she pays Gaelle and Michael and settles her designer dress bill. She also loves her Louboutin shoes, at £500 a pair, and accessories, especially designer handbags, usually Burberry, costing £2,000. It all adds up.

Adele is at pains to point out that she is not a recluse, and takes Angelo out to parks and museums around London, sometimes with Simon and always with her security. Occasionally, she is seen with other celebrities, having dinner with Alan Carr, for instance, at the Chiltern Firehouse in Marylebone. At one meal there, she was reported as having a blazing row with Simon, which resulted in them leaving separately. In New York, she ate with Jennifer Lawrence and Emma Stone at Cosme, a Mexican restaurant in the area of Lower Manhattan known as the Flatiron District. In Los Angeles, she met up with Jennifer again at Craig's on Melrose Avenue, where she also dined with Harry Styles. She was seen having sushi with Robbie Williams and Ayda Field at Nobu in Malibu. She doesn't do a lot of celebrity hopping, but when she does it is usually very much A-list.

The difficulty for Adele is finding the right balance between the fabulous lifestyle she can afford and the ordinary ones that her fans have. We want the Kardashians to lead a jaw-dropping existence because that reflects their image. It's not the same for Adele, who observed, 'No one wants to listen to a record from someone that's lost touch with reality. So I live a low-key life for my fans.'

She seldom gets it wrong, although she did upset many people when she moaned about having to pay 50 per cent income tax in 2011 after the success of *19*. She complained to *Q* magazine, 'Trains are always late, most state schools are shit and I've gotta give you, like, four million quid – are you having a laugh? When I got my tax bill in from *19*, I was ready to go and buy a gun and randomly open fire.' Jonathan Dickins must have choked on his cornflakes when he read that. She hasn't mentioned it again and has definitely not referred to any tax advantages gained by having a home in Los Angeles.

If money was something she didn't want to discuss publicly, then her father was an even more taboo subject. She doesn't even refer to him as Dad these days. Her steely resolve hasn't weakened and he still hasn't been invited to meet his grand-child: 'I am distraught about it,' he said simply. Adele hasn't taken Angelo to see his great-grandmother in Penarth, but Nana has been up to London to meet him.

Marc, it might be argued, has brought the situation on himself by selling a story to a newspaper in the first place. He put his head above the parapet and has had to face the consequences of that. Adele has no idea, however, that as a direct result of becoming visible, he was badly beaten up.

He had been in his local pub when four paratroopers started picking on him for being Adele's dad. It was a witty bar-room conversation: 'Yeah, I'm her fucking auntie,' one of them said when they heard who he was. It was nothing more than nasty banter until he was walking home and they pulled up as he was thumbing a lift. He recalls, 'I thought, "Oh no."' The fight was rather one-sided and, as Marc puts it, 'They hit shit out of me. I was lucky because two women pulled up and they were beeping the horn shouting, "What are you doing to that man?" God knows what would have happened if they hadn't.'

The biggest of the four men caught Marc with his ring and cut his face underneath his left eye. He was a complete mess. The worst thing was that when the swellings went down and his face returned to normal, his eye wouldn't stop sagging. In the end, he had to have an operation at a clinic in Cardiff to fix it, and he still has a scar.

According to Marc, not a day goes by when he isn't hassled about his famous daughter. Usually it's little more than friends phoning up and singing 'Hello, it's me' to him down the phone. The newspapers carried a story that he had reconciled with Adele following a cancer scare, but that wasn't the case.

. Her brother Cameron is continually hassled as well, especially when the paparazzi take pictures of him walking his dog near his home in South Wales. When Adele realised that she hadn't actually seen him for a couple of years, she rectified it by inviting him to her concert in Birmingham.

The demand for tickets to *Adele Live 2016* was extraordinary. According to Ticketmaster, four million fans applied for tickets to her six shows at Madison Square Garden, New York, in September; only 100,000 were available. In total, Ticketmaster reported ten million people wanted tickets to the five-month American leg.

Two weeks before she began the world tour in Belfast on 29 February 2016, she once again attended the Grammys at the Staples Center in Los Angeles. She hadn't been nominated for an award, because *25* was released after the deadline. She had agreed to perform because it was excellent publicity so close to the concerts. It didn't go to plan. She looked stunning in an intricate red Givenchy gown, but her fashion was overshadowed by sound issues during her performance that made it seem as if 'All I Ask' was out of tune. Apparently, a microphone fell onto the strings of a piano, so it appeared as if she were being accompanied by a noisy guitar. Afterwards, she wished she had stopped the song. 'All I Ask' is a difficult one to manage at any time, without mishaps like this. In a rare tweet, she responded in robust fashion, 'It made it sound out of tune. Shit happens.'

Adele doesn't really do social media. She isn't on Facebook and generally doesn't write her own tweets, claiming she is banned from posting because in the past she tweeted drunken messages. That may be the case, but the Adele Twitter is very half-hearted. She only averages fifty tweets a year. Kim Kardashian, meanwhile, has written on Twitter well over 20,000 times.

Her belligerent attitude to a rare performance disaster was soon replaced by dismay. 'I pretty much cried all day yesterday,' she told chat-show host Ellen DeGeneres a couple of days later. She then sang the song again and it was perfect.

Adele ditched 'All I Ask' in favour of 'When We Were Young' at the BRIT Awards eight days later, which seemed a sensible move. She wore a vibrant burgundy chiffon dress by Giambattista Valli, with matching red lipstick, when she won Best British Female Solo Artist. Her acceptance speech was unintentionally hilarious to those watching on television when ITV attempted to censor any use of the F-word. They failed miserably and muted the wrong word, so she could clearly be heard saying 'I bet you're fucking bored of me' to the audience in typical Adele fashion. Hosts Ant and Dec had to apologise to any viewers who might be offended.

The 107-date world tour, which was expected to generate receipts of more than £100 million, opened at the SSE Arena in Belfast. She set the tone for the rest of her concerts by balancing breathtaking singing with maintaining a constant stream of bawdy chat. 'My kid was being a nightmare,' she confided to the audience. 'And then there was a spillage at Gatwick and I thought my boyfriend wasn't going to get here – I thought the whole tour was doomed.' It's the contrast between bar-room banter and her fabulous voice that is so compelling. 'I've been shitting myself,' she announced. 'But I've had an Imodium.'

She was determined that Angelo would be part of the experience. Adele commissioned a specially kitted-out tour bus complete with nursery and a mini fire station. Beyoncé had advised her to take the same bed with her everywhere she went, so her child would have familiarity and feel safe. Her tour rider was distinctly unrock 'n' roll with no alcohol. Instead, she asked for mini pizzas, Jammie Dodgers and custard creams.

Angelo is with her the whole time and Simon joins them when business allows. He is wearing his hair and beard longer these days and looks like he should be playing guitar for the Grateful Dead. At various stops, they were pictured together, although publications were careful not to show her boy's face in any articles. They took him to the Artis Royal Zoo in Amsterdam and the following day enjoyed a bike trip round the cycle-friendly city, flanked by two bodyguards, who were also on bicycles.

She made no comment about reports the same week that she had signed a Gareth Bale-style transfer deal from XL Recordings to Sony for £90 million. The financial details were unconfirmed, but if the figure was correct, it eclipsed the previous record held by Robbie Williams, who signed with EMI for £80 million.

Sony already had a stake in Adele's US market through her arrangement with Columbia, but they now had secured the rights to her future recordings worldwide. It remains to be seen whether XL will have any future involvement with Adele. The label can congratulate itself on nurturing such a successful artist from scratch. In return, she has made a fortune for Martin Mills, Richard Russell and many others.

The new deal was good business for Sony. Adele had been widely credited with single-handedly saving the music industry in 2015. The 17.4 million global sales of *25* were more than the next five sellers combined. The second best, Ed Sheeran's *X*, sold 3.5 million.

Adele had already been named as Britain's richest-ever female musician in the 2016 *Sunday Times* Rich List with an £85 million fortune, a rise of £35 million on the previous year. That figure is expected to rise to more than £200 million in 2017. She will almost certainly top the Young Music Rich List for the sixth consecutive year.

She finished the European section of her tour by headlining the main Pyramid stage at Glastonbury at the end of June. She had been to Worthy Farm with Simon the previous year to watch Kanye West. Simon was there again, enjoying the chance to roam about unrecognised with his camera, have a quiet smoke in the hospitality area or queue to use a portaloo without being bothered by his wife's fans. Penny, too, was able to wander around unnoticed. She was staying in the luxury Greenfields campsite so that she could feel part of the whole festival experience.

Adele had once said she would never appear at such an event, frightened of performing in front of such a large audience. But here she was, striding onto the stage in front of 160,000 people in a fabulous bespoke dress, a hand-woven gown that took 200 hours to create. It was designed by Clare Waight Keller, the British designer at Chloé, as homage to the Seventies and the era when Janis Joplin was queen of the festivals.

Warnings were issued beforehand for the television audience that she might use some bad language, even though she wasn't on until 10.15 p.m., well after the watershed. She didn't disappoint and used the F-word thirty-three times during her hour-long performance. There were many tuts of disapproval in the papers, but the funniest thing about it was that some poor soul had to count the number of times she said 'fuck' rather than listen to some glorious music. Afterwards, the BBC had just eighteen complaints about the use of bad language.

If ever she was going to have stage fright, then this would be the occasion. The announcer introduced her as the 'biggest star on the planet', and she proved it as she managed to recreate her homely, mates-in-the-pub atmosphere on this great stage. Robbie Williams and James Corden were in the crowd watching. Simon was there, too, of course but, most fittingly, her mother Penny looked on, perhaps remembering all those years ago when she had taken her little girl to Glastonbury for the first time. 'This is fucking amazing,' Adele gasped, scarcely believing what she could see in front of her. Movingly, she remembered her late grandfather. 'This is for my granddad,' she announced, before beginning 'Make You Feel My Love' … and we did.

LAST THOUGHTS

Brockwell Park is like many other London parks – a green space to be treasured, but one that's a bit scruffy and could do with some more tender loving care. If you live in this part of South London, however, it's an enchanting oasis in the urban jungle. Watching the world go by on a sunny afternoon, I can easily understand why it holds a special place in Adele's heart. She has said that 'Hometown Glory' is not about a particular place but, if it were, this should at least be the location of the 'short skirts, shorts and shades'.

The song doesn't talk about young mothers with pushchairs, but there are plenty of those, sitting in the shade of a tree or watching their children cause havoc in the play area, where they scream and shout on swings and climbing frames. Adele could probably join them and not be recognised. In fact, she could hold an annual picnic for Team Adele in the park and none of them would be recognised. She could invite her mum, stepfather, cousins, aunts, nephews and nieces, safe in the knowledge that they, too, could remain incognito.

She doesn't look like *the* Adele when she's out and about in sweatpants and trainers, her hair fine and unkempt, her famous eyes hidden behind an oversized pair of her favourite sunglasses. The fashion conscious might wonder how a mum in this neighbourhood could afford Linda Farrow designer eyewear at £500 a pair. Adele can easily afford different ones for every day of the week.

We all know she is fabulously wealthy, but the important thing is she doesn't rub our noses in it. It would ruin her authenticity if she suddenly started sporting a Koh-i-Noor-sized rock on her finger. She knows how important it is that she is still one of us.

Even when she had a moan about the tax man, Adele was simply voicing what most people feel, which is what she always does. It is a large part of her charm.

Honesty and genuineness are important in our appreciation of Adele. Much has been written by experts trying to fathom her extraordinary appeal. I thought BBC Arts Editor Will Gompertz came close to working it out when he wrote that her personal investment in the narrative of her songs is both 'persuasive and palpable'. The lyrics are specific and vague at the same time, which allows the listener to interpret the words in any way that applies to them.

She sings about love and loss, of vulnerability and hurt, and of a sentimental yearning for the past. These are simple emotions to which everyone can relate, no matter what age, gender or sexual orientation they might be. Adele is often acknowledged as a leading gay icon and I can see the similarities between her and Kylie Minogue in this respect – they both sing in an emotional and sensitive way about their betrayal by men.

Some critics believe her lyrics lack penetration and fore-sight, but that completely misses the point for me. Most people don't need Plath and Kafka all the time – or even Bob Dylan and Leonard Cohen. They just want someone to chat to over a coffee about how relationships suck. Adele had that cracked right from the start.

She was encouraged to be herself at the BRIT School and thank goodness she was. It gave the green light to all the larger-than-life characteristics she has – the straight-talking, super-swearing, funny lady with the big laugh and even bigger voice. I would add sentimental and surprisingly sensitive to those qualities.

The media are always looking to catch her out as a closet diva, like the time it was reported she sent staff at an Oxfordshire hotel on a 140-mile round trip to London to fetch a pizza from her favourite takeaway in Kensington. At least it was a pizza (no anchovies) and not beluga caviar, but I don't believe the story for one minute. She is so careful about that sort of thing. She has her own team to look after her and doesn't need to ask hotel personnel to cater to her every whim. Her image is micromanaged and neither Team Adele nor their employer is going to make such a crass mistake.

She has admitted that she can be a diva to people she knows, but wouldn't dream of acting in that manner with someone she didn't. She used to be a waitress and is fully aware of how difficult it can be to deal with rude customers who feel they are entitled.

She doesn't want to insult her fans by parading around in a chauffeur-driven Rolls-Royce. When she went back to West

Norwood for an interview, she drove about in a Mini, while her bodyguard followed behind in a posh four-by-four.

Of course Adele has an image. You can't be in the public eye without one, whether you are a pop star, a politician, a sporting hero or someone who hosts cookery programmes on television. Her public face is as carefully managed as any of the more obvious ones in the world of entertainment. Ostensibly, she is the polar opposite of Kim Kardashian, yet she is exactly the same in presenting to us the image that works best for her.

Kim is apparently letting you in to every nook and cranny of her life, while Adele reveals as little as possible. Kim will endorse anything and everything; Adele plugs nothing. She was even rumoured to have turned down a deal to be the face of L'Oréal that was worth £12 million. She gets asked all the time to say how much she enjoys a particular kind of burger or always wears the latest shade of nail varnish. Thankfully, she is quick to say no. She does have favourite designers for her couture dresses, shoes and handbags, and so fashion houses like Burberry and Chloé receive much welcome publicity through their connection to a woman who has become – some might say surprisingly – a fashion icon of our times.

Ironically, both Kim and Adele are very similar in drawing a line between what they are prepared to reveal and what remains completely closed off. We never see inside their homes. We don't go through the keyhole to Kensington or Calabasas, where Kim lives in a closely guarded gated community.

I can see the attraction of moving to Los Angeles for Adele. These gated communities are like Fort Knox. She loathes the paparazzi and is very careful to protect her son. It will be interesting to see where she sends him to school. He is far more likely not to be bothered in LA, where they are used to dealing with the children of very famous people.

At least in Simon Konecki Adele has found someone who is unfazed by celebrity. He may be an old Etonian, but seems refreshingly ordinary despite his privileged upbringing. His business and charitable concerns have made steady if unspectacular progress. Anyone who monitors the drop4drop Twitter feed can admire the pictures mainly of women and children smiling happily at the provision of fresh water to their communities, whether in Asia or Africa. My favourite is of boys and girls learning how to wash their hands. According to drop4drop, women and children around the world spend 125 million hours each day collecting water. Adele supports the charity, of course, but not in a shouty celebrity way. She mentioned World Water Day in 2014, but little since then. It is Simon's mission in life.

Adele doesn't shy away from making her left-wing political views known. She called the former Prime Minister David Cameron 'a wally' and is happy to describe herself as 'Labour through and through'. She made it clear she had not given permission for Donald Trump to use 'Rolling in the Deep' at his campaign rallies, and she was uncomplimentary about Sarah Palin.

She is also happy to speak about controversial issues. At the 2016 BRIT Awards, she publicly gave her support to Kesha, the rap star who had accused her producer of drugging and raping her. She dedicated an entire show in Antwerp to victims of the gay nightclub massacre in Orlando, and showed her support of the LGBT community by wearing the rainbow flag. She told the audience, 'I'm going to dedicate this song to all my gay friends who lost their lives. I can't stop thinking about it. It's completely broken my heart.'

Adele is a very intelligent woman, however much she may try to hide the fact through her liberal use of the F-word and Queen Vic chortling. She hates that everyone shuts up when she walks into a room. She wants to talk to people and find out about their lives, but they shy away from her as if they can't possibly be as interesting as she is.

I decide to walk back to West Norwood from Brockwell Park. The lido where Adele used to swim is at the Herne Hill gate, and the Norwood Road entrance is about twenty minutes away, past the ponds. On the way, I think about what Adele might do next.

She finds that her world is shrinking – as many famous people do. They retreat behind burly bodyguards and electronic gates, where they can play safely with their children and, in Adele's case, watch movies or reality TV shows.

She says she doesn't like touring and is only doing it for the fans, so I don't expect her ever to be one of those performers who appear on stage year in and year out. Nor do I think she will perform in Las Vegas for months on end.

My guess is that she will go dark again now for a year or two. She will get on with her life, focus on raising Angelo and possibly add to her family away from prying eyes and lenses. I don't believe she will give up England at all, but could well see her spending more time in Los Angeles. Her new deal is probably much like her old one: three albums, but definitely not one a year. Why fix something that isn't broken? Three in ten years is more likely.

Hopefully Adele won't follow a growing trend of producing albums by committee. In the old days, the best songwriters used to congregate in Tin Pan Alley and write songs to order. Now, they sit around pools in Los Angeles, available when the artist comes into town. A major star might flit between half a dozen writers in a day, working on songs for a new album. It might conceivably only take a weekend. Adele needs to ensure that she continues to keep her own individual stamp on her music and not take this easy option.

She was made an MBE in 2013 and I believe she will be made a Dame at a very young age. I can imagine Graham Norton announcing, 'Give it up for Dame Adele Adkins' and us hearing the famous cackle as she makes her way onto the studio floor.

There will definitely be a blue plaque outside the old address in Norwood Road. It may not be Beverly Hills, but the street probably has more personality. It was little more than ten years ago that she was here, full of dreams and ambition but, as she poignantly wrote in the title of a song, it was a 'million years ago'.

The area is finally coming up. You can always tell that by the number of smart coffee shops, antique places and galleries. The This, That and the Other store has been replaced by a trendy and lively new bar. Adele would definitely have been trying to sneak in here when she was underage. She could have had a row with her boyfriend, punched him in the face and gone straight upstairs to write 'Chasing Pavements'. She could have flung open a window and treated the world walking by on the pavement below to a burst of her magnificent voice.

Adele is arguably the best-loved performer in Britain today – and most of the world for that matter. Her triumph at the 2017 Grammys at the Staples Center in Los Angeles highlighted her universal appeal and the phenomenal success of her 'comeback', as she called it. Despite being surrounded by the superstars of modern music, including Beyoncé, Katy Perry, Bruno Mars and Lady Gaga, she managed to turn the occasion into 'Adele Night' by the sheer force of her personality.

She performed 'Hello' even before the host, James Corden, came on stage, as if the Grammys were just another Adele concert. She could have been back at the O2 as the spotlight lingered on her in the darkness and she began once again, 'Hello … It's me!'

Her immaculate floor-length, Egyptian-themed Givenchy gown revealed the care that Adele now takes to look a million dollars. According to *Vogue*, the heavily embellished dress took a squadron of dressmakers a combined total of 1,500 hours to make. Her stylist, Gaelle Paul, observed, 'It's about perfection.'

Not everything on the night was perfect, however. She messed things up for the second consecutive year when she reappeared on stage to pay tribute to George Michael, who had died seven weeks earlier.

She revealed that she had been left devastated by news of his death on Christmas Day and had gone for a walk by herself to come to terms with her sadness. She knew then that she wanted to perform in his honour. George's family and 'people' were very specific that they wanted only Adele to sing one of his classic songs.

She chose to do a highly personalised version of 'Fastlove', the 1996 hit that had first made her appreciate his music. Even as a young girl she had been struck by how good looking George was, but, more than that, she recognised that he was one of pop's 'truest icons'. He understood, as she calls it, the 'inevitable fakeness' of the business.

Adele provides a refreshing contrast to that false world. That's why we love her naturalness. And why nobody cared when she suddenly stopped singing 'Fastlove' in the middle of the song and announced dramatically, 'I know it's live TV. I'm sorry. I fucked up. I can't do it again like last year. I can't mess this up for him.'

She had turned 'Fastlove' into a slow-paced, heartfelt torch song and simply went back to the beginning and started again. Her emotion shone through and afterwards, looking drained, she made sure she apologised for swearing. The audience loved it and, importantly, so did the establishment.

Neil Portnow, the President of the National Academy of Recording Arts and Sciences, which puts on the Grammys, was full of praise: 'What I think was magnificent was it shows the humanity of live television, but it also shows professionalism.'

In any ordinary year, this would have been enough to guarantee Adele the headlines afterwards. But she hadn't finished. The Awards had been billed as a contest between Beyoncé and her album *Lemonade* and Adele and *25*.

If it had been a boxing match, the referee would have stopped it in the first round. Adele won all five awards she was nominated for, including the most prestigious of the night, Album of the Year.

During her acceptance speech, she spoke gushingly about Beyoncé, saying *Lemonade* was her album of the year and that she had voted for her: 'It was so monumental and well thought-out and beautiful and soul-baring.' She even broke the award in two to show the extent of her appreciation for her rival.

Afterwards, backstage, she remembered that she had fallen in love with Beyoncé's music when she was eleven, which must have made her rival feel very old. It was a reminder of the days when she and her friends would have sing-offs with Destiny's Child songs during school break time.

In typical fashion, Adele added stridently, 'I thought it was her year. What the fuck does she have to do to win Album of the Year?'

While her praise for Beyoncé filled column inches afterwards, the biggest news of the night was thrown in when she did her thank yous. She mentioned her 'husband' – her way of confirming the rumours that she and Simon had secretly married with no fuss or fanfare.

Simon, as ever, was there to support her in his unassuming way and spent the whole evening beaming. Afterwards, they didn't attend a glitzy party but had low-key drinks with Jonathan Dickins and various suits from Sony at Hotel Bel-Air. Duty done, it was a short limo ride home to kiss Angelo goodnight.

If asked, I couldn't sum Adele up any better than the young woman assistant in the Floral Hall flower shop in Norwood Road, where she used to buy a bunch or two for her mum. 'I love Adele,' she told me. 'She keeps it real.'

ADELE'S STARS

Enormous faith, an abundance of hope and plenty of charity – these are potentials clearly suggested by the birth chart of the prolific, inspiring performer Adele. A tight link between her Taurus Sun, planet of individuality and direction, and Jupiter, ruler of expansion, belief and good fortune, hints at the urge to reach out, gain wisdom and grow continuously.

Compounding this trait, a positive link with Neptune reveals a fundamental desire to connect with something greater and beyond the self. Sensitive, escapist Neptune longs for a sublime ideal. Those with the planet placed strongly have a natural instinct for beauty, harmony and compassion. While the first two qualities play a major role in her craft, it is compassion, the ability to identify with the pain of others, which allows her to act as a medium for the thoughts and feelings of us all. There is openness, loyalty, kindness and understanding of the non-rational here; she can be instinctively, readily in tune with the ethereal and all things other-worldly too. Alongside these rarefied fairy gifts, Adele has been granted some tough stuff as well. Planetary aspects that challenge a

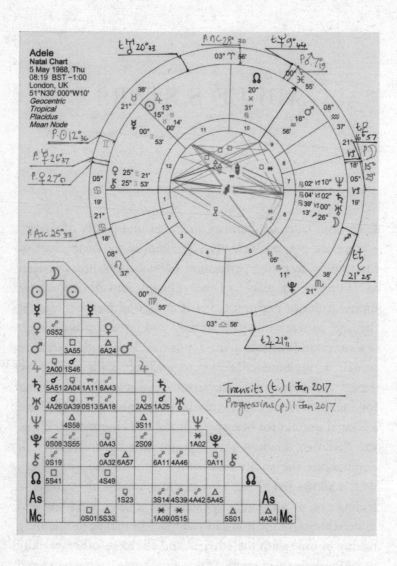

Adele
Natal Chart
5 May 1988, Thu
08:19 BST −1:00
London, UK
51°N30' 000°W10'
Geocentric
Tropical
Placidus
Mean Node

Transits (t.) 1 Jan 2017
Progressions (p.) 1 Jan 2017

soul and ground it in the real world, contribute, when mastered, towards solid achievements and great artistic strength.

Both the Sun and Moon, termed the luminaries, or the two lights, have discordant links with other planets. Her sensual, stability-loving Taurus Sun is opposite disruptive Pluto, planet of death and regeneration. Periodically, Adele will find herself in head-on power struggles, generally because she can be unwilling to let others have their way. This forcefulness and determination, which on occasion may be accompanied by questionable tactics or iffy justifications, can be invaluable when there is a clear vision of the future. Adele will then seek to bend the world to her rather than bend to the world – the mark of a true pacesetter. Not yielding can intensify opposition, attracting powerful forces, but Pluto is highly seductive, gifting Adele with enormous charm, agreeableness and general bewitchery. Opponents may not always see the trap instinctively set before it is too late. There is, of course, an additional value in such confrontation leading to self-understanding and a clearer sense of identity.

Long term, that need for change, the powerful instinct to break down structures and destroy, vital though it is in order for her to feel alive and essential for her creative evolution, will be wearing on the part of her that longs for peace and may impact on her health. The task here is to balance out those needs, focusing always through unselfish means on noble ends. There is no doubt she has been given the abilities to achieve these noble ends, and working for the greater good of the collective will dominate in her eventful life.

While a winsome combination of Venus and Mars supports Adele with the allure and appeal so helpful to popularity, fighting Mars links awkwardly to her Sun. There is a touchiness here – she may be over-quick to see a challenge in a relatively innocent situation and can be prone to impulsiveness. But this feisty planet makes for someone with the urge to win and the courage to engage – she has a big, vivacious personality. She is not the type to sit around, but will lead from the front, having a healthy sense of self-interest and appreciating the strategic importance of helping others from a position of strength.

One other problem that may arise is physical injury. With Adele's Sun, symbol of vitality, in the sign of Taurus, associated with the throat, and Mercury, the planet of communication, positioned at the exact degree linked to the trachea, there will always be the potential risk of damage.

A number of planets, including the Moon, in the area of the chart associated with well-being, highlight Adele's need to be vigilant about her health. Too much stress and nervous tension may weaken her defences and unresolved conflicts from the past can erode her vigour. She will constantly adjust daily commitments to accommodate priorities, including health, and will share discoveries about healing processes and medical treatments with her public.

Although the forceful, driving gifts of the Pluto and Mars contacts come with strings attached, they are a very good counterbalance to a contrary influence that can undermine Adele. There can be occasions where the needs of others are given too much priority over her own, often because she questions her worth. Then compliance is used as a means to avoid a struggle.

Adele's Sun is the planet found influencing her initial education. Its complex links suggest huge expectations that may not have been met early on. The picture is of a child excited by knowledge, able to gobble up experience, needing an environment with a singular and disciplined focus on creativity. Until her needs were met here, she could only have endured frustration.

Early family life might also have been erratic. The Moon, representing Mother in the birth chart, sits with rebellious Uranus and lonely Saturn in the freedom-loving, cavalier sign of Sagittarius. Adele's mother may have rejected societal norms in terms of family and decided to go it alone. The Sun, normally representing the Father, is joined to the ruler of the Moon, Jupiter, suggesting that Mother took both parental roles. This is a heavy burden and, no matter how necessary, well intentioned and heroically executed, will have had an impact on Adele primarily in terms of her emotional needs and self-worth. Communicating her needs would have been hard and using material acquisitions or embracing other means to gain comfort will have become a pattern. Clearly, songwriting is one enormously effective form through which to open up, but to do so will have needed the courage, vision and hope to move beyond inhibitions and security needs. Thank goodness for her spirited Mars. Hope is having that certainty the future will deliver, and Mother, although possibly swinging between a certain rigidity and unconventionality, would have provided that.

There may be a weakness around Adele's Father. The paternal symbols, Sun and Saturn, are tightly linked to confusing, elusive Neptune. This suggests absence and vulnerability. Perhaps this is a man who found it hard to deal with the realities of mundane life, seeking to escape through whatever means; someone who was not or could not set himself up to be the voice of authority. He may be, or may see himself, as something of a victim. However, given the very close association between Neptune and creativity, one must make the association of inherited talent or cultivation of that gift from the paternal side.

Despite the enormous protection that positive, generous Jupiter provides in inspiring and guiding Adele, it should be clear that she has had her trials and some of these go right back to her earliest days. The difficult links both luminaries pick up suggest she had to grow up and become emotionally self-sufficient at an early age. It is likely that beneath a protective exterior lie many defences and questions concerning her self-worth. Learning to love herself might require some understanding and validation of her lost or absent parent.

She will play a spokesperson role for her generation, her personal journey undertaken on behalf of thousands. Ultimately an examination of her own emotional needs may focus on the modern dilemma of shared parenting. With Venus, planet of femininity, linked closely to Chiron, the marker of our deepest wound, there is much fear around rejection, specifically rejection as a woman. Fear of rejection can prompt an impulsive defiance, helping a dread to become real. Adele needs to be careful of negativity that can self-sabotage, when thoughts take on a life of their own. For her and many others now there are questions. How do mothers meet their own needs for growth and success while maintaining a role for fathers? How do they make sure their partners meet them halfway?

In terms of personal relationships, Adele will seek partners who can offer status, stability and strength. She can be curious and flirtatious, but will be cautious and discriminating in her long-term choices. Problems may occur if she is pursuing some form of father figure. While this may help her consolidate her understanding of herself as an individual, there is a risk of disillusionment. There will be a natural appreciation of artistic men and visionary types. Quite possibly, too, she may find her nurturing qualities to the fore as she seeks to create a relationship that is compassionate and understanding.

Intimacy can best be achieved through like-minded ambitions with her partner – schemes and projects that will help the world. Here, her strong and spiritual personal resolutions will find brave solutions when confronting sensitive issues. For both parties, careers that keep them 'on the road' will be beneficial. This way she can accommodate her strong, contrary need for emotional freedom and space on a day-to-day level.

Since January 2014, Saturn, the Great Task Master, has been moving through an area of Adele's chart associated with work, health and well-being. It would have been a period of enormous effort and responsibilities, which even this model of perseverance would have found testing. With Saturn, you reap what you sow and rewards will always come for any application, discipline and enterprise expended with integrity during this time.

Difficulties would have accelerated for a while on the emotional front, with the movement of this planet of terminations and restrictions towards her Moon in February 2017. Issues with parents and her own responsibilities as a parent will be to the fore, leaving her feeling overly self-critical and introspective. There will be a focus on obligations and Adele must do what is demanded to make good any debt. It is a time of reckoning and there is a need for clear and wise communication.

There is a continuance of this quickening maturity, leading up to the astrological marker known as the Saturn Return. This planet returns in January 2018 to the exact position it occupied at her birth. The discipline and resilience imparted by the trials of her growing-up years will work greatly in her favour now, helping her to endure tests to her ambitions and authority, because on many fronts this is primarily a period of endings, so that firmer foundations can be established for future potential.

In February, June and November 2018, Adele will need to be careful with her health and all close relationships. She may meet opposition from those who might appear to want to hold her back, but the task now is to understand the real nature of the agreement she has entered into with any significant other. She will ride any storms, provided she lives up to her obligations.

Although there are challenges over the next few years, indicated by Saturn's links, other planetary movements suggest a period of flourishing creativity and success for Adele. December 2017 looks especially promising as expansive Jupiter meets regenerative Pluto in her chart. It will be hard for Adele not to work almost compulsively towards greater achievement and recognition.

This is also an indicator that she may add to her family and in her private world will gain increasing pleasure from her present child, meeting developmental needs in a way that feels naturally satisfying. As a mum, Adele is likely to be intuitively ahead of her time. Provided her own personal world is in order and she is productive, she can live very happily with creative chaos and will be inspirational to her child in allowing him to feel comfortable with change and adventure. She will be supportive of tolerance and appreciative of a child's needs for peer friendships and his own space, working hard to create a family environment on the job, with strong ties to co-workers. Her Sagittarius Moon suggests she will be endlessly enthusiastic about sharing her passions and will be a champion of justice. Instinctively, caring full time for a baby would make Adele restless – she has been lucky in that success has enabled her to delegate aspects of childcare easily so that both parties thrive. She is a role model in many respects for contemporary motherhood. The challenge of maintaining a stable family life lies ahead.

Finally, in February 2018, there is a very positive link between transiting Pluto and a point called the North Node in Adele's chart, triggering her sense of destiny – the lure of great public success. This again speaks of her need to climb the ladder to the top. There will be times when she does feel that prioritising herself will conflict with the need to do things for others, most especially family. During these very important years, however, personal self-betterment – honing her creative talent – must come first.

Madeleine Moore

LIFE AND TIMES

5 May 1988: Adele Laurie Blue Adkins is born at the North Middlesex Hospital, Edmonton. Her mum, Penny, aged nineteen, is living in emergency accommodation for unmarried mothers in Finsbury Park. Her Welsh father, Marc, has a window-cleaning round in Crouch End.

April 1992: Is smuggled into the Brixton Academy inside Penny's trench coat to see The Beautiful South, her first concert. Her father has returned to Penarth; mother and daughter are living in a flat in Tottenham.

June 1993: Attends her first pop festival when her mother takes her to Great Xpectations in Finsbury Park. They watch The Cure, Penny's favourite band. Adele goes to the local Coleraine Park Primary School, where she says she was the only white face in class.

Sept 1995: Her half-brother Cameron O'Sullivan is born in Cardiff.

June 1997: Her mum takes her to Glastonbury for what was labelled the year of the mud. She sees The Prodigy and Radiohead on the main stage.

May 1999: Is inconsolable when her beloved Grampy, John Evans, dies from cancer at a hospital in Cardiff. She attends the funeral, aged eleven.

Sept 2000: Begins Year 7 at the Chestnut Grove School in Balham, a couple of miles from her new home in Streatham. She doesn't enjoy her time there, claiming she is surrounded by apathy and negativity. She prefers to hang out with her friends in Brockwell Park after school.

Jan 2002: Sings 'Free' by Stevie Wonder and plays the clarinet at her admissions interview for a place at the BRIT School in Croydon. Passes with flying colours and spends the next four years at the school.

May 2004: Obtains a distinction in her music GNVQ (General National Vocational Qualifications).

May 2006: Sings her own song 'Daydreamer' at final BRIT School concert and steals the show. Celebrates eighteenth birthday at a pub in Brixton, where she performs a few numbers. She has already attracted the attention of A&R man Nick Huggett after posting three songs on Myspace. Meets Jonathan Dickins, who agrees to manage her and then negotiates her first deal with indie label XL Recordings.

July 2006: Features in the fourth edition of *Platforms* magazine, an online culture monthly. There's a link to her songs 'Daydreamer' and 'My Same'.

Aug 2006: Makes professional debut at the 12 Bar Club in Soho, singing 'Painting Pictures' at Jamie T's monthly Panic Prevention night.

Sept 2006: Plays 'Painting Pictures' at a concert in St James's Church, Piccadilly, and again at the second birthday of Blue Flowers, a music venue at the back of the George IV pub in Chiswick.

Dec 2006: Performs at Troubadour in Earl's Court, opening for her friend Jack Peñate.

May 2007: Begins recording her first album, working primarily with Arctic Monkeys producer Jim Abbiss and the songwriter/producer Eg White.

June 2007: Meets acclaimed DJ/recording artist Mark Ronson at the XL offices in Notting Hill. By the time he arrives for their meeting, she is 'pissed off her face'. He produces 'Cold Shoulder'. Makes television debut on *Later … with Jools Holland*, despite not having released a record. She performs 'Daydreamer' and 'Hometown Glory' and is petrified when she is placed between Sir Paul McCartney and Björk. Paul tells her he 'really enjoyed' her songs.

Oct 2007: Features for the first time on a record as a backing vocalist on Jack Peñate's song 'My Yvonne' from his album *Matinée*. Her debut single, 'Hometown Glory', is released as a seven-inch vinyl limited edition of 500 copies on Jamie T's Pacemaker label. The track is played on Radio 1 and Radio 2.

Nov 2007: Supports Will Young at the Little Noise Sessions in London, a series of annual charity concerts in aid of Mencap, and tells him she voted for him 5,000 times on *Pop Idol*.

Dec 2007: Named the winner of the first-ever Critics' Choice Award, which she will receive at the following year's BRITs. Wins the BBC Sound of 2008 poll. Sings new single 'Chasing Pavements' on *Friday Night with Jonathan Ross*. On New Year's Eve, she is mentioned positively by the US celebrity blogger Perez Hilton.

Jan 2008: First album *19* is released and debuts at number one. 'Chasing Pavements' reaches number two in the UK charts.

Feb 2008: Collects first BRIT Award from Will Young. Performs Coldplay's 'God Put a Smile upon Your Face'. Calls Arctic Monkeys 'fucking idiots'.

March 2008: Makes her US debut at Joe's Pub, a 184-seat venue in Manhattan. Tickets cost $12. The following night, signs her American deal with Columbia in her dressing room before her second show. Flies to California for LA debut at The Hotel Café.

April 2008: Denies that she ever dated the musician known as Slinky Sunbeam. The Welsh side of her family turn out for her concert at St David's Hall, Cardiff. She points out Cameron and waves to Nana Rose. Backstage, it is the last time her father sees her in person. Sets up her own company, Melted Stone Ltd, which makes a net profit of £562,000 in its first year.

May 2008: 'Hometown Glory' features in the season finale of the popular US show *Grey's Anatomy*. Begins first proper American tour, *An Evening with Adele*, at the Roxy on Sunset Strip in LA.

July 2008: Sings in St John's Smith Square at the Black Ball event, a fundraiser for Aids charity Keep a Child Alive. The evening is hosted by Alicia Keys. Cancels US tour dates for the next two months to be with new boyfriend in London.

Oct 2008: Performs first US single 'Chasing Pavements' and 'Cold Shoulder' on *Saturday Night Live* in New York. The same episode features vice-presidential candidate Sarah Palin and is watched by 17 million Americans. Flies home to London, and by the time she lands, *19* has climbed from number forty to number one on the iTunes chart.

Jan 2009: Buys her first flat on the corner of Kensington Park Road in Notting Hill for £380,000.

Feb 2009: Sings 'Cracklin' Rosie' at a fundraiser honouring Neil Diamond and declares, 'I was shit'. Wins first Grammy for Best New Artist and Best Female Pop Vocal Performance. She wears a black satin dress designed by Barbara Tfank. Ignores the after parties and celebrates with Team Adele at the In-N-Out Burger on Venice Boulevard.

April 2009: Represents 'curvy' in the Annual Shape Edition of American *Vogue*. The leading photographer Annie Leibovitz photographs her wearing a Michael Kors evening coat, lying on a bed.

May 2009: Plays herself in an episode of *Ugly Betty* called 'In the Stars', in which she sings 'Right as Rain'. Calls herself 'the worst actress of all time'. Spends her twenty-first birthday in concert at the Roseland Ballroom in Manhattan. Her mother wheels a huge cake on stage and leads the audience in a chorus of 'Happy Birthday'.

Oct 2009: Buys a spacious apartment across from Battersea Park for £890,000 and invites her mother to move in. The location is ideal for walking her new dog, a dachshund, called Louie in honour of the jazz great Louis Armstrong. Learns that her former boyfriend has become engaged and writes 'Rolling in the Deep'.

May 2010: Filmed at the Shangri-La Studios in Malibu, where she is working with legendary producer Rick Rubin on her second album.

Dec 2010: Sings 'Rolling in the Deep' at her first Royal Variety Performance at the London Palladium in front of the Prince of Wales and the Duchess of Cornwall.

Jan 2011: *21* is released and is currently the fourth bestselling album of all time in the UK. It becomes the longest-running number-one album by a female solo artist in the history of the British and US charts and the biggest selling album of the twenty-first century. So far, it has sold more than 30 million copies.

Feb 2011: Gives a life-changing performance of 'Someone Like You' at the BRITs. The following week, the song is her first single to reach number one in the UK. Her album *19* and previous single 'Rolling in the Deep' both climb back into the top five.

May 2011: 'Rolling in the Deep' becomes her first US number one on the *Billboard* Hot 100 chart. Cancels concert in Minneapolis when her voice 'switched off like a light' during an afternoon sound check. Scraps rest of tour a few weeks later when things don't improve.

Aug 2011: Relaunches North American tour in Vancouver and dedicates 'Make You Feel My Love' to Amy Winehouse, who died a few weeks earlier.

Oct 2011: Voice problems again force the cancellation of her US tour dates. Flies to Boston for operation to remove polyps on her vocal cords. Advised not to speak for two months.

Nov 2011: Releases *Live at the Royal Albert Hall*, which will be the biggest selling DVD of 2011, despite being on sale for only two months.

Dec 2011: *Billboard* names Adele Artist of the Year. Posts a tweet stating that @drop4drop is a wonderful charity.

Jan 2012: Gets all-clear from surgeon in Boston. Pictured at the Everglades National Park in Florida embracing a new boyfriend, an old Etonian former investment banker called Simon Konecki, who founded drop4drop. He is fourteen years older and divorced, with a young daughter.

Feb 2012: Simon accompanies her to the Grammys where she cleans up, winning all six awards for which she had been nominated. She sings for the first time since vocal surgery, performing 'Rolling in the Deep'. She gives the finger to the 'suits' at the BRIT Awards after her acceptance speech for Best Album is cut short by host James Corden. Karl Lagerfeld faces a backlash when he says Adele is a 'little too fat'.

March 2012: Buys a house in a millionaire's row on the Brighton waterfront for £2 million. It's near Simon's company's HQ. Her neighbours include Zoe Ball and Nick Berry.

April 2012: *Time* magazine lists Adele as one of the 100 most influential women in the world. Presents Jonathan Dickins with Manager of the Year trophy at the *Music Week* Awards, telling him he 'fucking smashed it'. Tops the *Sunday Times* Rich List of young British musicians with a fortune of £20 million.

May 2012: Named Songwriter of the Year at the prestigious Ivor Novello Awards in London. 'Rolling in the Deep' also wins an award for Most Performed Work.

June 2012: Announces on her website that she and Simon are expecting their first child together and are over the moon at the news. The site promptly crashes due to volume of traffic.

Oct 2012: Her Bond theme 'Skyfall' reaches number two in the UK chart. Gives birth to her first child, a son called Angelo. A few days later, she has to miss the movie's world premiere in London. 'Rolling in the Deep' is named Song of the Year at the BMI Awards – the most played song on US radio and TV.

Dec 2012: 'Skyfall' is named Best Original Song at the Golden Globes. *21* is the biggest selling album of the year in the US for the second year running.

Feb 2013: Another year, another Grammy award – this time 'Set Fire to the Rain' wins Best Pop Solo Performance. Sings 'Skyfall' at the Oscars and wins Best Original Song. Adele wears a crystal-encrusted Burberry dress weighing thirty-three pounds.

June 2013: Awarded an MBE for services to music in the Queen's Birthday Honours. Renowned New York tattooist Bang Bang inks the word Paradise on her left hand.

Oct 2013: Passes her driving test at the first attempt and is thrilled that she can drive her son about herself. Splashes out on a £100,000 Porsche Cayenne SUV.

Dec 2013: Has a fit of the giggles at Buckingham Palace when she receives her MBE from the Prince of Wales. Puts award in frame and places it in the loo at home.

Feb 2014: 'Skyfall' takes her Grammy tally to ten when it wins Best Song Written for Visual Media.

July 2014: Wins a High Court legal action taken out in her son's name against a picture agency that published photos of Angelo's 'milestone moments'.

June 2015: Adele and Simon attend Glastonbury as pop fans, watching Kanye West and Burt Bacharach and staying in the VIP area at the site.

Oct 2015: During an *X Factor* ad break, a teaser for her new song 'Hello' appears without warning on the screen. The video, directed by Xavier Dolan, is viewed more than 27.7 million times on YouTube within its first twenty-four hours – a record.

Nov 2015: Makes her television comeback in an hour-long special hosted by Graham Norton. Guest edits the first edition of the revived *Observer Music* magazine and features on its cover. Her third studio album, *25*, debuts at number one, breaking first-week sales records with 800,000 in the UK and 3.38 million in the US.

Jan 2016: Sings 'Wannabe' by the Spice Girls, as well as a Nicky Minaj rap and some of her own hits, during 'Carpool Karaoke' with James Corden. 'Hello' becomes the fastest video to reach one billion views on YouTube in ninety-three days.

Feb 2016: Singing 'All I Ask' at the Grammys, she is strangely off-key. Apparently the piano mic fell on the strings and sounded like a twangy guitar. 'Shit happens', said Adele. Wins four BRITs, including the Global Success Award, presented from outer space by astronaut Tim Peake.

March 2016: Her third major tour, *Adele Live 2016/17*, opens at the SSE Arena, Belfast. She will play 122 shows, ending in spectacular style with four nights at Wembley Stadium in the summer of 2017.

April 2016: Named Britain's richest-ever female musician, with an £85 million fortune.

May 2016: Reportedly signs to Sony for £90 million – a record for any artist.

June 2016: Headlines the main Pyramid Stage at Glastonbury for the first time and announces, 'This is fucking amazing.'

Feb 2017: Becomes the first artist to win the three biggest Grammy Awards – Record of the Year, Album of the Year and Song of the Year – twice. Stops and restarts 'Fastlove', her tribute to George Michael. Tells audience: 'I fucked up'. Thanks her manager, her husband and her son.

ACKNOWLEDGEMENTS

There's been much talk in this book of Team Adele, the group of talented people that surround the star and have done so much to develop and support her. Now it's the time for Team Sean to take a bow. Quite simply, I could not write these books without their help and expertise.

First, my long-standing agent Gordon Wise has transformed my career and continues to do so. I think this is our fourteenth book together. Gordon was deservedly named Agent of the Year at *The Bookseller* Awards of 2015. This year he has been elected President of the Association of Author's Agents (AAA). Thanks also to Richard Pike, his assistant at Curtis Brown, who manages to deal cheerfully with all manner of hopeless enquiries from me.

My research squad has been marvellous as always. Thanks to Emily-Jane Swanson, who sensibly did most of her work from beside a pool in Ibiza, and to Alison Sims, Jo Westaway and Sophie Sims. They all find Adele as fascinating as I do. That is also the case for astrologer Madeleine Moore, who once again has produced a brilliant birth chart.

I've no idea how she does it, but her insight never ceases to amaze me.

Obviously, fashion played a considerable role in my last book on Kim Kardashian. It was a big surprise, however, to appreciate its significance in the Adele story. I relied on my fashion guru, Alison Jane Reid, who brought her knowledge and critical eye to proceedings. Her ethical-hedonist.com website is well worth a visit. Talking of things online, don't miss tvkev.co.uk, run by my old friend Kevin O'Sullivan, the best television critic in the country. I enjoyed meeting up with Patrick Humphries to get his astute thoughts about the music business.

Thank you to Jen Westaway for transcribing my interviews so expertly. I don't know how she coped with the tape of the former BRIT School student who managed to sit right next to a loud coffee machine during our chat. I am grateful to Arianne Burnette for her outstanding work as copy editor on yet another book.

I had better not include HarperCollins as part of *my* team – I am a very small part of theirs! Sincere thanks to my publisher, Natalie Jerome, for suggesting Adele as a subject and commissioning this book; my editor, Kate Latham, for her enthusiasm and kind words about the manuscript; Isabel Hayman-Brown and Holly Kyte for project editing; Claire Ward for her striking cover design; Dean Russell in production; Isabel Prodger and Jasmine Gordon for looking after publicity and marketing.

You can read more about my books at seansmithceleb.com or follow me on Twitter @seansmithceleb and facebook.com/seansmithcelebbiog.

SELECT BIBLIOGRAPHY

Hudson, Alice, *Adele: Songbird*, Flame Tree Publishing, 2012

Newkey-Burden, Chas, *Adele: The Biography*, John Blake Publishing, 2015

Sanderson, Caroline, *Someone Like … Adele*, Omnibus Press, 2012

Shapiro, Marc, *Adele: The Biography*, St. Martin's Griffin, 2012

Simpson, Neil, *Adele*, Endeavour Press, 2015

PICTURE CREDITS

INDEX

INDEX